FIGHTING MEN
OF WORLD WAR II
ALLIED FORCES
UNIFORMS, EQUIPMENT AND WEAPONS

FIGHTING MEN
OF WORLD WAR II
ALLIED FORCES
UNIFORMS, EQUIPMENT AND WEAPONS

David Miller

CHARTWELL
BOOKS, INC.

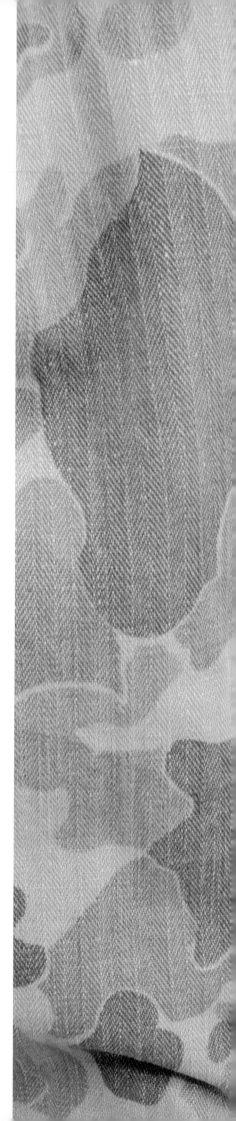

CONTENTS

INTRODUCTION

World War II was a watershed in terms of what had gone before and what was to follow. A changeover between lines of men in opposing trenches, dug in, or advancing across the muddy battlefield firing indiscriminately at the opposing side, to a more mobile, purposeful, global war, fought in the streets, the fields and hedges, pacific jungle and desert.

From the point of view of the average fighting man of the Allied Forces, a lot had changed. He was now required to jump out of an aircraft over enemy lines, provide support columns of armored vehicles, fight from an armored jeep or perhaps wade ashore from a specially designed landing craft. The challenge of fighting in all terrains and climates meant that armies had to have different equipment and clothing to succeed in each. Uniforms and equipment issued to men fighting in the Western Desert looked very different to that of those fighting in the bitter winter of the Russian Front.

Despite this, however, the same considerations that fighting men have always had still applied: was the uniform comfortable to fight in and were the weapons and other equipment good enough to do the job? How could life be made bearable in terms of food, cigarettes, medical treatment, and letters home; and would there be entertainment in moments of leisure?

These issues would have made up much of a soldier's conscious thought during the bitter conflict.

In these pages we show how the average Allied fighting man fared in all the main armies, from the mighty Soviet Red Army, to the United States, the British, their Dominions and Commonwealth, and including those other nations like the French and Polish who fought on, despite being overrun at the beginning of the war.

David Miller's carefully researched text is tempered by his own experience as a serving soldier in the British Armed Forces, and shows both the structure of each army and describes in detail the equipment, weapons, uniforms, and personal items carried by its fighting men.

Specially commissioned color photography obtained in museums and private collections worldwide shows genuine wartime items. The book also uses extensive archival photography to show that equipment in use during the conflict.

This highly illustrated book is designed to present a rich selection of information and images to the general reader, budding collector, military enthusiast, re-enactor, and modeller.

!EXTRA!

THE STARS AND STRIPES

MEDITER

Vol. 1, No. 170, Tuesday, June 6, 1944

INVA

Allies Hit

30,000 Po

WHERE THE BLOWS AR

Eisenhower's Folks A

Order Of Day Gradua

EUROPEAN EDITION

YANK

THE ARMY WEEKLY

10¢ FEB. 23 1945

VOL 1. NO 47

By the men... for the men in the service

PHILIPPINE FRIENDSHIP

What Jap Prisoners Think About the War and Us

UNITED STATES

During World War II the United States Army had to expand beyond anything envisaged in peacetime and to fight in two very different environments and against two very different enemies: the Japanese in the Pacific, and the Germans in Europe. As with other armies, at the heart of all these campaigns was the infantryman, who found himself fighting in countries he had never heard of or, in the Pacific, on islands whose importance was not at all clear.

Also of great importance was the system behind the lines which supplied everything the fighting men needed, from rifles and ammunition through boots, socks, food and drink to surgical treatment and hospitalization. When war broke out much of this materiel and many of these systems were, primarily due to pre-war parsimony, distinctly second-rate; but by late-1943 the American soldier was among the best armed and equipped in the world, with logistic support that was the envy of all others.

US INFANTRY

Until the late 1930s the US infantry was scattered around the continental United States and a number of overseas territories. Almost every unit was short of manpower, equipment and funding, while training was piecemeal and lacking in realism. Many of the divisions and regiments were "paper" units with a limited regular component, making them dependent on reinforcements to bring them up to combat strength. Expansion started in 1938, gradually picked up momentum, then between 1941 and 1945 proceeded at a breakneck speed.

INFANTRY DIVISIONS

At the end of the war there were 67 active infantry divisions. Of these, all were conventional infantry, except for five airborne

below A line of US infantrymen on a typical *bocage* embankment in Normandy. They are lucky enough to wear the M1943 field jacket with four front pockets, an item which wasn't in widespread use during the Normandy campaign. They also have M1943 boots with built-in buckles around the ankles.

left An officer wearing a hooded parka with reversible white color inside. He has the dark woolen OD (Olive Drab) trousers and brown "combat shoes", although in this case he doesn't have the usual gaiters. A brown leather pistol holster hangs from his belt and he is wearing thick, fur-backed winter mittens.

left Men from Coy I, 331 Infantry Regiment move cautiously through the streets of St Malo in August 1944. The man in the middle of the street is carrying an M1919 light machine gun while the rifleman following him has ammunition belts draped over his shoulder. This man also has his overcoat tucked into his belt at his back.

Below As the war progressed, a range of colorful badges and patches appeared on US combat uniforms. Many men wore their divisional badge at the top of the arm, such as the patch for the 69th division seen here. The rank badge shows this man is a 5th Grade Technician.

divisions (11th, 13th, 17th, 82nd and 102nd), one mountain division (10th) and the 1st Cavalry Division, which turned in its horses in 1942 and became a light infantry division (but still with its cavalry title). Of these divisions, 25 served in the Pacific and 42 in North Africa, Italy and Northwest Europe.

The World War II division was commanded by a major-general, with a brigadier-general as his assistant commander. The primary combat capability lay in the three infantry regiments. The divisional artillery, commanded by a brigadier-general, comprised four 12-gun battalions (three "light" with 105 mm guns and one "medium" with 155 mm howitzers). There were also a cavalry reconnaissance troop and support troops, including engineers, communications, medical, transport, etc.

An infantry regiment comprised three line battalions, one cannon company, one anti-tank company, a service company, a headquarters, and a headquarters company.

At its full strength, a division had a total of 14,253 personnel.

AIRBORNE DIVISIONS

Going to war by parachute or glider was novel and exciting, and the newly-formed airborne divisions underwent a number of major changes during the war. They originally comprised one parachute regiment (three battalions), two glider infantry regiments (each two battalions), three artillery, one anti-tank and one engineer battalion, plus the usual support services. But, when first fielded in North Africa and Italy this organization proved unbalanced and after several modifications the division ended up with four regiments (two parachute, two glider), with an increase in strength from some 8,500 to just under 13,000 men.

above Men from an Airborne unit hook their parachutes onto the static line in the aircraft. When the men jump out the door the fabric strips stay hooked to the wire and pull the parachute out of its pack to open.

MOUNTAIN DIVISION

The 10th Light Division was formed in 1942 but was subsequently redesignated 10th Mountain Division. It was an all-volunteer formation and after deploying to Alaska it went to Italy. The infantry organization was the same as for an infantry division, but there was no medium artillery battalion. For transportation, there were many fewer trucks, but some 6,000 horses and mules were required for off-road operations in the mountains.

left The United States produced a range of equipment for mountain and winter warfare, such as the large bergen-style backpack seen here.

right Many men improvised winter camouflage from "liberated" sheets and such like, but some, like this man, were lucky enough to be issued with specialized winter clothing. The reversible parka and white overtrousers were worn over the normal uniform, providing extra warmth as well as camouflage.

left Visible here is part of the frame of the rucksack as well as an M1943 folding entrenching tool in its carrier.

RANGERS

There were six Ranger battalions, five of which deployed to Northwest Europe and one to the Pacific. The 1st, 3rd and 4th Ranger Battalions suffered such heavy casualties at Anzio that they had to be disbanded, but the other three served through to the end of the war.

below There were many special units in the army, mainly created for specific roles and purposes. But some were also formed from various cultural, national and racial groups. These men are from the 100th Infantry Battalion, a unit comprised of *Nisei* (US citizens of Japanese extraction).

SPECIAL SERVICE FORCE

The First Special Service Force (FSSF) was raised as a result of a proposal from the Chief of (British) Combined Operations to undertake an operation against the hydroelectric facilities in German-occupied Norway. An all-volunteer mixed US/Canadian force, it was commanded by Colonel Robert T. Frederick. In the event the Norwegian operation was canceled, but the force remained in being, deploying first to the Aleutians and then to Europe, where it was disbanded in December 1944.

right Many men kept personal record books such as this, listing details of their service, their deployments, qualifications gained and general service history. While unofficial, they formed an enduring personal record.

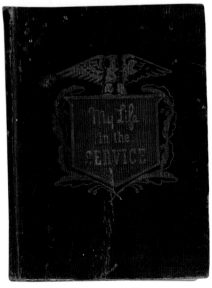

THE INFANTRYMAN

The United States infantryman was tough and resolute, and fought with distinction in every theater in what turned out to be a global war. The expansion of the infantry between 1938 and 1945 was unprecedented, but was achieved by a robust enlistment and training system. The organization, weapons and equipment of the Field Army at the start were not really adequate and initial operations, for example in North Africa, were not as successful as had been hoped. But, the American armed forces have always been ready to face up to shortcomings and failures, identify the problems and then to take urgent and ruthless corrective action. As a result, the armies that fought their way across France and Germany and, in cooperation with the Marine Corps, from one island to another across the Pacific, were more than equal to their enemies.

above Pages from a commercially-printed personal book for soldiers, showing a range of rank insignia and specialist trade badges used in the early years of the war.

above As well as the Thompson sub-machine gun, grenade and hurricane lamp, this table holds personal items such as air mail letters, Camel cigarettes, gum, matches and French phrasebook.

RANKS

When wearing service dress officers had their rank badges on jacket epaulettes or shirt collars. When wearing combat or working dress rank badges were sometimes worn on shirt collars or were often not worn at all. Painted bars and symbols on the front of steel helmets were also often used to indicate rank in combat.

NCOs wore their rank badges on their sleeve on both service dress and combat uniform. Sometimes formation badges or even the national flag were worn at the top of the arm.

Until January 1942 there was an NCO group designated "specialists" who were graded similarly to the command ranks. In that month, however, the title was changed to Technician, with

Shoulder (Officers)

Warrant Officer

Chief Warrant Officer

2nd Lieutenant

1st Lieutenant

Captain

Major

Lieutenant-Colonel

Colonel

Arm (NCOs)

Private 1st Class

Corporal

Sergeant

Staff Sergeant

1st Sergeant

Master Sergeant

Arm (Technicians)

Technician 5th Grade

Technician 4th Grade

Technician 3rd Grade

Technical Sergeant 2nd Grade

T/5 equivalent to a corporal, up to T/2 which came between Staff Sergeant and Master Sergeant. For several months they wore the same rank insignia as their command equivalent but in September a letter "T" was added below the angle of the lowest chevron.

Group	Rank	Insignia	Where Worn
General officers	General of the Army (inst Dec 1944)	US Eagle plus five stars in circle	Shoulders
	General	Four stars	
	Lieutenant-General	Three stars	
	Major-General	Two stars	
	Brigadier-General	One star	
Field officers	Colonel	Eagle	Shoulders
	Lieutenant-Colonel	Oakleaf, silver	
	Major	Oakleaf, bronze	
Junior officers	Captain	Two silver bars, horizontal	Shoulders
	Lieutenant	One silver bar, horizontal	
	Second Lieutenant	One gold bar, horizontal	
Warrant Officers	Chief Warrant Officer	Horizontal red lozenge; with gold center, backed in gold	Above cuff
	Warrant Officer Junior Grade	As for Chief Warrant Officer but . with vertical gold stripe	Above cuff
NCO Grade 1	Master Sergeant	Three chevrons, inverted over three arcs	Upper sleeve
	First Sergeant (Grade 2 until 1942)	Three chevrons, inverted over three arcs with lozenge	
Grade 3	Staff Sergeant	Three chevrons, inverted over one arc	
Grade 4	Sergeant	Three chevrons, inverted	
Grade 5	Corporal	Two chevrons, inverted	
Grade 6	Private First-class	One chevron, inverted	
Grade 7	Private	None	

far left Technician grades were introduced in 1942 to give equivalent NCO status to specialists in infantry units.

left Colors of individual badges varied considerably, especially as uniforms became weathered. This Private 1st Class also has the "Big Red One" badge of the 1st Infantry Division on his sleeve.

THE INFANTRY BATTALION

Like other armies the US Army's primary fighting strength lay in its infantry battalion. As with those others, this underwent various reorganizations as lessons were learnt and new equipment replaced the old. The last major reorganization came in 1943, but this was amended slightly in mid-1944, resulting in a strength of 35 officers and 825 enlisted men, for a total of 860. The battalion was commanded by a

right This man is wearing an ammunition carrier vest over his woolen OD shirt and woolen trousers. Such vests supposedly allowed men to carry heavy loads with the weight evenly distributed over their back and shoulders.

lieutenant-colonel with captains commanding companies, and the basic organization was triangular, with three rifle companies, each of three platoons, each of three squads, but with headquarters and support weapons at each level. It should be noted that there were a large number of 2.56 in rocket launchers (bazookas) and M2 0.5 in heavy machine guns which were issued to squads and personnel in the various headquarters to bolster the battalion's air defense and anti-tank capabilities. The great majority of the infantrymen still marched, but the battalion had a substantial motor pool of some 40 Willy's Jeeps and trailers, Dodge WC-51 cargo trucks/troop transporters/weapons carriers and Ford G8T cargo trucks.

BATTALION HQ

The 4 officers in Battalion Headquarters (4 officers, 13 men) were the commanding officer (lieutenant-colonel), executive officer (major), adjutant (captain) and intelligence officer (lieutenant). The 13 men who were the drivers, clerks and orderlies for the officers, were nominally "Battalion HQ Section" of Headquarters Company but in reality their full-time employment was with Battalion HQ.

HEAVY WEAPONS COMPANY

The Battalion had a Heavy Weapons Company (8 Officers, 158 men) which provided one Mortar Platoon and two Machine Gun Platoons, although, rather surprisingly, the Anti-tank Platoon was part of HQ Company. The Mortar Platoon (4 officers, 56 enlisted men) was commanded by a 1st lieutenant and divided into three sections, each commanded by a 2nd lieutenant and equipped with two 81 mm mortars. The two Machine Gun Platoons (each 1 officer, 35 enlisted men) were armed with four .30 cal

Browning M1917 machine guns with a Jeep and trailer for each weapon. Company Headquarters (2 officers, 26 enlisted men) was commanded by a captain with a 1st lieutenant as Executive Officer and, like the Rifle Company HQ had a surprisingly large number of men, although most of these were involved in ammunition resupply.

HEADQUARTERS COMPANY

The Battalion Headquarters Company (5 officers, 117 enlisted men) provided the usual clerks, cooks, and supply specialists, but also had three functional platoons. The Communications Platoon (1 officer, 22 enlisted men) operated the various radio, wire and telephone systems within the battalion and to the unit on its right. Ammunition & Pioneer Platoon (1 officer, 26 enlisted men) was divided into three squads of 7 men each under command of a sergeant. It combined the functions of light engineer tasks with ammunition resupply to the rifle companies which, in view of the many automatic and semi-automatic weapons was a demanding task. The Anti-tank Platoon (1 officer, 32 enlisted men) was commanded by a 2nd lieutenant, with a sergeant and driver. There were three 10-man squads, each

above Men of the 3rd Battalion, 132 Infantry Regiment, belonging to the "Americal" Division come under fire as they land on the beach near Cebu City in the Philippines. Armored amphibious tracked carriers come ashore behind them. Note the variation in finishes on the men's M1 helmets.

left A column snakes ashore and inland from the Normandy beaches. They have the M1941 field jacket ("Parson's jacket"), woolen OD trousers and canvas gaiters. They are also wearing the M1928 backpack, an obsolescent design that served throughout most of the war.

armed with one 57 mm anti-tank gun (the British 6-pounder manufactured under license in the USA). Already mentioned above, the Battalion HQ Section of 13 enlisted men was permanently part of the Battalion HQ. HQ Company headquarters comprised 2 officers and 19 enlisted men.

THE RIFLE COMPANY

Three Rifle Companies (each 6 officers plus 187 enlisted men) were the ultimate combat strength of the battalion and were each organized into a headquarters, three Rifle Platoons and a Weapons Platoon. The Rifle Platoon comprised three squads of 12 men, each comprising a staff-sergeant, sergeant and 10 riflemen, which split into an assault group (7 men) and a BAR group (3 men), all of whom, except for the man carrying the BAR, were armed with the M1 Garand semi-automatic rifle, which gave them considerably greater firepower than, for example, a British section. Three men in the squad carried launchers for rifle grenades. Platoon HQ consisted of the platoon commander (1st or 2nd lieutenant), 2

above A pre-war exercise, with the men wearing World War I-style uniforms and wide-brimmed hats. They are equipped with the M2 .50 in heavy machine gun.

below For real this time, as an infantry squad cautiously tries to find a way forward in the Normandy *bocage*. One soldier is trying a "cunning ruse" with a helmet placed on his M1 carbine, while another gives overwatch, again with a carbine. Note the discarded German MG 42 machine gun in the foreground.

sergeants, a radio operator (SCR-36 "handie-talkie") and a runner. The Weapons Platoon (1 officer, 34 enlisted men) consisted of a Mortar Section of 17 men plus three 60 mm mortars, and a Machine Gun Section of 12 men plus two M1919 machine guns. Platoon HQ was 1 officer plus 5 men, mounted in two Jeeps, one of which mounted a .50 in Browning for local air defense. Company HQ was surprisingly strong, consisting of 2 officers (a captain and a 1st lieutenant), plus 33 men.

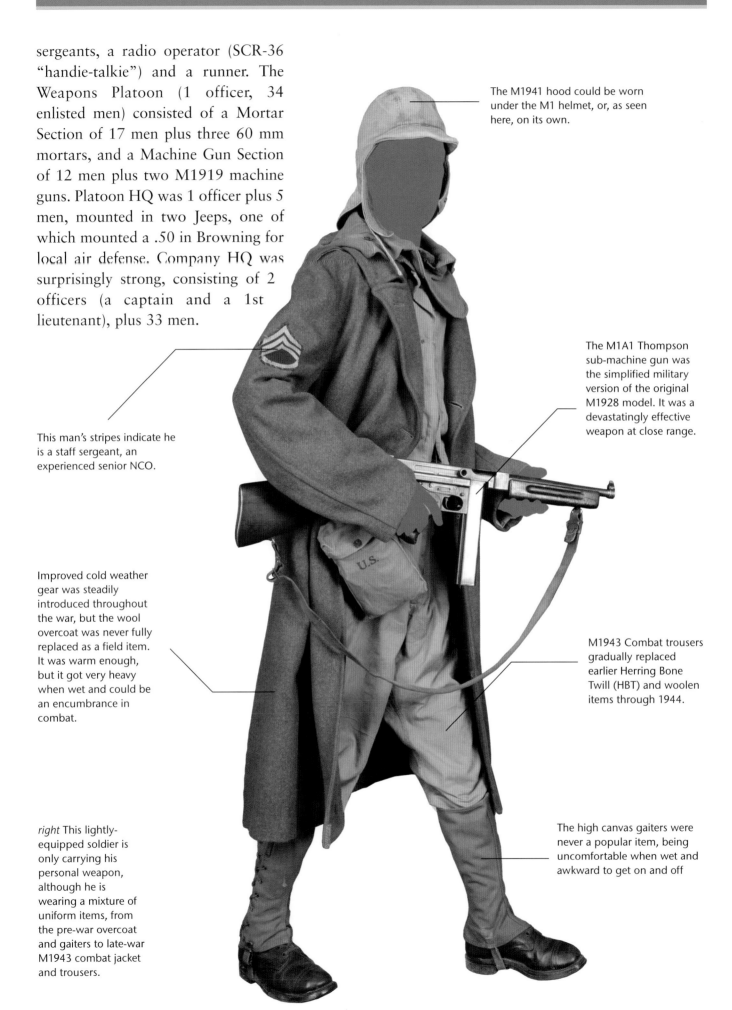

The M1941 hood could be worn under the M1 helmet, or, as seen here, on its own.

The M1A1 Thompson sub-machine gun was the simplified military version of the original M1928 model. It was a devastatingly effective weapon at close range.

This man's stripes indicate he is a staff sergeant, an experienced senior NCO.

Improved cold weather gear was steadily introduced throughout the war, but the wool overcoat was never fully replaced as a field item. It was warm enough, but it got very heavy when wet and could be an encumbrance in combat.

M1943 Combat trousers gradually replaced earlier Herring Bone Twill (HBT) and woolen items through 1944.

right This lightly-equipped soldier is only carrying his personal weapon, although he is wearing a mixture of uniform items, from the pre-war overcoat and gaiters to late-war M1943 combat jacket and trousers.

The high canvas gaiters were never a popular item, being uncomfortable when wet and awkward to get on and off

MEDICAL SERVICES

The Battalion Surgeon was a key man, responsible for treating casualties as soon after their wounding as possible. Usually working under adverse conditions and often under fire, his job was one of the most demanding in the entire medical profession. The equipment and facilities available to a US Army battalion surgeon were probably the best in any army in the war, but that did not make his task any easier or less demanding.

right Medics usually had the red cross symbol painted onto their helmets as seen here. Although in the chaos of combat they couldn't necessarily rely on their enemy respecting the symbol.

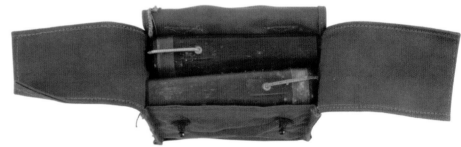

right Known as "Medical Kit B", these pouches have a range of immediate use items. They would be held at squad or platoon level.

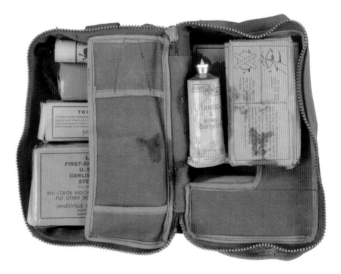

left Serious casualties would be repatriated to theater-level medical facilities or even back to the United States. Clean sheets, first-class medical treatment and care from American Red Cross Nurses such as this one would go a long way towards helping the injured soldier recuperate.

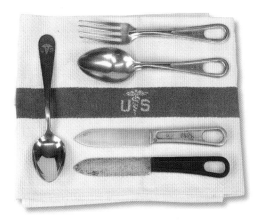

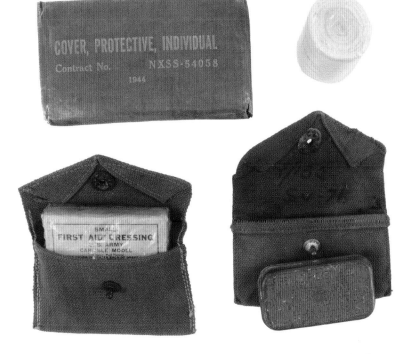

above A cutlery set and napkin bearing the crest of the medical service, as found in military hospitals.

right the pouches are typical of those carried on the soldier's belt, and contain his emergency field dressing. Above and below are a range of items from "Medical Kit A", the immediate-use equipment carried by many soldiers, including quinine tablets, bandages and scissors.

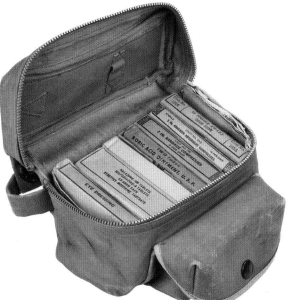

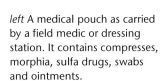

left A medical pouch as carried by a field medic or dressing station. It contains compresses, morphia, sulfa drugs, swabs and ointments.

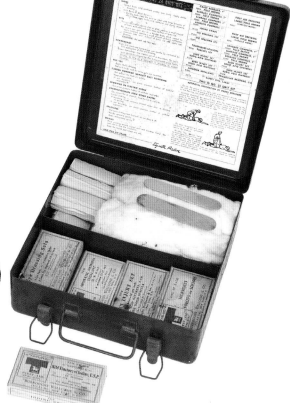

right A large medical kit box with an array of dressings, splints and other items.

THE ARMORED INFANTRY BATTALION

When the US Army entered World War II its armored divisions consisted of two Armored Regiments, each of six Armored Battalions (four medium, two light) and an Armored Infantry Regiment of three battalions. This proved too large and unwieldy and in 1943 division was made smaller and the regimental level of command was removed leaving the division with three Armored and three Armored Infantry Battalions. A new level of headquarters was introduced called a "Combat Command" to which tank and armored infantry battalions were allocated as the tactical situation required. There were originally two such HQs, designated Combat Commands A and B, with a third, Combat Command Reserve, added in 1944. This structure proved much more flexible and remained in use for the rest of the war. In the armored infantry, when the regimental level of command was abolished some logistic assets were transferred to the battalions, leading to the creation of the Service Support Company and resulting in an increase in strength from 700 to around 1,000 officers and enlisted men. The huge increase in

below Combined arms in action. Smoke from a burning building provides cover as men from an Armored Infantry unit sprint forward, escorted by an M4 Sherman tank. Some men are wearing overcoats, the rest just the normal M1941 field jacket.

right The M3 half-track became the standard infantry armored vehicle throughout the war. There were numerous variants, including some mounted with howitzers and anti-tank guns, but the standard transport usually had one or two machine guns, either .50 in or .30 in Brownings. A squad could ride in relative safety, although with no overhead cover the occupants were vulnerable to airbursts and artillery fire.

vehicles led to a requirement for maintenance sections in all companies, while the requirement for gasoline and ammunition was considerable.

The Type 1944 Armored Infantry Battalion comprised 39 officers and 956 enlisted men, every one of whom was mounted in either a half-track or wheeled vehicle, most of which had some form of armored protection. The main fighting strength was the three Armored Rifle Companies, each of three platoons. The standard anti-tank gun was the 57 mm (British 6-pounder), but, in addition there were numerous bazookas to enhance point anti-tank defense. Many vehicles also mounted either .30 or .50 in Browning machine guns.

BATTALION HQ

Nominally part of HQ Company, the Battalion Headquarters (8 Officers, 21 enlisted men) was in reality separate, and, unlike that in the infantry battalion, included the communications personnel.

HEADQUARTERS COMPANY

Headquarters Company (6 officers, 134 enlisted men) was something of a misnomer because it was, by any standard, a heavy weapons company, armed with assault guns, mortars and a large number of machine guns. The Assault Gun Platoon (1 officer, 26 enlisted men) was equipped with three 75mm Howitzer Motor Carriage M8, essentially an M5 Stuart light tank with an open turret in which was mounted a short-barreled 75 mm howitzer, a developed version of the M1A1 pack-howitzer mountain gun. In late 1944 these were replaced by three 105 mm Howitzer Motor Carriage M7B1, an M4A3 Sherman chassis with a fixed open-top fighting compartment mounting a 105 mm howitzer. This was, without doubt, one of the most powerful weapons ever to be an integral component of an infantry battalion in any army. The Machine Gun Platoon (1 officer, 34 enlisted men) was armed with four M1917 belt-fed machine guns. There were two half-tracks, each carrying two machine guns, which could be fired either from the vehicle or dismounted and fired from a tripod on the ground. The Mortar Platoon (1 officer, 24 men) had three carriers, each with one 81 mm tube, which fired from a platform in the rear of the vehicle. The Reconnaissance Platoon (1 officer, 20 enlisted men) had four Jeeps, each with a four-man crew, commanded by a sergeant or corporal. Platoon headquarters had a Jeep and a half-track armed with a pintle-mounted .50 cal M2 Browning machine gun and a loose-stowed bazooka. Finally, there were company headquarters (1 officer, 5 enlisted men), the maintenance section (1 officer, 7 enlisted men) and an administrative section (18 enlisted men).

SERVICE COMPANY

The battalion had a Service Company (7 officers, 68 enlisted men), responsible for administration and logistics. It included: a Supply and Transportation Platoon (2 officers, 21 enlisted men); a Battalion Maintenance Platoon (3 officers, 23 enlisted men); a Personnel Section (1 officer, 5 enlisted men); a Mess and Supply Section (18 enlisted men), and a Company Headquarters (1 officer, 4 enlisted men).

below Another half-track, this time in the field ambulance role. Such a vehicle could get right up to the front line to extract wounded men and transport them to the field hospitals The US soldier generally had superb medical services backing him up.

ARMORED INFANTRY BATTALION c.1944

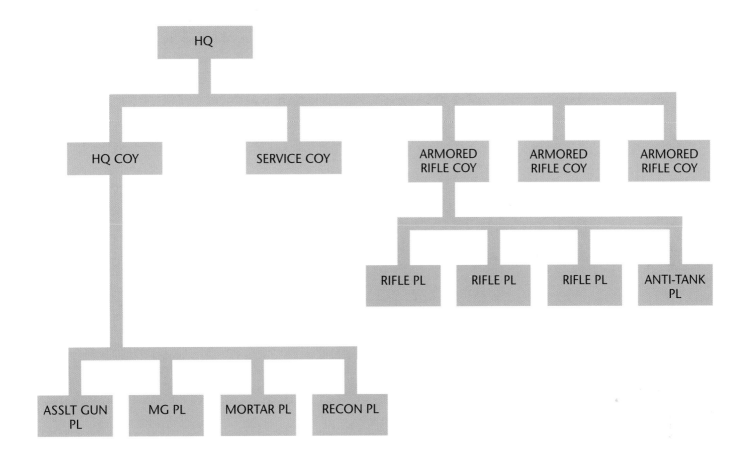

THE ARMORED RIFLE COMPANY

The fighting strength of the Armored Infantry Battalion was in its three Armored Rifle Companies, each comprising three Rifle Platoons and an Anti-tank Platoon (6 Officers, 245 enlisted men in total).

The Rifle Platoon HQ consisted of 1 officer (lieutenant), 2 sergeants and 9 men who functioned as a third rifle squad. The platoon's two rifle squads were each 12 strong, comprising a staff-sergeant, sergeant and 10 men. The Mortar Squad had a single 60 mm mortar and 8 men, while the Machine Gun Squad had 12 men and two M1919 Browning machine guns. The platoon was mobile in five M3A1 half-tracks, one per section, with 1 man being the designated driver. The Platoon HQ and the mortar squad halftracks both mounted a 0.5 in machine gun, the remainder a .30 in machine gun, while all vehicles carried a Bazooka. The Anti-tank Platoon (1 officer, 32 enlisted men) had three squads, each with a half-track towing a 57 mm gun and, in addition, mounting either a .30 cal or M2 .50 cal machine gun. The platoon commander had a Jeep. Finally, the company headquarters included a maintenance section and an administrative section.

COMBAT UNIFORMS

The US Army entered World War II with a variety of outmoded and unsuitable designs for combat clothing. Three years later it had the most advanced combat clothing system of any army – a remarkable transformation. Prior to the outbreak of war there were five types of uniform on general issue.

• **Class A** intended for wear in cold and temperate climates, consisted of a garrison cap, four-button jacket, trousers and shirt, all in olive-drab woolen material. The ensemble was completed by a khaki cotton tie and Service Shoes (actually, ankle boots) in russet-brown leather.

• **Class B,** or garrison uniform, was as for Class A but minus the jacket.

left and below An enlisted man's service cap for wear in the rear areas and in non-combat roles.

left A "garrison cap", a soft, comfortable hat worn in a "fore and aft" style. The top has a "V" indent when the hat is on the head and the pale blue piping indicates the wearer is in the infantry.

• **Class C** was for hot climates and was made of a material known as "chino" in the US which was virtually identical to the British "khaki drill."

• There was also a very smart and popular outfit which consisted of a shirt, tie and trousers, made of beige materials which were perceived to have a slightly pinkish tinge, with a service jacket, which was slightly greener than its predecessor. Thus, the outfit was known throughout the Army as "pinks and greens."

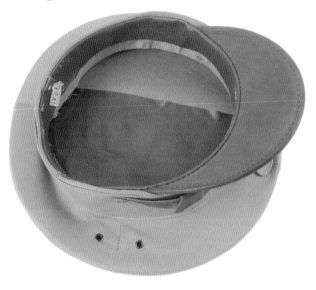

above and below Another service cap, this time in light tan material and intended for wear in summer and warm weather conditions.

left A Military Policeman dressed for keeping order in a rear zone or garrison town. He wears the "Ike" jacket, a short jacket which finishes at the waist and has hidden front buttons, based on the British battledress tunic. He also has high brown boots and a pistol holster. Note the slung bag containing his gas mask.

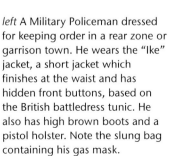

right This wide-brimmed Herring Bone Twill (HBT) hat was popular wear in tropical conditions in the Pacific theater.

left Originally designed as work wear for fatigues, the olive green Herring Bone Twill (HBT) saw widespread use as a combat suit, especially in the Pacific theater.

right Men from Company A, 119 Infantry Regiment, taking cover in a thick hedgerow near Mortain in northern France. The nearest man has an ammunition bandolier around his shoulder and a folding entrenching tool at his waist.

• Finally, there was the "work fatigue" uniform, which consisted of a jacket with twin pockets and trousers, together with a wide-brimmed fatigue cap, all made of a strong cotton olive-drab material.

JACKET, FIELD, OD (PARSON'S JACKET)

The Jacket, Field OD (olive-drab) had been designed by Major-General Parsons and was often referred to as the "Parson's Jacket," but, following the introduction of the Jacket, Field 1943 (see below), it became retrospectively known as the M1941 Field Jacket. In general concept the M1941 Jacket was similar to contemporary civilian-style wind-breakers, but in olive-drab cotton/poplin mix with a flannel

above Combat in Brest in September 1944. One man is wearing a camouflaged suit, an item that was soon withdrawn in Europe as being too easily confused with SS camouflage patterns.

left The M1941 hood, a cold-weather covering that could be closed around the face with a drawstring. It could be worn with or without the M1 steel helmet.

liner. It had a short skirt, front zip covered by a buttoned flap, buttoned collar and wrists, epaulettes, and two vertical pleats at the back to make it easy to wear. There were a number of pockets although they were not particularly capacious. This jacket was considered by troops to be insufficiently warm in winter and too hot in the tropics, on top of which it had insufficient pocket capacity. Despite all that – and even though a replacement appeared in 1943 – the M1941 remained in use until the end of the war.

MACKINAW

One pre-war item that retained its popularity throughout the war was the "Coat, Mackinaw, OD" usually known as either the Mackinaw Jacket, or, more widely, as the "Jeep Coat." First issued in 1938, the design was based on that of a jacket developed in Mackinaw, Michigan, an area between Lakes Huron and Michigan with a particularly bleak winter. This jacket was made of water-repellant cotton duck, lined with a woolen

right This man wears a late-war double-breasted winter jacket with a woolen scarf underneath. His trousers are the M1943 pattern while his boots are the high M1942 Airborne style.

left A pre-war despatch rider wears a fur-lined hat, high riding boots and an early-pattern Mackinaw jacket. Note the fur lining around the collar and the two rows of buttons at the front.

above and right An officer's garrison cap in the winter/temperate material. It has a brown leather peak and the large officers' badge at the front.

below and right The obsolescent M1911 service hat could still be seen in training depots and rear zones. This one has the yellow cords which indicate the cavalry branch.

blanket material which extended over the shawl collar so that it could be turned up to keep the wearer's neck warm. The coat was of double-breasted design and did not have any breast pockets, although there were large pockets in the skirt, which extended halfway down the thighs. There was a built-in cotton belt.

A slightly revised pattern appeared in 1942, which was a little lighter and easier to wear, and the woolen lining did not extend over the collar. The third and last military version appeared in 1943, and was cut more generously to enable it to be worn over other clothing; the belt was deleted and the shawl collar replaced by a more conventional notched type. The whole range of Mackinaw Jackets was superseded by the 1943 pattern OD jacket.

M1943 CLOTHING ENSEMBLE

Faced with rapid expansion and a global commitment, the US Army needed a more logical and coordinated approach to clothing and equipping the soldier. In addition, many of the existing items were proving inadequate, lacking sufficient protection at elbows and knees, and with stitching giving way under stress. This led to the Model 1943 Uniform Ensemble which was based on the layering principle. The design was the source of much internal argument in the development phase, although all was eventually resolved and the outcome was an excellent outfit.

The M1943 Field Jacket was a loose-fitting, single-breasted, olive-drab garment, made from water repellent, windproof cotton sateen, which was longer than the M1941 (Parsons) jacket, extending down to the wearer's mid-thigh. It had a drawstring waist and four pleated and strengthened cargo pockets: two on the chest, two below the waist. There was a detachable hood of the same material but with a fur lining.

Normal headgear was the M1943 Field Cap in olive-drab cotton, or the M1 Helmet system. Further layers could be added underneath as the temperature dropped, including a high-necked

left An officer dressed for northern Europe, with the M1943 jacket and trousers ensemble. The M1943 introduced the concept of a layered system for combat dress and a water-resistant combat jacket with four large pockets on the front. Notice the large gas mask pouch on the left.

above and left The M1943 field cap had a fold-down ear and neck flap. It could be worn under the helmet and was intended to replace the earlier knitted woolen cap.

pullover, but the most important was the Pile Field Jacket.

Field trousers, of the same material as the jacket, were tucked into M1943 Combat Service Boots. Other items in the M1943 range included a Field Pack, an Entrenching Tool and Carrier, and either a Shelter Half, or, for the lucky few, a waterproof Poncho. There were also a set of M1943 Goggles, but these were replaced by a modified design the following year.

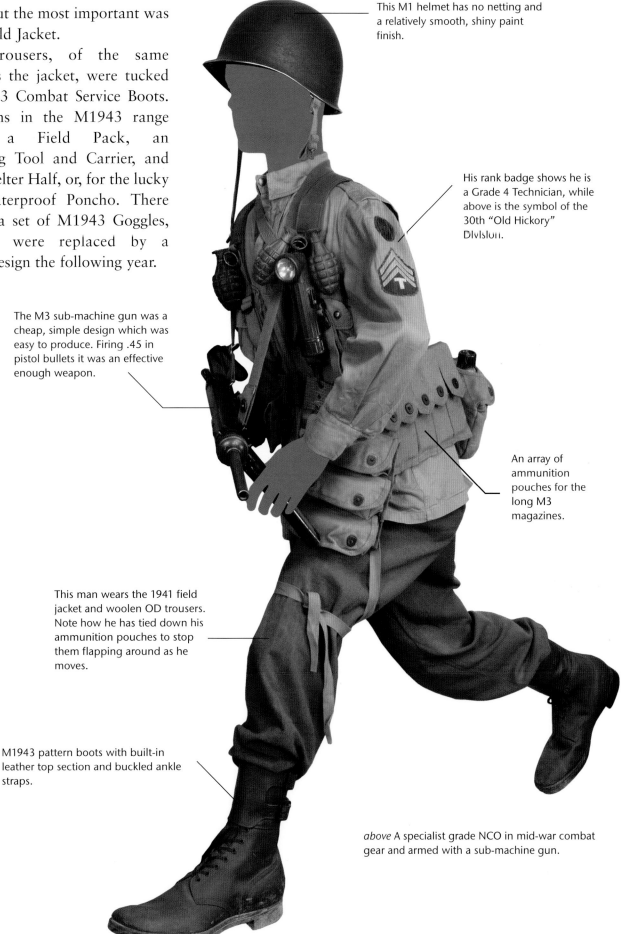

This M1 helmet has no netting and a relatively smooth, shiny paint finish.

His rank badge shows he is a Grade 4 Technician, while above is the symbol of the 30th "Old Hickory" Division.

The M3 sub-machine gun was a cheap, simple design which was easy to produce. Firing .45 in pistol bullets it was an effective enough weapon.

An array of ammunition pouches for the long M3 magazines.

This man wears the 1941 field jacket and woolen OD trousers. Note how he has tied down his ammunition pouches to stop them flapping around as he moves.

M1943 pattern boots with built-in leather top section and buckled ankle straps.

above A specialist grade NCO in mid-war combat gear and armed with a sub-machine gun.

M1 HELMET

The US Army entered World War II wearing the M1917A1 steel helmet, which was virtually identical to the British World War I Brodie helmet. This was, however, rapidly replaced, from 1942 onwards, by the M1 Helmet System, whose characteristic and instantly identifiable shape made it one of the defining images of the US Army in the war. There were four components to the M1. The suspension system, which held the device on the wearer's head, was formed from a series of straps made from white rayon (early production) or OD cotton (later production), and a partial or full leather headband. This suspension system fitted inside the liner, which was originally made from heavily compressed paper fiber, but when this proved very susceptible to damp it was replaced by high-pressure plastic. Then, fitting snugly over the liner was the steel pot, which was made from a single piece of pressed, non-magnetic steel with a narrow, upturned rim lined by a crimped stainless- or manganese-steel band. The only attachments to the steel pot were two bales for the leather chinstrap. Finally, came the helmet covers and netting to camouflage the helmet. It should be noted that while the liner could be worn without the outer shell, it was impossible to wear the shell without the liner. Of necessity, soldiers are an inventive breed, devising uses for their equipment which were never envisaged by designers and staff officers, which in the case of the steel pot included a wash-basin, entrenching tool, seat, hammer for tent pegs, and even a cooking pot.

below and right The US Army began the war mainly equipped with World War I vintage uniforms and equipment. The standard steel helmet was the M1917 shown here, based on the British "Brodie" helmet worn by them through both world wars.

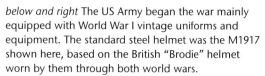

above The infantry were very quickly issued with the M1 helmet, one of the most effective designs ever, and iconic of the American soldier at war.

right and below Inside the steel shell of the M1 was a liner, originally made from compressed paper but later, as shown here, from plastic. The view below shows the outside of the liner, finished in green paint and with a formation badge on the side. The view right shows the strap and suspension system and the unusual "stripe" pattern inside.

left An M1 helmet with a netting cover and with strips of colored hessian attached as camouflage. The inner strap for the liner is wrapped over the front rim.

below A close-up of the straps, suspension system and liner for the M1 helmet.

below Mosquito nets were issued for tropical theaters. They were worn over the helmet and could be rolled down to protect the face and neck.

above Rear view of an M1 helmet. It was common practice, as shown here, to paint a rank indicator on the back of the helmet. Men could see at a glance who the leader was and who to follow.

BOOTS, SERVICE, COMBAT M1943

By mid-1945 the Army's Quartermaster-General was providing footwear for some 8,300,000 soldiers in the US Army, of which 5,000,000 were overseas. He also supplied 100,000 pairs of footwear per month to the US Navy and met all the footwear needs of the Free French and Filipino forces. There were 30 identifiable types of footwear, but by far the majority were the Service Shoe and the Combat Boot, which were provided in every size from 3 to 15? (8.3 in/21.2 cm/ to 12.5 in/31.7 cm) and in widths from AAAA to EEEEE. The scale of issue was two pairs per soldier, and each pair had to be resoled twice before being replaced, with average lives of five months in combat zones and twelve months in the Continental United States.

Up to 1943, the US soldier wore an ankle-high Service Shoe with russet-colored uppers and rubber soles, which was worn in conjunction with canvas leggings. The Service Shoe continued to be worn after the introduction of the Combat Boot, but the design was slightly modified by removing the hardened toecap and using nylon in place of cotton laces. The leggings were laced using a vertical array of hooks and grommets and had a securing strap that passed under the instep.

The Model 1943 Boots, Service, Combat were created by extending the ankle of the Service Shoe upwards with an upper section that was closed by a pair of buckles. Among other benefits, this ended the need for the much-disliked leggings. The leather was reversed with the rough side outermost, which was not only better able to absorb waterproofing oils but was also more durable than a polished leather. The one-piece sole and heel were made either from molded synthetic rubber, or from rubber reclaimed from worn-out boots.

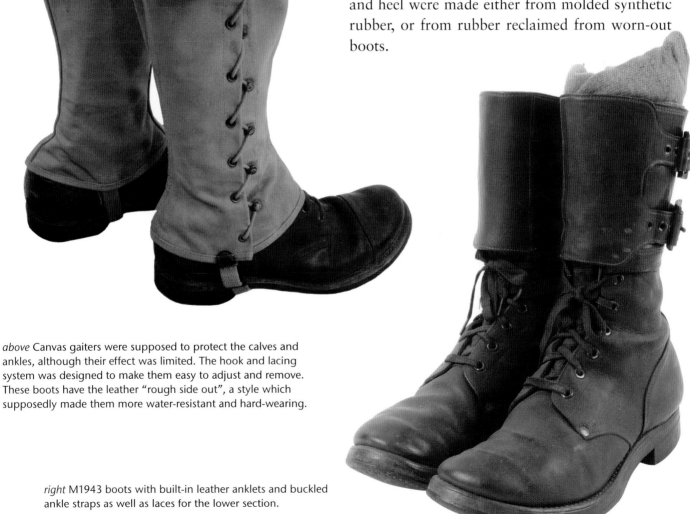

above Canvas gaiters were supposed to protect the calves and ankles, although their effect was limited. The hook and lacing system was designed to make them easy to adjust and remove. These boots have the leather "rough side out", a style which supposedly made them more water-resistant and hard-wearing.

right M1943 boots with built-in leather anklets and buckled ankle straps as well as laces for the lower section.

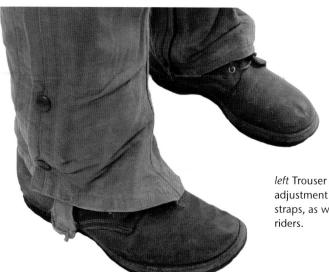

left Trouser bottoms with adjustment studs and boot straps, as worn by despatch riders.

below Pre-war high laced boots, also worn by despatch riders and others.

below High boots with straps and spurs, worn by cavalrymen and as a fashion statement by some general officers.

right White overboots could be issued for winter and mountain conditions.

OTHER ITEMS

right While equipped with webbing belt, steel helmet, grenades and BAR ammunition pouches, this man is really dressed for rear area service. He has the short "Ike" jacket, woolen trousers and boots with no gaiters or other ankle protection.

right An Army soldier dressed in the M1942 camouflage suit. Mainly worn in the Pacific theater it was made in Herring Bone Twill woven material. Both one-piece and two-piece patterns existed, and while at first glance this was similar to the USMC combat suit, unlike the Marines' version it was not reversible.

The M1943 Ensemble was for general issue and was supplemented by a number of more specialized items. One of these was a two-piece oversuit in a camouflage pattern which was issued to some Army troops for the June 1944 Normandy campaign. While this was effective as camouflage, it turned out that it was very similar to the patterns worn by the *Waffen-SS* and after several tragic accidents it was withdrawn.

An item which proved very popular among troops in the European Theater of Operations (ETO) was a long-sleeved, open-collar blouse, which had two pockets and a built-in belt. Introduced in 1944, it was known after its originator as either the "Eisenhower" or the "Ike-jacket" and was made of a slightly darker material than the usual OD. There was a standard pattern for GIs, but officers and their tailors devised many minor variations.

A white snow smock was developed and issued to 10th Mountain Division in Italy in 1944/45. Single-breasted, it was knee-length and buttoned from top to bottom. There was a built-in hood but no pockets. These troops were also issued with Sleeping Bags, Mountain M1942, the first US troops in history to be given anything more than blankets to sleep in.

below Men of the US Ninth Army take cover in Julien, Germany. They are lightly laden, having left their packs with unit transport.

above This man is wearing the winter parka with reversible white lining. He has an officer's despatch case over one shoulder and a small pack over the other.

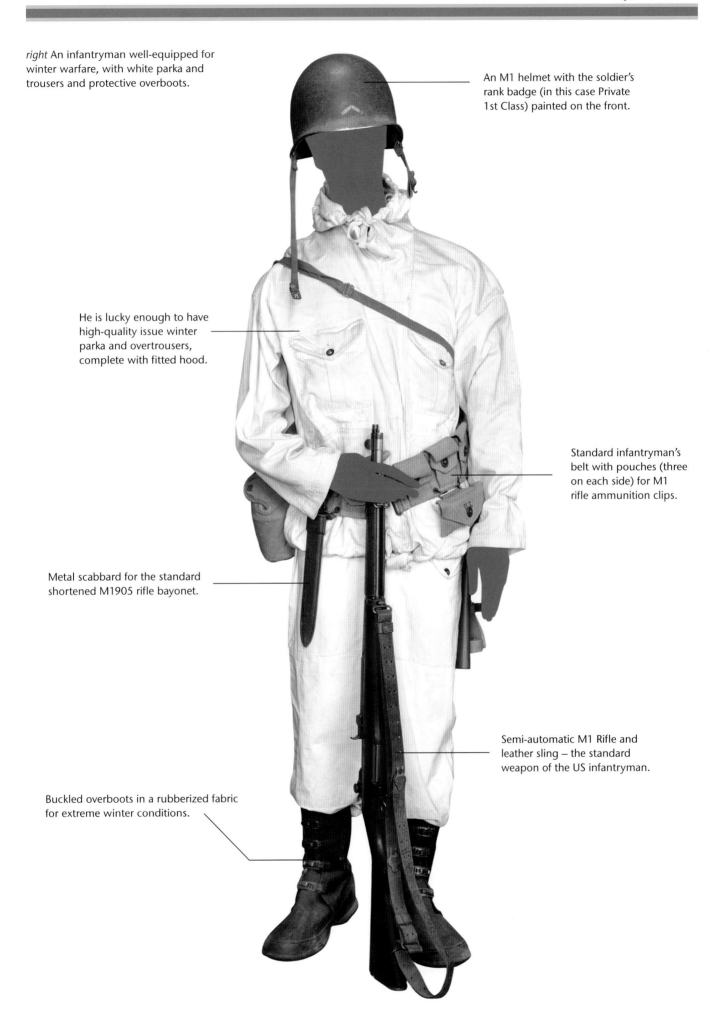

right An infantryman well-equipped for winter warfare, with white parka and trousers and protective overboots.

An M1 helmet with the soldier's rank badge (in this case Private 1st Class) painted on the front.

He is lucky enough to have high-quality issue winter parka and overtrousers, complete with fitted hood.

Standard infantryman's belt with pouches (three on each side) for M1 rifle ammunition clips.

Metal scabbard for the standard shortened M1905 rifle bayonet.

Semi-automatic M1 Rifle and leather sling – the standard weapon of the US infantryman.

Buckled overboots in a rubberized fabric for extreme winter conditions.

PERSONAL EQUIPMENT

The US Army did not have a unified webbing outfit on the same lines as the British 1937 Pattern, but an array of individual items which achieved the same result. These were made of a strong, woven, web material, which was khaki in color until 1944, thereafter olive drab. All metal parts were of aluminum or cast alloy and painted black. All Army webbing items had the letters "U.S." stenciled in black on the outside.

For the enlisted infantryman, the basis of the system was the Belt, Cartridge, Cal .30, Dismounted, M1923. This had ten permanently attached pockets, five per side, each with a flap cover and stud. Each of these could contain two clips of 0.30 in ammunition for the M1 Garand rifle. The belt and pockets all had eyelets for attaching the suspenders, haversack, or other items of equipment. For soldiers carrying the Browning Automatic Rifle there was a different pattern, the Belt, Magazine for BAR, M1937, which had six pockets in total, three each side of the buckle.

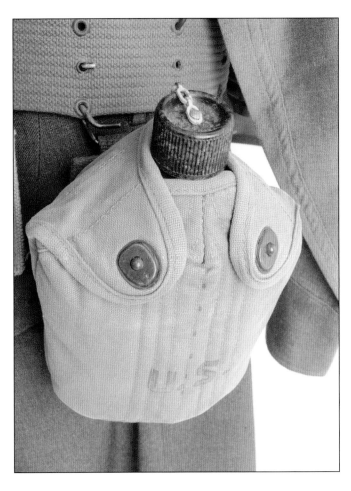

above Metal waterbottle (canteen) and padded fabric carrier.

above Light bags such as this were useful for carrying all sorts of personal and military items.

left A close-up of the standard belt array, with M1 rifle ammunition pouches and field dressing pouch.

right The individual soldier's field dressing was carried in this small M1942 pouch, suspended from his web belt. It allowed a soldier's comrades to quickly find the dressing to use it on the man should he become a casualty.

right An M1944 load-carrying packboard with two packs tied to it. The larger one is the M1944 cargo pack while the smaller is the M1936 pack known as the "musette" bag.

below The standard suspender system had shoulder straps which supported the weight of the belt plus allowing a haversack to be mounted on his back. This man has a Mk 2 grenade attached to one strap.

below A standard shelter half. Two of these could be tied together and pegged out to make a lightweight tent shelter for two men.

Next came the Suspenders, Belt, M1936 with two wide shoulder straps, which provided support for the belt, and on which were mounted D-rings for the haversack straps. Each of the two shoulder straps terminated in four, thinner, adjustable straps, each with a snap-hook to attach to a top-row eyelet on the belt.

There were a number of different sized pockets designed to accommodate magazines for squad and platoon weapons, most of which had a large tunnel loop to enable them to be slid onto the belt. These included pockets for two 0.30 in magazines for the M1 Carbine, two .45 in magazines for the Colt M1911A1 pistol, or five 0.45 in sub-machine gun magazines. There was also a pocket for the first-aid packet, with a double hook for attaching to the belt.

The Haversack, M1928 was the large pack with straps and snap-hooks for attachment to the belt. Apart from the contents of the main compartment, the outside of the pack was used for attaching: bayonet; pouch for mess kit, pan, plate and cutlery; and a triangular extender which increased capacity so that a shelter half and a blanket could also be carried. The Entrenching Tool Cover (see below) could also be attached.

Made in khaki web, the Bag, Canvas, Field, M1936 (also known, for obscure reasons, as a musette bag) was intended for officers, drivers and paratroopers. It had two adjustable Cargo Straps, each with a snap hooks and could be hooked to the bottom of the bag or to the "D" rings of the suspenders.

above The M1944 pack system was seen as a great improvement over the M1928. It came in two parts, the upper combat pack and the detachable lower cargo pack which could be left with unit transport when going into action.

above The M1928 pack was unpopular for being too narrow and too small to carry enough equipment. This one has an M1910 T-handled entrenching tool and carrier strapped to it.

above Wooden case for 12 "K" field rations. Menus varied but each one contained meat plus a range of biscuits, cheese, gum, coffee, candy and other sundries such as toilet paper.

below Individual "K" ration packs. The whole day's ration was supposed to provide enough calories to maintain hard physical activity.

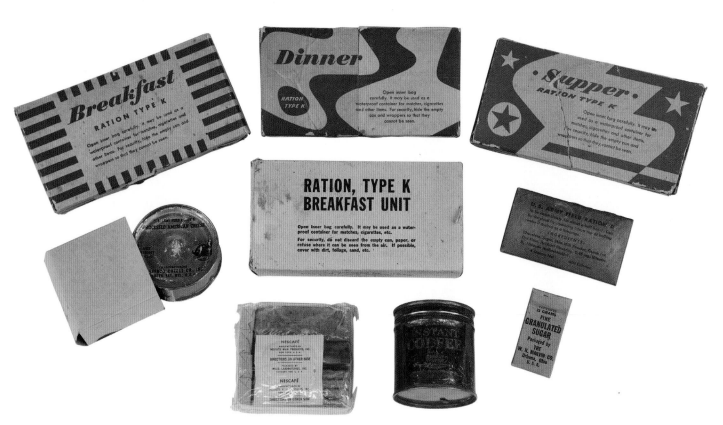

above and right As well as the "K" ration boxes there were individual tins. This one contains dried eggs, not a particularly popular concoction with most soldiers.

above Issue knife, fork and spoon for use with the canteen and mess tins below. The US managed to supply its troops with high-quality, nutritious field rations.

above and right Seen here are the steel canteen cup, an M1910 canteen (waterbottle), a M1942 canteen (with seam) and the two-part mess tin set, known as meat cans.

49

left Mountain warfare demanded specialist equipment such as this Bergen rucksack, a one-piece load carrier that sat firmly on the back.

below These crampons could be strapped onto mountain boots, the spikes underneath giving grip in snow and ice.

above The frame side of the rucksack, showing how it rested on the back yet kept the load reasonably high. A mountain soldier was supposed to be able to live and fight for a few days on the contents of this pack.

above Snow shoes spread the weight of a man and allowed him to traverse soft snow, although they were cumbersome to carry at other times.

right An array of protective goggles, used in dusty or icy conditions, some with glare filters fitted. While useful, such items only rarely found their way down the supply system to the ordinary infantryman.

below A M1910 aluminum canteen with metal cap and padded holder. Later models were enameled or made from plastic, some with Bakelite caps.

above and right Accurate navigation was critical in mobile operations and patrolling. This wrist compass is typical of those issued to officers and NCOs

Officers had a different pattern of belt, the Belt, Pistol, M1936, which had no permanently attached items, but had three continuous rows of eyelets; there were also two metal slides, and male and female buckles. The belt was 42 in (107 cm) long and could be adjusted in length with each of the two unused portions being turned back and hooked into the most appropriate in the central row of eyelets. Most officers also carried a Case,

Dispatch, Canvas, M1938, which, despite its name, was generally used as a map case. It had pockets for papers, notebooks, pencils, etc. It was carried on its own shoulder strap and did not attach to any of the webbing items. Another items for officers was the Compass, Lensatic, which had a lanyard around the officer's neck, and a Carrier Compass, Lensatic on his belt.

CARRYING

The unfortunate infantryman is always being asked to carry extra loads and some of these could be carried in webbing items such as the Bag, Spare Magazine, the Bag, Extra Ammunition, the Carrier, Pack, M1928 and the Grenade Pouch, M1945, whose titles are self-explanatory.

Sometimes, however, the simplest solutions are the best and the general-purpose manpack carrier used within infantry battalions was a brilliant innovation. The Packboard Plywood M1944 consisted of a plywood frame measuring 24 in (61.0 cm) long by 15.2 in (38.4 cm), a cotton backrest that was laced into position, three adjustable shelves, and carrying and securing straps. It was used to carry a wide variety of loads, including, as single loads: a Jerrican filled with either gasoline or water, a Browning M1919 machine gun or a 60 mm mortar. The M1917 MMG was carried as two separate loads – gun and tripod – and the 81 mm mortar in three loads – tube, bipod and baseplate. The packboard could also be used for anything else which would fit, such as radios, batteries, ammunition and so on.

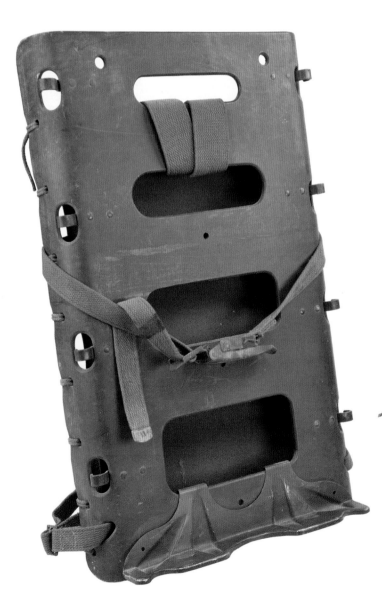

*left and above*The M1944 Packboard was a versatile aid for carrying heavy loads. Packs, heavy weapons, ammunition boxes or anything else could be strapped to it while the tied canvas liner and straps protected the back of the unfortunate carrier.

below The clothing bag or kit bag had both a handle and shoulder strap and was used to carry a soldier's possessions when moving duty station.

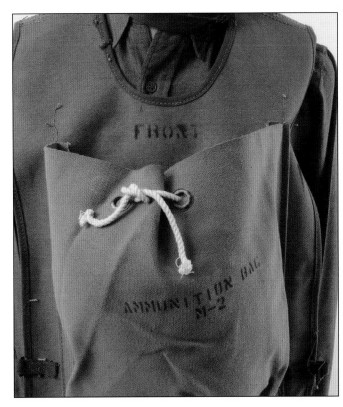

above The M2 ammunition carrying vest went over the top of the combat uniform and was used to carry mortar bombs or machine gun ammunition up to the front line, while leaving the soldier's hands free.

right A rear view of the ammunition carrier, its straps and rear pocket.

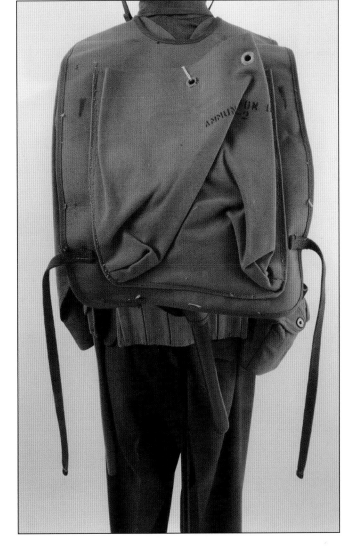

DIGGING TOOLS

At the start of the war, the infantry used the Entrenching Tool M1910, which was a grandiose name for a shovel with a metal blade, short, fixed wooden shaft, and cross-piece to form a handle. This was replaced by the Entrenching Tool, M1943 in which the blade was hinged to the end of the one-piece shaft, with a large nut for securing it in line with the shaft for use as a shovel, at 90 degrees for use as a hoe, or folded back along the shaft for carrying. With the endless and always urgent need for digging foxholes this was one of the most valuable items in the infantryman's kit. These two models each had

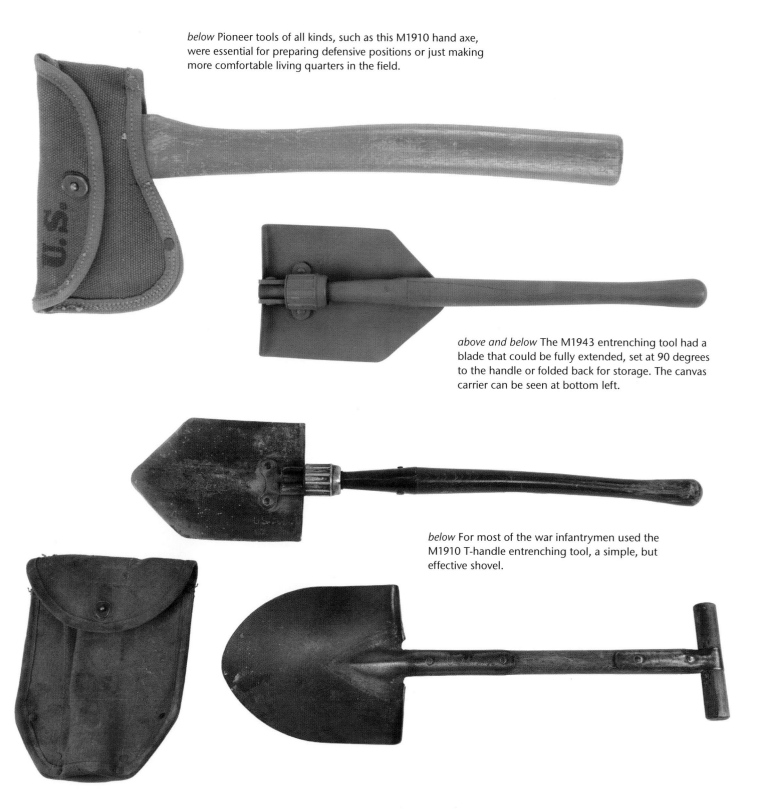

below Pioneer tools of all kinds, such as this M1910 hand axe, were essential for preparing defensive positions or just making more comfortable living quarters in the field.

above and below The M1943 entrenching tool had a blade that could be fully extended, set at 90 degrees to the handle or folded back for storage. The canvas carrier can be seen at bottom left.

below For most of the war infantrymen used the M1910 T-handle entrenching tool, a simple, but effective shovel.

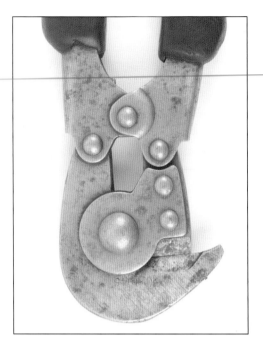

below The M1943 folding entrenching tool was held in this canvas carrier which was in turn strapped to the pack or web suspenders.

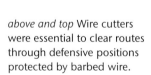

above and top Wire cutters were essential to clear routes through defensive positions protected by barbed wire.

their own web carrier which attached to the Haversack M1928 or, if that was not being worn, to the Suspenders. Similarly, several soldiers in each squad carried a Pick Mattock, M1910, while others carried an Axe, Hand, M1910, again each with its own purpose-made webbing carrier. Also carried by some of the men were the Barbed Wire Cutter, M1938 and the Mark 2 Machete each of which had their own webbing sheaths.

GAS PROTECTION

As described above, the design and production of military equipment for the US Army in World War II was generally a great success, with outstanding equipment being supplied in generous quantities. Unfortunately, this could not be said of its gas masks, which, despite being produced in vast numbers, were never fully satisfactory. Indeed, it was fortunate that they were never put to the test of combat. The problem – which was never properly solved – was to combine satisfactory anti-gas performance with comfort, lightness, adequate speech transmission and eyepieces that did not mist up.

The army entered the war with the M1A2 respirator, in which the facepiece was fabricated from stockinette covered in rubber sheets, and with eyepieces and sockets which were assembled by hand, using cement, adhesive tapes and vulcanization. As with other armies at that time, the filter was housed in a separate metal canister and was connected to the facepiece by a 27 in (70 cm) rubber hose. The M2 mask, initially designed

for use only in training as a cheaper substitute for the M1A2, had a molded facepiece and on the outbreak of war this was selected for production, although it was unpopular due to its heavy weight of 5 lb (2.2 kg) and was severely criticized in the Tunisian campaign. The next step was the M3, which was lighter at 3.5 lb (1.6 kg), had a smaller canister and shorter hose, and was virtually as effective as the M2; this entered production in 1943. Production problems with the facepiece led to a temporary solution, the M4 mask which was the M2 mask reconstructed with lightweight components, but still connected to a separate filter.

There were more complaints from field units, which led to the M5 mask, in which the canister and hose were replaced by a cheek-mounted filter. Due to a shortage of rubber, the M5 facepiece was made from neoprene and the particularly severe 1944/45 winter in Northwest Europe revealed that this material became rigid in cold weather. Production of the M5 then had to be halted and a

left A fearsome lineup during a training exercises in October 1942 wearing old-style gas masks with separate filters.

right US Army Chemical Mortar Battalions were equipped with the 4.2 in heavy mortar, designed to fire gas-filled projectiles at ranges of up to 5000 yd. Thousands of such projectiles were made but were never used in action. Instead this highly-accurate rifled mortar became a popular source of fast-reacting explosive firepower. It's most common use, however, was to create smoke screens, mainly by firing White Phosphorus (WP) bombs. WP could create a thick white smoke screen very quickly, the effect begin enhanced by by the choking effect of the smoke and burning fragments of phosphorus being showered around the target area.

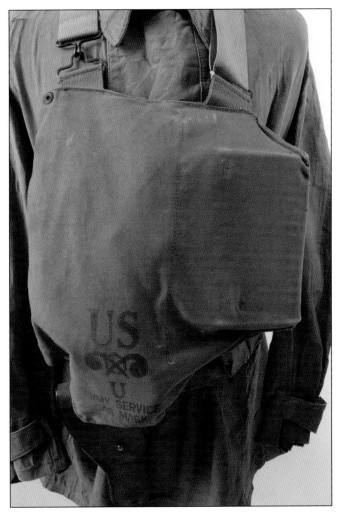

left Bulky carrying case for M1 or M2 gas mask. Combat in gas conditions would have been a desperately difficult affair, with cumbersome masks hindering movement, visibility and shooting.

new mask devised, with the M2 and M3 facepiece coupled with a new adapter to accommodate a chin-mounted filter canister.

Other items of anti-gas equipment included an eyeshield which gave protection against enemy aircraft spraying mustard gas, and the British gas cape and hood which enveloped both the wearer and his equipment.

Fortunately, this equipment, although tested in laboratories and "gas-chambers" was never used in combat, where it might well have been found lacking. The one item that did prove of real use, although not for its intended purpose, was the waterproof bag designed to carry the complete anti-gas outfit. This was worn on the chest and proved to be a very satisfactory lifebelt when some landing-craft were sunk during the D-Day landings, saving a number of lives in the process!

MAKING LIFE EASIER

above While hardly field items, devices such as this gramophone could help while away the monotony of barracks existence.

left Where possible, personal hygiene was important for morale and the health of the troops. Seen here is an array of soaps, cleaning and shaving gear and a personal metal mirror.

left A neat shaving kit complete with razor and fresh blades in its canvas pouch.

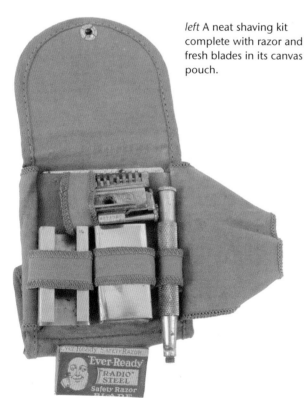

above Delousing powder and two brands of tooth powder cover both external and internal hygiene needs.

right An issue metal soap dish complete with army identifying label.

above Cigarettes such as these became a form of currency in the front line and between soldiers and civilians.

above Small comforts become incredibly important in the field. For many, tobacco was a vital morale booster and this array of cigarettes, matches and loose leaves would have gladdened the hearts of most GIs.

right Tobacco is useless without a means of ignition, and here we show both safety and water-resistant matches.

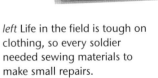

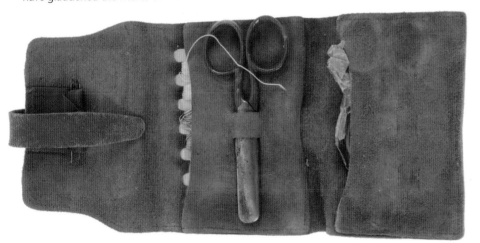

below Prophylactic cream could be issued to soldiers, although as far as sex was concerned the army had to walk a fine line between pragmatism and setting an acceptable moral tone.

left Life in the field is tough on clothing, so every soldier needed sewing materials to make small repairs.

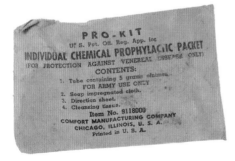

right Gum was probably as iconic to the US soldier as the M1 helmet and the Garand rifle. It was also popular with Allies, civilians and captured prisoners alike.

below The *Stars and Stripes* newspaper was produced army-wide and was an attempt to keep the American soldier informed as to what was going on in the war.

above Two booklets providing background information on France and Japan alongside an "uplifting" army song book.

left Yank magazine was a glossy, well-illustrated production showing the work of the army.

left This personal service mail or "V" mail would have been highly-prized by the recipient.

above A Christmas parcel of "goodies", one of millions sent out to make life slightly easier for the boys at the front.

right Humorous and illustrated postcards were popular both with civilians and soldiers.

below Glamour pinups were (and still are) popular with lonely young men, thousands of miles and many months away from home.

below Playing cards were easily carried and provided a way of passing many hours of otherwise boring time. Below the packs shown here are some army currency used for purchases in France and occupied Germany.

COMMUNICATIONS

The US Army conducted only limited development of military electronic communications during the 1920s, because interest in military matters was low and funds limited. Some equipment began to reach units in the late 1930s but by 1940 the predominant means of communication in the forward areas remained cable telephones, messengers and visual signaling. Once it was clear that war was coming, however, US industry became involved and the pace of progress was rapid.

RADIO

In the 1930s, radio sets were bulky and heavy, which meant that they had to be carried in a vehicle, on the backs of the still widely-used mules, or split into two- or even three-man loads. A particular, but now often forgotten problem, was that of power supplies. Vehicle-borne radio stations could use wet (secondary) cells charged from the vehicle engine, while static sets could use mobile generators. More portable sets depended on dry (primary) batteries, which were heavy, bulky, had a short life and could not be recharged.

At the start of America's war in December 1941, tactical radio communications extended as far as battalion command posts, but once viable man-portable radio sets began to appear they were soon extended forward to company and then platoon level. There was also an early desire to achieve what would later become known as "interoperability" so that artillery, tank and infantry units could all talk to each other on the battlefield, as well as to ground support aircraft.

The battalion command post was linked to superior headquarters, to the artillery unit in direct support and forwards to the company command posts. By 1944 the rifle companies each had six radio sets to provide a company net, with one station at the company command post, one each at each of the four rifle platoons, and one for the company commander to use when away from his HQ.

The most commonly used set was the SCR-538, which was issued in various forms, all providing voice only communications in the 20-28 Megacycle range. The first "walkie-talkie," SCR-195, appeared in 1938 but although intended for use by infantry at company/platoon level, was both large and heavy. This was succeeded in 1942 by the first "handie-talkie", the SCR-536. A significant advance in the war years was the gradual transfer from HF up to the VHF range, and from amplitude modulation (AM) to frequency modulation (FM) both of which resulted in more reliable and much better quality communications.

right The SCR-536 "walkie-talkie" was introduced towards the end of the war for company-platoon communications. It contained five tubes, had 50 crystal-controlled channels, and was powered by a dry battery. A masterpiece of design, it was the world's first really portable radio system.

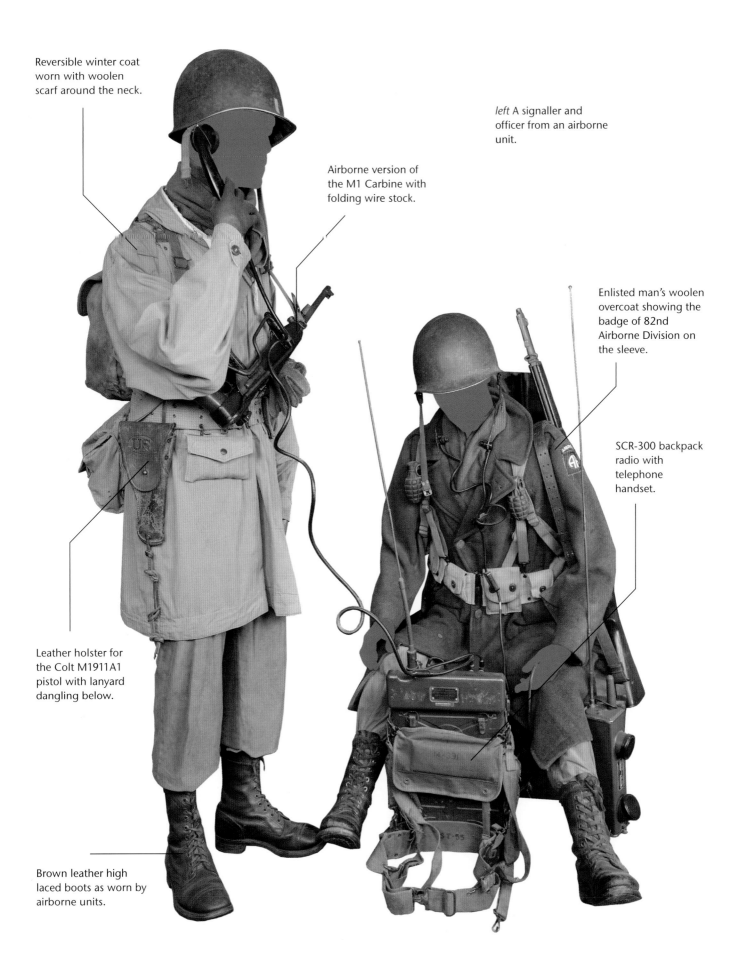

Reversible winter coat worn with woolen scarf around the neck.

left A signaller and officer from an airborne unit.

Airborne version of the M1 Carbine with folding wire stock.

Enlisted man's woolen overcoat showing the badge of 82nd Airborne Division on the sleeve.

SCR-300 backpack radio with telephone handset.

Leather holster for the Colt M1911A1 pistol with lanyard dangling below.

Brown leather high laced boots as worn by airborne units.

MESSENGERS

Messengers provided relatively fast and secure communications, and could, where necessary, carry bulky documents, maps, and so on. Such men needed to be skillful, intelligent and determined, and able to find their way from one command post to another, often on their own and at night, and sometimes under fire. Pools of such men were maintained at company and platoon level, until the widespread use of radio rendered them unnecessary.

above and right Even with effective portable radios, signal flags could be a useful, silent form of communication – in daylight anyway.

right Whistles were also useful for signaling and could often cut through the sounds of combat.

left Over longer distances signal flares fired from pistols such as this could be used to give instructions or identify the firer's location to other units.

LINE

Line provided secure communications, but required time to lay, and both cable and drums were heavy. As soon as command posts halted wiremen had to lay cable around the headquarters and forward to subordinate command posts, all of which took time. Then, once they had been laid the routes had to be maintained and breakages repaired, then when the next move took place the lines had to be reeled in, cleaned and prepared for reuse. A particularly valuable use for telephones was for Observation Posts (OPs) and Listening Posts (LPs). The main telephone in use in the forward areas was the EE-8 which entered service in 1938. It was lighter than its predecessor and had much better range, and was originally delivered in a leather carrying-case. Once military operations in the Pacific started, this case was found to rot in the humid atmosphere and had to be replaced by a canvas bag.

The CE-11 was a small frame device which was carried by the operator on by a strap around his neck and used for laying 1/4-mile lengths of assault cable or the slightly heavier W-130. Rather larger was the RL-16, a two-wheeled handcart, which carried two DR-4 drums. Speed was always required and the "back-room boys" produced some sophisticated devices including the MX-301/302 dispenser which could be used to lay assault cable from a vehicle at speeds of up to 60 mph, or from liaison aircraft such as the Piper L-4 Cub.

right Where technical means weren't suitable there was always the despatch rider who could deliver a written message on a motorcycle or by any other transport he could get hold of. This one has his gas mask in its bag on his chest.

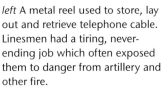

left A metal reel used to store, lay out and retrieve telephone cable. Linesmen had a tiring, never-ending job which often exposed them to danger from artillery and other fire.

MESSAGE CENTER

Key to the communications at battalion level was the Message Center Chief, who coordinated access to communications systems and decided how messages were to be sent: whether by radio, telephone or messenger.

INFANTRY WEAPONS

Built by some of the most advanced arms manufacturers in the world, US infantry weapons were, on the whole, reliable and effective. There were very few failures, and the US soldier was lucky to be equipped with an excellent array of weapons, many of which served on for years after the war.

The military were lucky to benefit from the designs of John Browning, an engineering genius and probably the best weapons designer ever. His automatic pistol (the Colt M1911A1), automatic rifle (BAR), light machine gun (M1919), medium machine gun (M1917) and heavy machine gun (M2) provided the backbone of US infantry firepower throughout the war and beyond.

With the M1 Garand, the United States was the first major nation to equip its front-line forces with general issue automatic rifle. This decision could have risked America's fighting men going to war with an unreliable and overly-complex weapon, but the design proved to be an outstanding rifle which served with distinction all around the world.

The US military also had one of the first effective sub-machine guns in the shape of the M1928 (and later M1A1) Thompson. Other automatic weapons were less successful, such as the Johnson rifle and light machine gun.

Innovation was also apparent in the design of the first shoulder-launched anti-tank rocket, the M1 "Bazooka".

When you add the list of automatic weapons to effective mortar designs and other support weapons, it is apparent that a US infantry platoon or company could put down more firepower than almost any foreign equivalent.

left and below On the left is a box of .50 in rounds for the M2 heavy machine gun in a disintegrating metal-link belt. On the right is a box of .30 in rounds in a canvas belt for the M1917 or M1919 machine guns. In the centre are 8-round clips of .30 in as used with the M1 Garand rifle.

above Near Fontainebleau in August 1944, US infantry move up behind a tank destroyer. The figure nearest the camera has an M1 rifle, a 2.35 in Bazooka over his shoulder and his jacket tucked into his belt at the back.

right A Bazooka anti-tank team take cover behind a cut-down tree to cover the road. The loader is at the rear, although he will need to make sure he doesn't get caught by the blackblast when the rocket is fired.

RIFLES

RIFLE, .30 CAL M1903 (SPRINGFIELD)

Type: bolt-action rifle
Origin: US
Caliber: .30 in
Weight (empty): 8.7 lb (3.9 kg)
Barrel length: 24.0 in (610 mm)
Ammunition: .30-06 Springfield
Feed: 5-round internal box

At the end of the nineteenth century the US Army started a search for a new rifle using the Mauser-principle bolt-action. The first prototypes had a 30 in (762 mm) barrel but it was decided to reduce the length to a more manageable 24 in (610 mm). The new weapon from the Springfield Arsenal was type classified in 1903, but there were several further modifications, including, crucially, a newer, lighter and more pointed bullet,

before it entered service. Always known as the "Springfield rifle" it was in production and service for many years

The M1903A1 was a 1929 version with a pistol-grip butt stock and the M1903A3 was a Remington redesign in 1942 to facilitate production, while the M1903A4 was a sniper version, which lacked any iron sights and was fitted to accommodate a variety of telescopic sights.

above The M1903 Springfield was a popular, reliable and effective bolt-action rifle. This one was made by Remington.

above An M1903 produced by Smith-Corona.

above An M1903A4 equipped with a sniper scope.

above Another sniper variant, this time a Remington-made M1903A5. Note the protective endcaps on the sight.

RIFLE, .30 CAL M1 (GARAND)

Type: self-loading rifle
Origin: US
Caliber: .30 in
Weight (empty): 9.5 lb (4.4 kg)
Barrel length: 24.0 in (610 mm)
Ammunition: .30-06 Springfield
Feed: 8-round internal box

This outstanding rifle was designed by John C. Garand (1887–1974), who had been working at the Springfield Arsenal since 1919. Its design resulted from the US Army's experience in World War I and it competed with several other self-loading designs before being selected in 1936. Considering that it was the first self-loader to enter service with any army and the great enhancement it brought to squad firepower, it was remarkably simple, reliable and robust, although at 9.5 lb (4.4 kg) it was quite heavy. The Garand was gas-operated with an internal eight-round magazine, which could only be loaded using a

above An early-production M1 Garand, probably the best general-issue rifle of the war.

above A later M1 with the more common barrel and foresight configuration.

below A Springfield-made M1 with the leather sling attached.

right The large can contains "rifle grease" for applying to moving parts while the smaller contains light oil, used to lubricate and preserve metal parts from corrosion.

special clip filled with eight rounds in two staggered rows of four each. When the final round had been fired the empty clip was automatically ejected and the bolt remained open, telling the firer that the magazine was empty and he had to reload. The rifle was fully stocked, with exposed barrel and gas cylinder, and equipped with a neat, double-edged bayonet which fitted onto a bayonet bar beneath the barrel.

Various developments were designed and tested, including the M1E1, -E3 and -E4 with changes to the mechanism and the M1E5 and -T26 with shorter barrels, but none ever went into production. However, a number of sniper versions did see service use.

above and left An M1 rifle configured for sniping, with the Griffin & Howe side mount, M82 sight and leather cheek pad.

below This sniper variant has a conical flash hider on the muzzle to prevent the firer being temporarily dazzled, especially in dim light.

RIFLE, .30 CAL M1941 (JOHNSON)

Type: self-loading rifle
Origin: US
Caliber: .30 in
Weight (empty): 9.7 lb (4.3 kg)
Barrel length: 22.0 in (558 mm)
Ammunition: .30-06 Springfield
Feed: 10-round rotary, internal

Melvin Johnson, a captain in the US Marine Corps Reserve, designed two weapons, which, despite their ingenuity, never gained wide acceptance. The first was this rifle, which was passed to the Army testing authorities in 1938. The Garand was already in service and not encountering problems, so in 1940 the Ordnance Committee ordered all effort to be concentrated on the Garand and to ignore the Johnson. The company then won an order for 70,000 rifles from the Dutch government-in-exile for supply to their forces in the Dutch East Indies, but this became null-and-void when the islands fell in the Japanese onslaught in early 1942. Some 30,000 of the Dutch weapons were taken on by

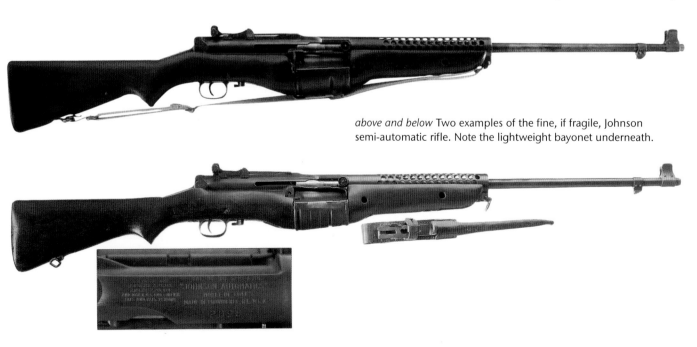

above and below Two examples of the fine, if fragile, Johnson semi-automatic rifle. Note the lightweight bayonet underneath.

the US Marine Corps, with whom it saw limited service in Europe and the Pacific.

The Johnson rifle used short recoil in combination with an eight-lug rotating bolt. The magazine was built into the weapon, and was semicircular in shape; the rifle could be reloaded, even if the bolt was closed. The rear half of the barrel was sheathed in a pierced sheet-steel jacket to assist cooling. The return-spring was housed in a tube which ran through the narrow wrist and then along the full length of the butt. Since the barrel reciprocated backwards and forwards when firing, there was a particular problem in firing the weapon with a fixed bayonet. As a result the existing bayonet could not be used and a special lightweight spike bayonet had to be designed.

Compared to the Garand, the Johnson had a larger magazine capacity and less recoil. On the other hand it was larger, less reliable and had a multiplicity of small parts which could be lost when stripping and cleaning in the field. Had the weapon been accepted for widespread service and developed properly these could probably have all been cured, but it was not to be.

CARBINE, .30 CAL M1

Type: carbine
Origin: US
Caliber: .30 in
Weight (empty): 5.5 lb (2.5 kg)
Barrel length: 18.0 in (458 mm)
Ammunition: .30 US Carbine
Feed: 15/30-round removable box

The M1 carbine stemmed from a US Army 1930s requirement for a weapon for junior officers and non-commissioned officers, which would be lighter and easier to carry than the Garand, but with more firepower than a pistol. It was also intended for mortarmen, drivers and wiremen, for whom the M1 Garand was too awkward. The result was the Winchester M1 carbine; in effect, a light self-loading rifle, but, it is important to note that it was not a development of the Garand, nor, indeed, did it fire the same cartridge.

above Light, handy, yet reasonably powerful, the M1 carbine was a popular weapon, especially with drivers or men who had to carry something else, such as a radio, mortar or machine gun.

right The .30 in M1 cartridge had a blunt-nosed bullet and was shorter and less powerful than the .30-06 of the Garand rifle.

DO NOT USE AS FOOD CONTAINER
600 CARTRIDGES
CAL .30 CARBINE
BALL M1
IN IORD CLIPS BANDOLEERS
LOT WRA 22753

above and below The upper carbine has a bayonet attached and an ammunition pouch strapped to the butt, while the lower has the folding wire stock

Cartridge	Type	Length		Bullet weight
		Complete Round	Case Only	
.30-06 Springfield	Rimless necked	8.36 mm	6.1 mm	9.72 g
.30 US Carbine	Rimless straight	4.25 mm	3.28 mm	7.0 g

Some five-and-a-half million M1s were produced and they fulfilled an obvious need, although technically the carbine fell between a self-loading rifle and a sub-machine gun.

The M1A1 Carbine designed for airborne forces had the same action as the M1, but with a folding, skeleton stock and a pistol grip which enabled the weapon to be fired with the stock folded. Approximately 150,000 of these were manufactured. There was also the M2 which entered service in 1944, which had a selective fire lever on the left side of the action and the 30-round magazine as standard.

below A carbine with early night-vision equipment, comprising an infra-red searchlight, battery pack and infra-red scope. A few of these systems saw service before the end of the war.

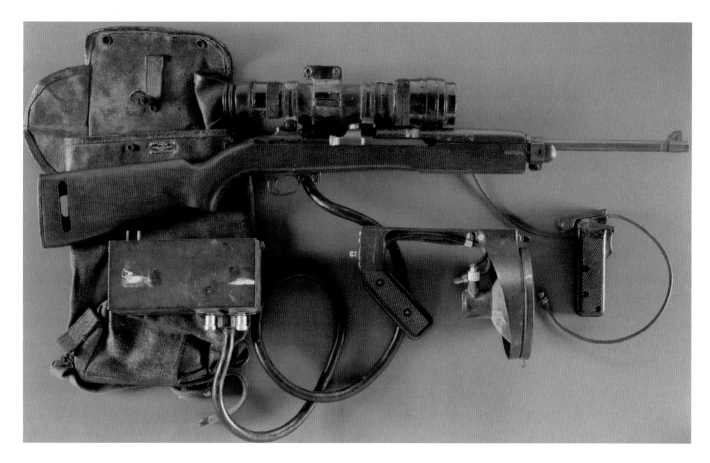

TRAINING RIFLES

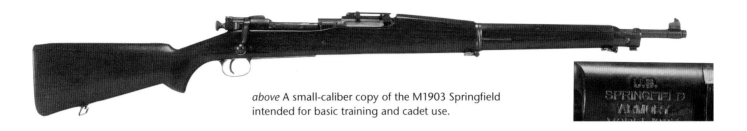

above A small-caliber copy of the M1903 Springfield
intended for basic training and cadet use.

above Training rifles such as this allowed handling
skills to be gained without the cost, recoil and sound
of full-caliber rounds.

above A civilian target rifle stamped as "US Property"
and used as a training aid.

above Training weapons such as this Stevens rifle
would have given many young men their introduction
to military shooting.

PISTOLS

COLT M1911A1

Type: automatic pistol
Origin: US
Caliber: .45 in
Weight (empty): 39 oz (1.1 kg)
Barrel length: 5.0 in (127 mm)
Ammunition: .45 ACP
Feed: 7-round removable box

above The Colt M1911, the iconic US military pistol.

Some officers may have carried their privately owned handguns in combat – General George Patton had a variety of such weapons at his disposal – but these were few in number and the vast majority carried the excellent Colt M1911A1. The original Model 1911 was produced in huge numbers and used by the US Army throughout World War I. In 1921 various modifications were made, incorporating the lessons of the recent fighting. These included a longer horn on the grip safety, a shorter hammer, and the chamfering away of arc-shaped grooves behind the trigger to make it more comfortable to operate.

There were four main components. The receiver was the main body and included the grip, trigger and ribs. The barrel, machined out of high quality steel, was locked in position when forward and then withdrew only a very short distance on firing before disengaging from the third component, the slide, which continued rearwards to eject the empty case and chamber a new round. Finally, there was the magazine, which held seven rounds. Now designated the M1911A1 this remained in production for many decades and was standard throughout the US Army during World War II and beyond. It was a single-action weapon, using the Browning swinging-link lock, and had a grip safety. It was well balanced, very reliable and easy to use, but, like all handguns, its accuracy was more up to the shooter than to the weapon itself.

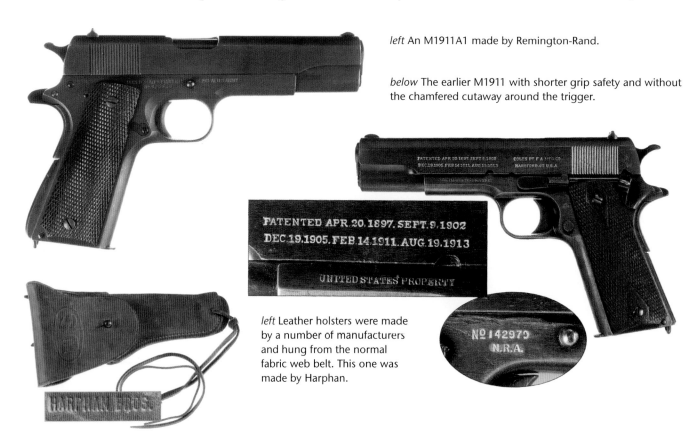

left An M1911A1 made by Remington-Rand.

below The earlier M1911 with shorter grip safety and without the chamfered cutaway around the trigger.

PATENTED APR. 20. 1897. SEPT. 9. 1902
DEC. 19. 1905. FEB. 14. 1911. AUG. 19. 1913

UNITED STATES PROPERTY

№ 142979
N.R.A.

left Leather holsters were made by a number of manufacturers and hung from the normal fabric web belt. This one was made by Harphan.

above An M3 shoulder holster made Enger-Kress, sometimes worn by officers, especially in airborne units.

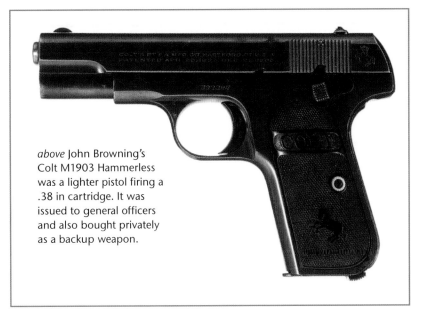

above John Browning's Colt M1903 Hammerless was a lighter pistol firing a .38 in cartridge. It was issued to general officers and also bought privately as a backup weapon.

SMITH AND WESSON M1917 REVOLVER

Type: double-action revolver
Origin: US
Caliber: .45 in
Weight (empty): 2.25 lb (1.02 kg)
Barrel length: 5.5 in (140 mm)
Ammunition: .45 ACP
Feed: 6-round cylinder

The Colt M1911 had ostensible replaced revolvers as the US Army's standard handgun, but production couldn't keep up with demand in both World War I and II. Various version of Colt and Smith and Wesson revolvers were put into production and found their way into the hands of front line soldiers as well as those in support and service arms. many revolvers were used in their original .38 in caliber but thousands were also produced chambered for the same .45 in ACP as the M1911.

Hundreds of thousands were made and also served in British and Canadian forces.

left A short-barreled Smith and Wesson in .38 in calibre and issued as an army weapon.

below A Colt Army Special from World War I and brought out of retirement for World War II.

left A Colt Army special with army markings and a 1917 date stamp.

SUB-MACHINE GUNS

THOMPSON M1928A1

above The original M1928 Thompson, with top cocking handle, pistol grip fore-end and the ability to take a 50-round drum magazine.

Left: A three-way magazine pouch for the 20-round box used by the Thompson.

above The M1 Thompson with 30-round magazine and simpler fore-end and mechanism.

Type: sub-machine gun
Origin: USA
Caliber: .45 in
Weight (empty): 10.8 lb (4.9 kg)
Barrel length: 10.5 in (267 mm)
Ammunition: .45 ACP
Feed: 50-round clockwork drum; 20-round box.

For millions of moviegoers around the world in the 1930s, the Thompson sub-machine gun ("Tommy-gun") was not only an archetypical gangster weapon, but also *the* sub-machine gun. It was relatively small, easy to handle, did not require much skill and had a devastating effect at close quarters. In addition, its unique shape gave it an instantly recognizable appearance. Invented and developed by Colonel J.T. Thompson during World War I, the gun was ready too late to enter large-scale

production. Money remained tight throughout the 1920s, but even so it was produced in small numbers for law enforcement agencies, and, as Hollywood noted, some found their way into the hands of gangsters.

The original version had a rectangular receiver, removable butt, partially finned barrel, muzzle compensator, and two well-raked pistol grips. It could be served by either a spring-driven 20-round box magazine, or, more usually, by a 50-round, clockwork-driven, drum magazine. It was chambered for .45 in ACP, the standard US Army pistol round. It worked by the usual blowback system but with a built-in momentary delay to prevent the bolt opening until the pressure inside the barrel had dropped slightly after firing. This kept the cyclic rate down to a manageable 800 rpm

and aided accuracy. The Tommy gun was not adopted by the US Army until 1938 when it was accepted as the M1928A1. It was then produced in vast numbers and widely used by US armed forces and many of their allies.

In 1942 the improved M1 version was introduced, primarily in order to ease production. This had the delayed blowback system replaced by simple blowback, was given a wooden fore-end in place of the forward pistol grip, could only use the box magazine and had a butt that was no longer removable. The barrel was the same length as before but overall the weapon was 1.75 in (43 mm) shorter. This was quickly followed by the M1A1, in which the separate firing pin and hammer of the M1 were replaced by a fixed firing pin.

REISING MODEL 50

Type: sub-machine gun
Origin: US
Caliber: .45 in
Weight (empty): 6.18 lb (3.1 kg)
Barrel length: 11.0 in (280 mm)
Ammunition: .45 ACP
Feed: 12- or 20-round box.

right Two Marine Corps paratroopers pose in 1943 with their Reising sub-machine guns across their emergency parachutes.

Acceptance trials for new weapons are so demanding, particularly in the US armed forces, that it is unusual for a weapon to fail in service, but that is what happened to the Reising Model 50. It was developed in the late 1930s by Eugene Reising (who had once worked with legendary John Browning), patented in 1940 and entered production at Harrington & Richardson in late 1941. It was accepted by the US Marine Corps and used in a small number of actions, including Guadalcanal and Bouganville, where many Marines threw it away in disgust. It proved to be far too complicated which led to it being particularly susceptible to dirt and thus to frequent stoppages, none of which were endearing characteristics in a close-quarter weapon.

The Model 50 had a Cutts compensator and fired either semi-automatic or fully automatic at about 500 rpm. The Model 55 was intended for Marine paratroopers and had a wire stock and pistol grip, while the compensator was removed in order to shorten the barrel. Both versions were equally unsuccessful.

M3A1 "GREASE-GUN"

Type: sub-machine gun
Origin: US
Caliber: .45 in
Weight (empty): 8.2 lb (3.7 kg)
Barrel length: 8.0 in (203 mm)
Ammunition: .45 ACP
Feed: 30-round box.

above Cheap and easy to make, the M3 sub-machine gun was an industrial solution rather than a tactical one.

As with the British and the Sten gun, the US Army set out to develop a really cheap and effective sub-machine gun which would combine ease of manufacture with limited use of strategic metals. Design started in 1941, prototypes were under test by late 1942 and it was accepted in 1943. It used stampings and spot welds, had a cylindrical receiver, a short barrel, operated on the blowback principle and fired automatic only. It was chambered for the US standard .45 in ACP round, but could be easily adapted to fire 9 mm Parabellum. Its resemblance to the grease-gun familiar to every automobile owner led to its famous nickname and was produced in its millions, replacing the Thompson as the standard US sub-machine gun. The first version, the M3, had a cocking handle but this was removed in the M3A1 version and replaced by a simple finger-hole in the bolt.

SHOTGUNS

uring World War I privately held shotguns were found to be effective in close-range combat in and around trench positions. A number of designs, known as "Trench Guns" were developed as military issue weapons, although many were too late to see much service.

Surviving guns were pressed into service in World War II, while production was restarted by various manufacturers. Some were to exactly the

same design as before but others were updated for this war. The weapons were usually modified civilian weapons, often with a shorter barrel, perhaps with handguard and a bayonet fitting.

Shotguns once more proved themselves to be simple, tough, reliable and deadly effective at close ranges, especially in and around entrenchments and fortifications.

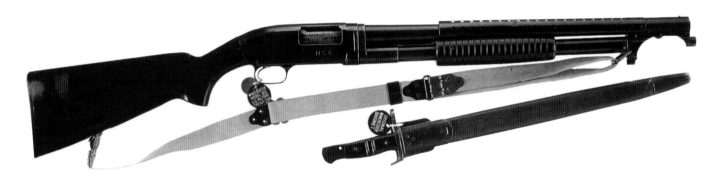

above The Winchester M12 combat shotgun was made during World War II. This one has a woven canvas sling and bayonet.

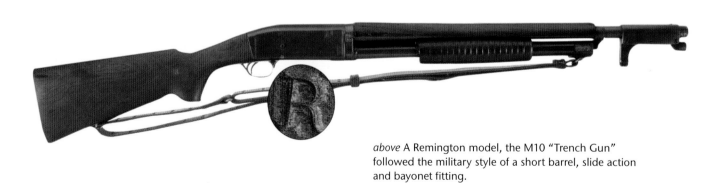

above A Remington model, the M10 "Trench Gun" followed the military style of a short barrel, slide action and bayonet fitting.

above An army model of the Remington M11 semi-automatic shotgun.

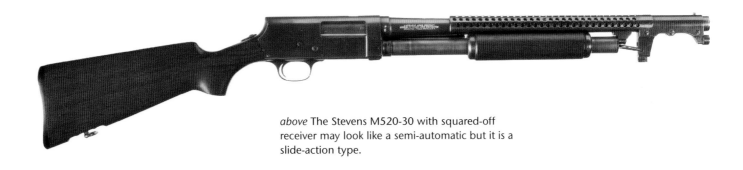

above The Stevens M520-30 with squared-off receiver may look like a semi-automatic but it is a slide-action type.

above The Stevens M620 was a World War I design brought back into production for World War II.

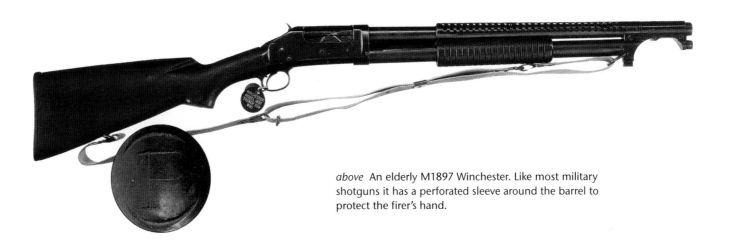

above An elderly M1897 Winchester. Like most military shotguns it has a perforated sleeve around the barrel to protect the firer's hand.

MACHINE GUNS

BROWNING AUTOMATIC RIFLE M1918A2

Type: light automatic rifle
Origin: US
Caliber: .30 in
Weight (empty): 19.5 lb (8.9 kg)
Barrel length: 24 in (610 mm)
Ammunition: .30-06 Springfield
Feed: 20-round box.

Although not strictly speaking a machine gun, the BAR was employed mostly in the light machine gun role in infantry squads, so is covered here rather than in the rifle section. The famous BAR was developed by John M. Browning, a genius and patriot of the first order, who identified the need for a squad-level light automatic weapon well before the United States entered World War I. It was designated a rifle from the start and, in fact, the models used in World War I did not have a bipod and could only be fired from the shoulder or the hip. Development went smoothly and manufacture started in early 1918 but only a few had reached US units in France before the war ended

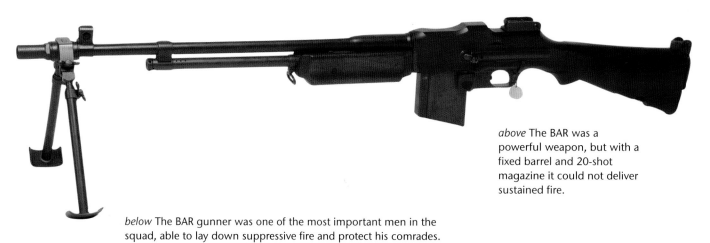

above The BAR was a powerful weapon, but with a fixed barrel and 20-shot magazine it could not deliver sustained fire.

below The BAR gunner was one of the most important men in the squad, able to lay down suppressive fire and protect his comrades.

(although one of those to use it was Lieutenant Valentine Browning, the designer's son). The Model 1918A1 introduced a light bipod and in 1940 a further version appeared, the M1918A2.

The M1918A2 was a gas-operated weapon which only fired bursts, but there was a selector enabling the firer to vary the rate – either 350 rpm or 600 rpm. The weapon was not, however, capable of sustained automatic fire and could not, therefore, be described as a machine gun. Some of the BARs produced in World War II had a butt rest, which could be used to maintain the weapon in a roughly horizontal position, as well as a butt-strap, a hinged length of metal on the heel of the butt which could be raised so that the weapon was held in the firing position ready to fire. Both butt-rest and butt-strap were subsequently omitted. Every infantry squad had at least one BAR.

BROWNING MODEL 1919A4

Type: machine gun
Origin: US
Caliber: .30 in
Weight: gun – 31 lb (14 kg);
tripod – 14 lb (6.4 kg).
Barrel length: 24 in (610 mm)
Ammunition: .30-06 Springfield
Feed: 150-round belt, air-cooled.

Another of John M. Browning's masterpieces, the Model 1919 was originally developed as a general purpose machine gun for the US Cavalry, for use in tanks and armored cars, or in the ground role with a tripod. It worked by recoil power with the brief rearward thrust unlocking the breechblock and sending it to the rear, ejecting the empty case as it did so, until it had compressed the return spring sufficiently to send it forward again,

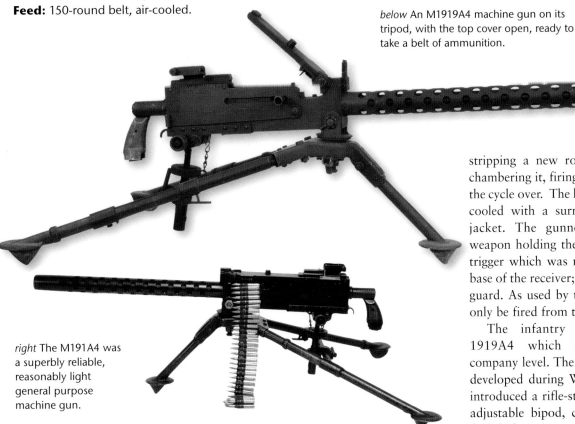

below An M1919A4 machine gun on its tripod, with the top cover open, ready to take a belt of ammunition.

right The M191A4 was a superbly reliable, reasonably light general purpose machine gun.

stripping a new round from the belt, chambering it, firing it and then starting the cycle over. The heavy barrel was air-cooled with a surrounding perforated jacket. The gunner sat behind the weapon holding the pistol grip and the trigger which was mounted at the rear base of the receiver; there was no trigger guard. As used by the infantry it could only be fired from the tripod.

The infantry liked the Model 1919A4 which was deployed at company level. The Model 1919A6 was developed during World War II, which introduced a rifle-style butt, pistol grip, adjustable bipod, carrying handle and flash hider.

BROWNING MODEL M1917A1

Type: medium machine gun
Origin: US
Caliber: .30 in
Weight: gun – 33 lb (15 kg);
tripod – 53 lb (24 kg)
Barrel length: 24 in (610 mm)
Ammunition: .30-06 Springfield
Feed: 250-round belt, air-cooled.

When the United States decided to join World War I John M. Browning had a medium machine gun design which had actually been ready since 1910, but only now was officialdom ready for it. It was rigorously tested, quickly accepted and ordered into production as the M1917. During what remained of that war US industry produced some 43,000, but few ever reached front-line units in France. Like all Browning's designs it was elegant in its simplicity. When the round was fired the barrel and breechblock recoiled together for about half-an-inch (1.3 cm) and when the pressure had reached a safe level

they separated with the block continuing to the rear, taking with it the

below A fabric belt with.30-06 cartridges as used by the M1919 and M1917 machine guns.

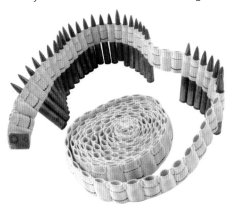

empty case until it hit the ejector and was thrown out of the gun. The breechblock picked up a new cartridge from the belt, continued rearwards until the return spring forced it forwards again, chambering and then firing the round. Like the British Vickers, the gun was water-cooled.

There was one major development

which entered service in 1930 as the M1917A1. This had various improvements such as a new cooling system and a stronger feed mechanism.

above The M1917 heavy machine gun had a metal water-jacket around the barrel to allow sustained fire without over-heating.

M1941 JOHNSON LIGHT MACHINE GUN

Type: light machine gun
Origin: US
Caliber: .30 in
Weight: 12.7 lb (5.7 kg)
Barrel length: 22 in (558 mm)
Ammunition: .30-06 Springfield
Feed: 20-round box

Melvin Johnson, an officer in the US Marine Corps Reserve, developed two weapons in parallel: a rifle and a light machine gun, which had many common components and operated on the same principle of short recoil and a rotating bolt. In the machine gun, Johnson's concept was for the working parts to move in a direct line with the firer's shoulder, minimizing muzzle rise and resulting in a much more accurate

weapon, an idea novel in the late 1930s but very common today. The weapon could fire either single rounds with a closed bolt, or in automatic with an open bolt, when the rate of fire was adjustable from 200 to 600 rpm. Because the butt was not cranked, the sights were higher than on a more conventional weapon. Feed was from a curved 30-round magazine on the left side of the gun and it was normally replenished by changing magazines, but the weapon could also be loaded by rounds fed singly through the ejection port on the right. There was a second version, the M1944, in which the wooden butt was replaced by a butt made of two steel tubes and a butt-pad. Somewhat curiously, the bipod was replaced by a monopod and shoe. In addition, the weapon was issued with a 30-round magazine.

Johnson LMGs were adopted in limited numbers by the US Army, where they equipped the First Special Service Force, and the US Marine Corps where they were used by the Paramarines. The weapon had many good points but the

left Firing a Johnson LMG with its distinctive, curved, side-mounted 30-shot magazine.

magazine sticking out made it difficult to carry, especially when running, – a problem made worse in the M1944 – and with hindsight it would have been relatively simple to produce a double-row design which would have greatly shortened it. One very unusual feature was that if a half-empty magazine was removed, some 3–5 loose rounds were left in the magazine port and the weapon had to be tilted and shaken to remove them.

BROWNING 0.50 IN M2

Type: heavy machine gun
Origin: US
Caliber: .50 in
Weight: gun – 84.0 lb (38.1 kg);
             tripod – 44.0 lb (19.1 kg)
Barrel length: 45.0 in (1,143 mm)
Ammunition:
Feed: 250-round belt, air-cooled.

The great John Browning's M2 heavy machine gun appeared in 1933 and was primarily intended for aircraft, although there were also versions for tanks and ground use. It worked on the Browning principle of short recoil, so that when the cartridge was fired the barrel and breechblock, securely locked together, recoiled for just under an inch, at which point the barrel was stopped by an oil buffer. By this point the pressure had dropped sufficiently for the breechblock to unlock and continue to the rear, extracting and ejecting the empty case and extracting the new round from the belt. Once the rearward action had stopped the compressed return spring took over and drove it all forward again, chambering the round, locking the breechblock and firing the cartridge. The first model tended to overheat but this was overcome by a new, heavier barrel and the weapon gave outstanding service through World War II and beyond. It is still in widespread use in the 21st century.

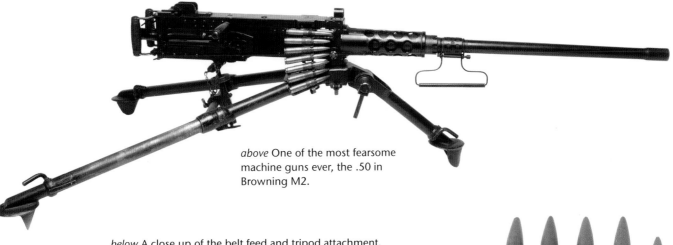

above One of the most fearsome machine guns ever, the .50 in Browning M2.

below A close up of the belt feed and tripod attachment. Gun and tripod came to some 128 lb (57 kg)

above A few .50 in caliber rounds in a section of metal disintegrating-link belt.

GRENADES

The standard fragmentation grenade throughout the war was the Mark II, universally known, due to its shape, as the "Pineapple." This weapon had a body 3.5 in (90 mm) long [4.5 in/114 mm including the safety/arming housing] and 2.25 in (57 mm) in diameter. It weighed 1.3 lb (640 g) and contained 2 oz (57 g) of TNT explosive. Like the British No. 36 Grenade, the US Mark II had a safety-handle, which was held in place by a split-pin, with a ring through the loop. The thrower grasped the grenade firmly in one hand, put a finger from the other hand through the ring, pulled the split-pin clear and threw the grenade. As soon as it was released the safety-handle flew off, thus arming the fuse. Also like the British No. 36, the surface of the cast-iron body was serrated, in this case in eight vertical rows of five, in order to ensure that it could be gripped properly, regardless of weather.

The danger area of the Mark II was a nominal 10 yd (9 m) but the base-plug could fly far beyond that and the thrower was well advised to be behind cover when the device went off. An alternative load was 0.74 oz (0.21 g) of EC blankfire powder, which broke the casing into fewer fragments. If filled with TNT the fuse was a detonating type; if filled with EC blankfire it was an igniting type.

MARK III

The standard concussion grenade was the Mark III which was cylindrical in shape and contained 8 oz (227 g) of explosive – four times that in the Mark II. Its primary purpose was to produce a large overpressure in closed environments, such as bunkers, rooms and foxholes, thus temporarily stunning any occupants. This grenade appeared with a variety of fuses.

below On the left is a smooth-finish grenade, in the center a Mk III concussion grenade and on the right is the standard Mk II "pineapple".

M1 FRANGIBLE GRENADE

The British were well-known for their "weird" weapons but the US had some, too. One was the M1 Frangible Grenade which was a one-pint capacity glass bottle which could be filled with various liquids, one of which was sculpture trioxide chlorosulfonic acid, or FS, for short. The grenadier was required to get close enough to a tank to break the bottle on its air intake, whereupon the liquid reacted in air to produce a dense black smoke which was sucked into the

intake. This, so the theory ran, made the fighting compartment uninhabitable, so that the crew emerged coughing and spluttering to be dealt with by rifles or machine guns in the traditional manner. This is the sort of weapon which sounds much more menacing to staff officers sitting round a table than to the unfortunate soldier who has to put it into operation. It was, of course, a US equivalent of the Red Army's Molotov cocktail, but as far as is known it was never used by US troops in action.

GRENADE LAUNCHERS

Hand grenades were valuable weapons but their range and accuracy was, by definition, limited to the thrower's throwing ability. This was overcome, in part, by grenade launcher attachments, which could be clamped over the muzzle of a standard issue M1 Garand rifle and fired using a ballistite cartridge. The projectile consisted of a fin, a tube and a warhead. The warhead could be integral with the tube, such as

on the M9A1 anti-tank grenade; alternatively, a hand grenade could be attached by spring-loaded claws at the front-end of the tube. The kick from this device was such that the firer had to kneel, holding his rifle at an angle and with the butt resting on the ground. Early versions had a simple empty tube but later a small propellant charge was added increasing the range to a maximum of about 250 yd (230 m).

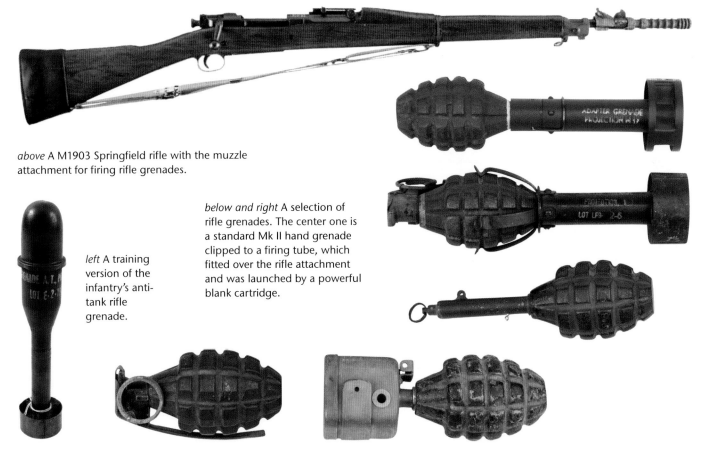

above A M1903 Springfield rifle with the muzzle attachment for firing rifle grenades.

left A training version of the infantry's anti-tank rifle grenade.

below and right A selection of rifle grenades. The center one is a standard Mk II hand grenade clipped to a firing tube, which fitted over the rifle attachment and was launched by a powerful blank cartridge.

MINES AND MINECLEARING

As with most armies, mine warfare had been given little priority before the US entered the war. And for much of the war, mineclearing was a case of soldiers carefully poking the ground with a bayonet or wire prodder, then gently defusing and lifting any mines that were found. American industry came up with a technological solution in the shape of an electronic mine detector, which made it much easier, quicker and safer to find metal-bodied mines.

The US dep;loyed a series of mines for both anti-tank and anti-personnel use. By the time reasonable quantities had been produced and sent to the troops, however, the Allies had largely switched to the offensive, and had little use for large defensive minefields.

SCR-625 MINE DETECTOR

The SCR-625 Mine Detector was a device which used electronics to achieve its purpose. The operator carried the battery and an electronic pack and held the detector, which consisted of a 6 ft (1.8 m) pole at the end of which was an 18 in (46 cm) diameter wooden disc with, underneath, a cylindrical search coil. The entire device weighed 7.5 lb (3.4 kg) and could detect metallic mines up to a maximum of 12 in (30 cm) below the surface. By chance, the first operational use of the SCR-625 was in North Africa following the TORCH landings where the dry, sandy soil was particularly

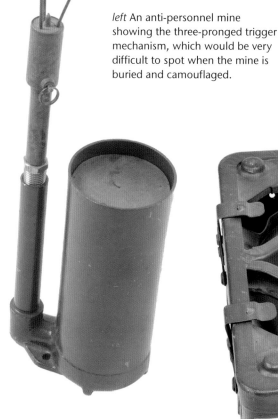

left An anti-personnel mine showing the three-pronged trigger mechanism, which would be very difficult to spot when the mine is buried and camouflaged.

right An anti-tank mine in its transport crate. The fuse would be screwed into the top before the mine was deployed.

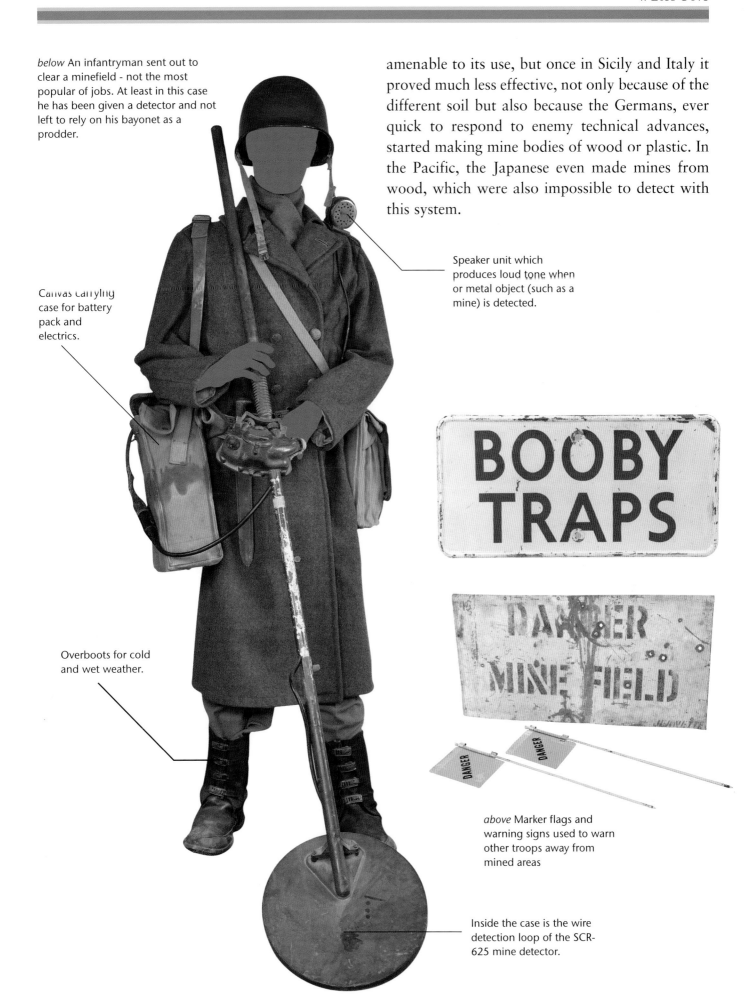

below An infantryman sent out to clear a minefield - not the most popular of jobs. At least in this case he has been given a detector and not left to rely on his bayonet as a prodder.

amenable to its use, but once in Sicily and Italy it proved much less effective, not only because of the different soil but also because the Germans, ever quick to respond to enemy technical advances, started making mine bodies of wood or plastic. In the Pacific, the Japanese even made mines from wood, which were also impossible to detect with this system.

Speaker unit which produces loud tone when or metal object (such as a mine) is detected.

Canvas carrying case for battery pack and electrics.

Overboots for cold and wet weather.

above Marker flags and warning signs used to warn other troops away from mined areas

Inside the case is the wire detection loop of the SCR-625 mine detector.

BAYONETS AND KNIVES

M1903 Springfield rifles were issued with the M1905 bayonet which had a massive 16 in (41 cm) blade, fullered for 80 per cent of its length and with a wood/metal handle. It was attached to the rifle by a ring on one end of the quillion which fitted over the muzzle and clipped onto a lug under the forward barrel-band. Many millions of these were made during World War I; those produced before 1917 having an untreated blade but thereafter being parkerized (i.e., given a phosphating protection). In 1942 large numbers of M1905s were reworked in government arsenals, with the wooden grips replaced by black plastic and, if not already done, the blades being parkerized. This version was known as the Model 1905/42.

From mid-1943 onwards a new bayonet was manufactured for the M1 Garand, which was identical in all respects to the M1905 apart from having a 10 in (25 cm) blade. This was much more useful, and as a result, from 1944 onwards most M1905 and M1905/42 bayonets were shortened from 16 to 10 inches, (41 cm to 25 cm); some being given spear points and the others having Bowie points. One result was that the fuller ran out to the end of the blade, a most unusual arrangement. All those reworked in this way were also given plastic grips in place of wood and were

designated Model 1905E1.

The original version of the M1 Carbine did not have a bayonet, but after some thousands had been produced this was changed, with a lug being added below the barrel for a new bayonet, the M4. Early models had leather grips but these were changed to black plastic. The bayonet was freed from the lug by simultaneously pressing two catches on the pommel.

M3 COMBAT KNIFE

This was the first combat knife to be issued in the US Army and was almost identical to the M4 bayonet for the M1 carbine, except that the quillion did not have a ring for the muzzle, nor was there a slot and retaining catch on the pommel.

V-42 STILETTO

The "Knife Fighting Commando, Type V-42" was designed by Colonel Robert T. Frederick, US Army, commander of the 1st Special Service Force, and his close-combat adviser Pat O'Neill, formerly of the Shanghai Police. The knife was manufactured by the Case Cutlery Company of Bradford, P.A. Overall length of the weapon was

left An Imperial-made M3 knife, a design originally based on the bayonet for the M1 Carbine.

right Many fighting knives were theater-made improvisations. This "D"-handle design was popular with airborne and other elite troops.

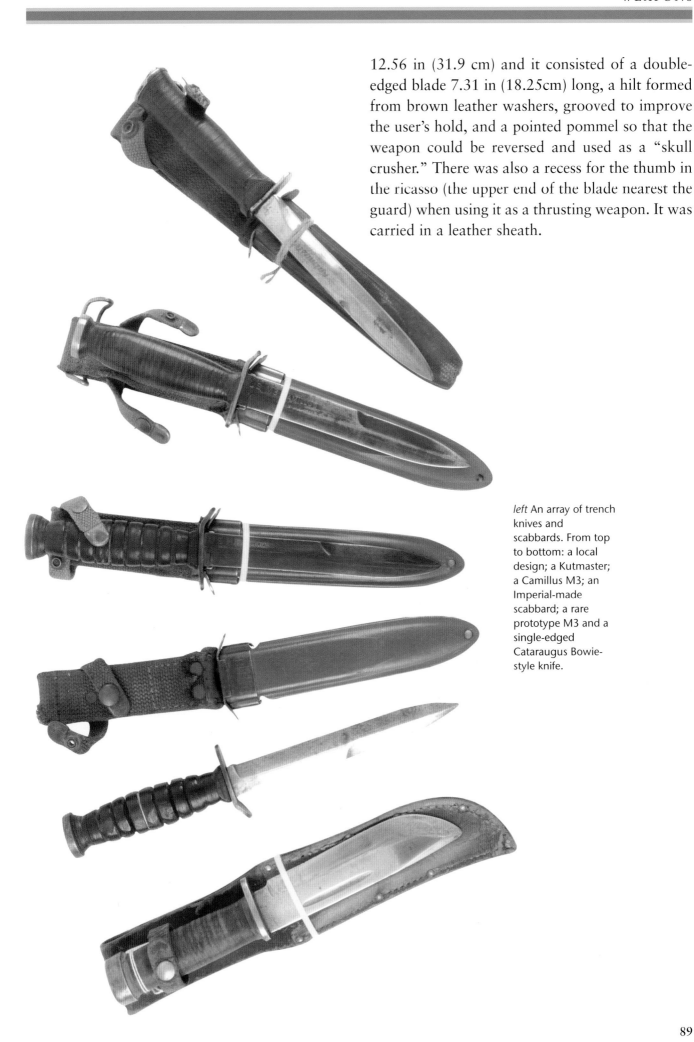

12.56 in (31.9 cm) and it consisted of a double-edged blade 7.31 in (18.25cm) long, a hilt formed from brown leather washers, grooved to improve the user's hold, and a pointed pommel so that the weapon could be reversed and used as a "skull crusher." There was also a recess for the thumb in the ricasso (the upper end of the blade nearest the guard) when using it as a thrusting weapon. It was carried in a leather sheath.

left An array of trench knives and scabbards. From top to bottom: a local design; a Kutmaster; a Camillus M3; an Imperial-made scabbard; a rare prototype M3 and a single-edged Cataraugus Bowie-style knife.

MORTARS

Mortars provided instantly available firepower under battalion control and only two models were deployed by the infantry during the war. Both were well up to the army's requirements.

LIGHT MORTAR

The 60 mm M2 Mortar had three major components: a 28.6 in (66 cm) long tube weighing 12.8 lb (5.8kg); a bipod at 16.4 lb (7.4 kg); and a baseplate at 12.8 lb (5.8 kg). It was a simple system for use at company and platoon level. It had an adjustable bipod and was aimed using a collimator sight, following which a bomb was dropped through the muzzle, where it fell to the base of the tube and hit a fixed firing-pin, thus igniting the propellant. The normal and sustainable rate of fire was 18 rounds per minute, although this could be increased to 35 rpm for a short period and with a well-trained crew. There were three types of round – see table. In some units the tube and bipod were carried already connected so that the weapon could be brought into action as quickly as possible.

left and below The US-made 60 mm M2 mortar was significantly more effective than the 50 mm light mortars of other nations such as Britain, Germany, Russia, Italy and Japan. Held at company-level it could deliver explosive, smoke and illumination rounds.

MEDIUM MORTAR

The 81 mm M1 Mortar had better performance than the 60 mm, but was also much heavier, its three major components being at the limits of man portability. The tube was 3 ft 9 in (114 cm) long, weighed 44.5 lb (20 kg) and sat on a baseplate weighing 45 lb (20.4 kg). The tripod and sight weighed another 46.5 lb (21 kg), giving a total, less ammunition, of 136 lb (62 kg). There were six types of bomb, all listed in the table.

left An 81 mm M1 mortar and crew with cardboard ammunition cases on the ground around them. Medium mortars such as this were usually the most powerful weapon the infantry battalion commander had under his direct control. Pound for pound, mortar ammunition has more explosive effect than artillery shells of the same caliber, while a good team could have bombs raining down on the enemy within a few seconds of the request. The kneeling figure has the M1942 paratrooper's jacket and is wearing a hood under his helmet. The standing figure has a woollen overcoat and is wearing the high-sided boots issued to airborne forces.

left Comprising a simple tube, bipod and baseplate, aimed using a dial sight, the 81 mm M1 mortar followed the same basic outline those of other nations.

above A metal ammunition case and individual cardboard tubes were used to transport this 81 mm M43A1 high explosive ammunition.

left To increase the range, extra discs of propellant charge could be placed around the tail of the bomb.

US Army Mortar Ammunition				
Caliber	**Round**	**Weight**	**Maximum Range**	**Remarks**
60 mm	M49A2 HE	3.1 lb (1.4 kg)	2000 yd (1830 m)	Maximum effective range approx 1000 yd (914 m)
	M302WP	4.0 lb (1.8 kg)	1000 yd (914 m)	white phosphorus
	M83 Illuminating	3.7 lb (1.7 kg)	1000 yd (914 m)	110,000 candle-power for 25 secs
81 mm	M43 HE Light	3.1 kg (6.9 lb)	3290 yd (3000 m)	Equivalent to 75 mm howitzer
	M45 HE Heavy	10.6 lb (4.8 kg)	2558 yd (2340 m)	Equivalent to 105 mm howitzer
	M56 HE Heavy	15.0 lb (6.8 kg)	1300 yd (1188 m)	
	M57 WP	10.7 lb (4.9 kg)	2470 yd (2260 m)	WP = white phosphorus
	M57 FS	10.7 lb (4.9 kg)	2470 yd (2260 m)	laid down dense white smoke.
	M301 Illuminating	9.1 lb (4.1 kg)	2200 yd (2011 m)	275,000 candle-power for 60 secs

ANTI-TANK WEAPONS

During the interwar years, the US infantry did not pay overmuch attention to anti-tank warfare until the Spanish Civil War broke out in July 1936 and quickly demonstrated that tanks were now a major threat. Having observed the early anti-tank engagements in that conflict, the US Army acquired two PaK 35/36 guns which arrived from Germany in 1937 and were examined in detail before being rigorously tested. Being in charge of the tests, the infantry was able to lay down the criteria for a future American weapon, among which were that the new weapon must be neither larger caliber nor heavier than the German gun. The result was the US-designed 37 mm M2 gun and by late 1941 every operational infantry battalion had its own anti-tank platoon armed with 4, while infantry regiments had a company of 12 guns and the divisional anti-tank battalion had two companies, also of 12 each (plus a company of 75 mm guns). In all cases, the prime mover was either a 3/4-ton Dodge or a 1/4-ton Jeep. In December 1941 the divisional anti-tank battalions were converted into independent tank destroyer battalions, with their towed guns being replaced by self-propelled weapons mounted initially on half-tracks and later on fully-tracked self-propelled chassis. Airborne troops initially liked the 37 mm and as of early 1943 an airborne division had 36 of these guns; they were also on issue to 10th Mountain Division in Italy.

When the Army realized that the 37 mm gun hadn't kept pace with developments in armor they replaced it with the 57 mm M1, this time based on a British design.

Both these guns were heavy weapons, used by specialized crews at battalion level and above.

There was also a need for some kind of light anti-armor defense for the rifle squad. The US Army met this with the development of a lightweight rocket launcher which became the most effective infantry anti-tank weapon in use. The army also led the way with the development of light, large caliber recoilless weapons: a technology which quickly spread to every army around the world.

37 mm Gun M1

Length (traveling): 12.9 ft (3.92 m)
Weight: 912 lb (413.7 kg)
Caliber: 37 mm (1.5 in)
Barrel length: 6.9 ft (2.1 m)
Crew: 4–6
Maximum range: 7,546 yd (6,900 m)

right The M1 37 mm anti-tank gun was a light, portable weapon, good enough for 1939 and 1940, but rapidly outclassed by German armor by the time the Unites States entered the war.

Following detailed study of the German Pak 35/36 the US Army developed the 37 mm Gun M1, which, while it bore some similarities to the German weapon was, in fact, a completely new design. The first weapons reached units in February 1940 and by the time production ended in 1943 some 186,700 had been manufactured.

The M1 was designed to be both low and light so that it could be employed and manhandled by front-line infantry. In general terms, it remained effective against Japanese tanks to the end of the war, but this was not too difficult as the Japanese Army did little to develop or improve its tanks. The M1 was definitely not so successful against the larger, better-protected, German tanks and was soon superseded by the 57 mm M1. The later M3 had a split-trail carriage with pneumatic tires.

M3s were deployed in the North African, Sicily and Italy campaigns and while they could deal with Italian and French tanks, they were no match for the new German tanks. Paratroop units favored the M1, mainly because of its lightness, but even they were pleased to finally turn them in exchange for 57 mm guns.

57 mm Gun M1

Length (traveling): 9.25 ft (2.82 m)
Weight: 2,520 lb (1,140 kg)
Caliber: 57 mm (2.34 in)
Barrel length: 117 in (2.85 m)
Crew: 10
Maximum range: 5,000 yd (4,600 m)

In 1941 the US Army was still equipped with the 37 mm gun, but their observation of the campaigns in France in 1940 and then of the British in North Africa showed that this was unlikely to be sufficiently powerful. Thus, when the British sent over two examples of their latest 6-pounder Mark 2 anti-tank gun for production in the US and then supply back to the UK under Lend-Lease, the weapon was studied with great interest, leading to a decision to adopt it as the infantry's battalion-level anti-tank gun. Designated the 57 mm Gun M1 it was virtually identical to the British weapon and the ammunition was fully interchangeable, but the US Army opted for a longer barrel – 117 in (2.85 m) as opposed to 96 in (2.45 m). The US gun also had a larger crew – 10 men compared to 6. Production started in 1942 and continued to 1945, by which time just under 16,000 had been made.

In US service the 57 mm fired AP (armor piercing), APCBC/HE (armor piercing, capped, ballistic capped/high explosive), HE (high explosive), and Canister rounds. The latter consisted of a mass of steel pellets to be fired against attacking infantry, and was only used at very short range and as a last resort, since the wear on the barrel was phenomenal.

2.36 in Rocket Launcher M1

above and left A 2.36 in Rocket Launcher M1 "Bazooka" complete with shaped-charge rocket and ammunition bag.

Length: 61 in (1550 mm)
Weight: weapon – 13.3 lb (6 kg);
  projectile – 3.4 lb (1.5 kg)
Caliber: 2.36 in (60.07 mm)
Penetration: 4.0 in (100 mm)

When the US Army entered World War II its anti-tank defense depended almost entirely on 37 mm towed guns and the 0.50 in Browning M2; there was not even a heavy caliber rifle such as the British Boys. In desperation the army adopted a Swiss-designed hollow-charge anti-tank warhead but without any means of delivering it to the target. At this point Lieutenant Uhl and Colonel Skinner suggested using a rocket-launcher they had developed and this was rapidly adopted. This led directly to the M1 "Bazooka," a tube 61 in (1.55 m) long and 2.36 in (60.07 mm) in diameter, with a simple wooden shoulder stock and pistol grip. The rocket was placed in the rear and connected up to two wires, linked to dry cells in the pistol grip. On pressing the trigger electric current passed to the rocket motor which ignited, driving the projectile out of the tube at considerable velocity. The only real problem was the backblast which could affect the firer and also indicate the position to the watching enemy. Nevertheless, with its shaped-charge HEAT (High Explosive Anti-Tank) warhead it was the best infantry anti-tank weapon of its time and was quickly copied by the Germans.

The later M9 was devised with the launch tube split into two parts to make the package easier to carry. They could be clipped together quickly, using a bayonet joint, to make the weapon ready to fire.

below The later M9 version could be split into two parts for easier carriage and was especially popular with airborne troops.

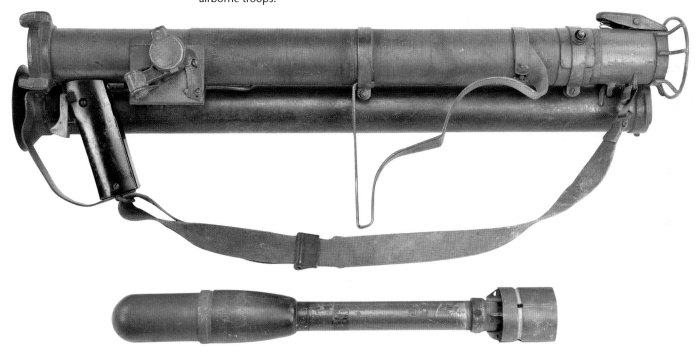

above and below A blunt-nosed practice rocket on top, and underneath, another M1 with a protective shield at the muzzle and different configuration of grip and shoulder rest.

M18 57 MM RECOILLESS RIFLE

Length (barrel): 5 ft (1.5 m)
Weight: 45 lb (20.4 kg)
Caliber: 57 mm (2.2 in)
Crew: 2
Maximum range: 4,300 yd (3,932 m)
Operation: ground mounted (bipod, shoulder) or M1917AQ1 mount.
Projectiles: HE (high explosive) 5.3 lb (2.4 kg); High Explosive Anti Tank (HEAT) 5.6 lb (2.5 kg); smoke 5.7 lb (2.6 kg)

The M18 manportable recoilless rifle (RCL) worked on the same principle as the M1 2.36 in bazooka but was slightly larger, considerably more powerful and had a much longer effective range. It could be fired from the ground, using a bipod or monopod, from the shoulder, or from an M1917A1 machine gun tripod.

below The 57 mm recoilless rifle was a useful source of high explosive fire as well as anti-tank capability. Clearly visible are the propellant vent holes around the projectile's "cartridge case".

M20 75 mm Recoilless Rifle

Above: The 75 mm recoilless rifle was much more powerful than the earlier 57 mm and remained in service for many years after the war.

Length (barrel): 6.83 ft (2.1 m)
Weight: 114.5 lb (52 kg)
Caliber: 75 mm (2.95 in)
Crew: 10
Maximum range: 7,000 yd (6,400 m)
Operation: Mounted on M1917A1 .30 caliber MG tripod
Projectiles: HE 21.9 lb (9.9 kg); High Explosive Anti-Tank (HEAT) 20.5 lb (9.3 kg); smoke 22.6 lb (10.3 kg)
Range: 7,000 yd (6,400 m)

Pound-for-pound this was one of the finest anti-tank weapons of World War II, being both accurate and very effective against even the most advanced German tanks, as well as having a very useful anti-personnel capability. Development started in 1943, prototypes were under test in 1944, production began in very early 1945, and the first models reached troops in both the European and Pacific theaters in March 1945. The M20 consisted of a 75 mm rifled tube, usually mounted on a standard M1917A1 .30 caliber machine gun tripod mount, which could, in turn be mounted on the ground, or on a light vehicle such as the Jeep. It could also be fired on the ground using a bipod or monopod, although this must have been very exciting for the gunner. Like all recoilless weapons, the M20 had a significant backblast, but could take on and defeat both Panther and Tiger tanks. It could also be used, to great effect, against pillboxes and, of considerable importance in the Pacific, cave positions.

AIRBORNE FORCES

In 1941 the US Army had a single airborne battalion, hastily formed after the successful German operations in 1940. By early 1944, just three years later, the army had raised, trained and equipped five complete airborne divisions. When the war ended, US paratroopers had carried out combat drops in North Africa, Sicily, France, the Netherlands, etc etc etc.

Carefully selected and highly-trained, the US Army paratrooper had much the same weapons and equipment as his infantry cousin, although there were some differences. As with the infantryman, his immediate unit was the battalion, organized on similar lines to the rifle battalion but smaller and with less organic support than the land-bound equivalent. We pick the 1945 version of this organization to look at in detail.

left An original combat jacket and badge of the 82nd "All American" airborne division, complete with bullet hole.

below Men of an airborne unit in a C-47 transport, June 1944. Note the cigarette, in a flimsy aluminum airframe filled with aviation fuel!

left Infantrymen and MP from the 82nd Airborne with a Jeep locally-modified with armor plate and used as a light reconnaissance vehicle.

TYPE 1945 PARACHUTE INFANTRY BATTALION

Despite their successes in the D-Day landings and Operation Market Garden it was clear that the organization of the US parachute battalion could be improved and this was implemented in late 1944, being ready for the crossing of the Rhine and other operations in 1945. The improvements mainly involved increases in the rifle platoons – in old-fashioned terms, added "bayonet strength." The result was a unit of 37 Officers and 669 enlisted men.

BATTALION HEADQUARTERS

The headquarters group (6 officers plus 15 enlisted men.) comprised the commanding officer, executive officer, adjutant, intelligence officer and two others. There were also 15 enlisted men who, for bureaucratic reasons, were shown as the Battalion HQ Section of Headquarters Company, but who, whether in barracks or in combat, formed an integral part of battalion headquarters and are shown as such here.

HEADQUARTERS COMPANY

Headquarters Company (7 Officers, 150 enlisted men) included two weapons platoons. The Mortar Platoon (3 officers, 42 enlisted men) had four 81 mm mortars, while the Machine Gun Platoon (1 officer, 46 enlisted men) had four M1919 Brownings. The Communications Platoon (1 officer, 27 enlisted men) provided radio facilities, but much less wire than a normal battalion. Finally, the Supply Section (13 men) was responsible for logistic missions, including, most importantly in a parachute unit, control of and removing stores from a drop zone. Company Headquarters consisted of 2 officers and 22 enlisted men.

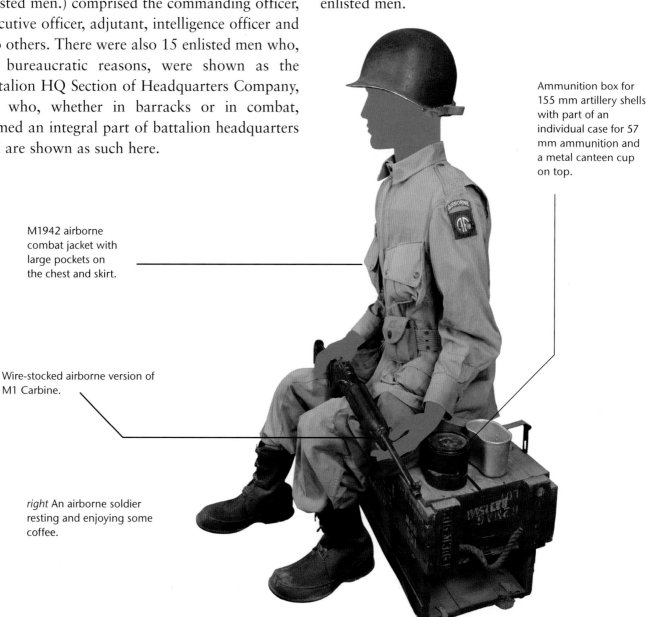

Ammunition box for 155 mm artillery shells with part of an individual case for 57 mm ammunition and a metal canteen cup on top.

M1942 airborne combat jacket with large pockets on the chest and skirt.

Wire-stocked airborne version of M1 Carbine.

right An airborne soldier resting and enjoying some coffee.

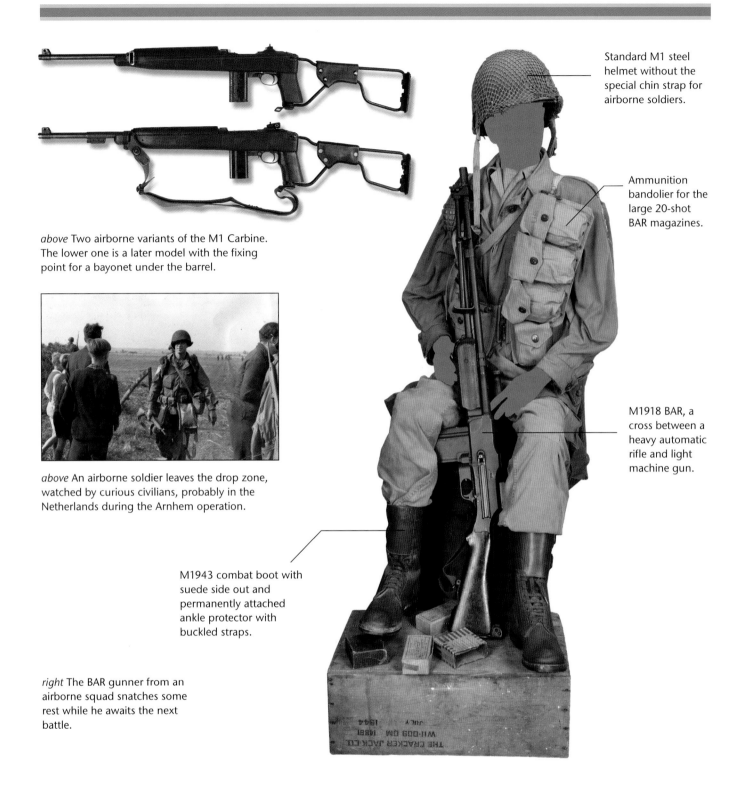

above Two airborne variants of the M1 Carbine. The lower one is a later model with the fixing point for a bayonet under the barrel.

above An airborne soldier leaves the drop zone, watched by curious civilians, probably in the Netherlands during the Arnhem operation.

right The BAR gunner from an airborne squad snatches some rest while he awaits the next battle.

Standard M1 steel helmet without the special chin strap for airborne soldiers.

Ammunition bandolier for the large 20-shot BAR magazines.

M1918 BAR, a cross between a heavy automatic rifle and light machine gun.

M1943 combat boot with suede side out and permanently attached ankle protector with buckled straps.

PARACHUTE RIFLE COMPANY

Three rifle companies (each 8 officers, 168 enlisted men) formed the core of the battalion, each being formed of three rifle platoons. Company headquarters was large (2 officers, 27 enlisted men), but included administrators (clerks, armorer, cooks, storemen) as well as two radiomen and messengers. The component rifle platoons each comprised two officers and 43 enlisted men, grouped into three 12-man squads (the addition of a third squad was the main change in the 1945 reorganization). The remainder of the rifle platoon were in the Mortar Section (6 men plus one 60 mm mortar) and Platoon Headquarters (two officers, staff-sergeant, sergeant, radio operator, messenger).

AIRBORNE UNIFORM

Paratroopers were issued with their own M1942 Paratrooper Uniform, which was made from light green cotton twill. The jacket had four front pockets and the trousers two cargo pockets. This was not found satisfactory, however, especially as the jacket tended to tear at the elbows, while the trousers not only tore at the knees but the stitching tended to break in the crotch. The paratroopers tried to fix this by sewing canvas patches on the elbows and knees, and also had further cargo pockets added to the trousers, but by 1945 they had found that the standard infantry

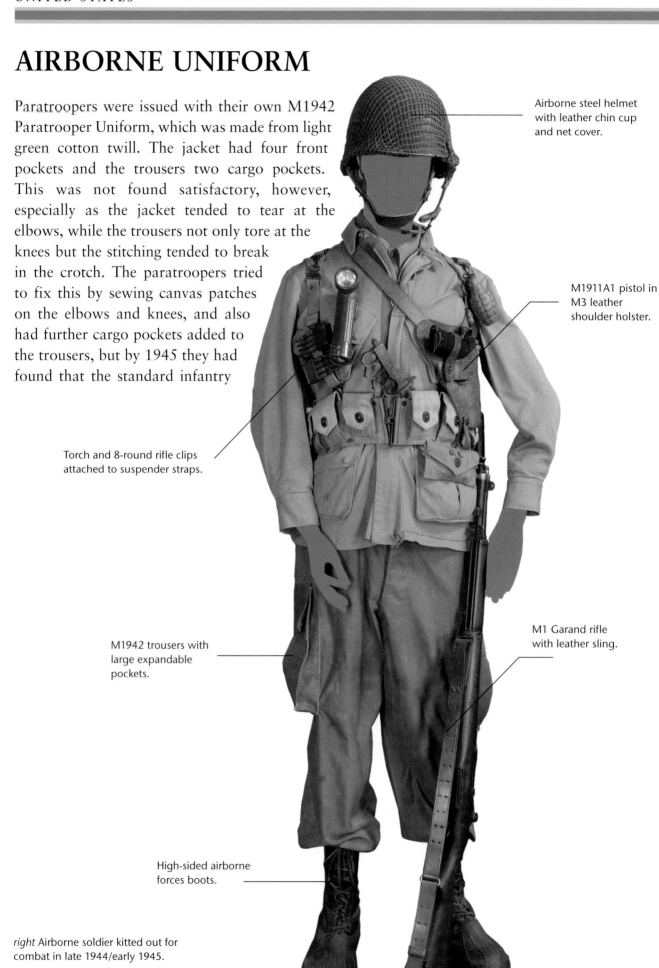

Airborne steel helmet with leather chin cup and net cover.

M1911A1 pistol in M3 leather shoulder holster.

Torch and 8-round rifle clips attached to suspender straps.

M1942 trousers with large expandable pockets.

M1 Garand rifle with leather sling.

High-sided airborne forces boots.

right Airborne soldier kitted out for combat in late 1944/early 1945.

M1943 outfit suited their needs and stuck with it.

One peculiarity of US paratroopers' combat uniform was that prior to boarding the aircraft all items which might become entangled with the rigging were strapped to the wearer's body by lengths of webbing strap, resulting in a "trussed-up" appearance. Once on the ground, however, such straps were quickly discarded.

A special design of boot was developed for the paratroops, the primary need being to combine a comfortable and durable marching boot with protection for the ankles, especially at the moment of landing. After several unsatisfactory designs, the M1942 pattern was accepted, which was a tall boot with lacing all the way to the top, with eleven to thirteen sets of eyes according to the foot size, together with reinforced toe and heel caps. This also satisfied another paratrooper requirement, which was that it was different from the normal army boot and instantly recognizable.

right and below Interior and exterior view of airborne forces helmet. The same shape and design as the standard helmet, it had a slightly different strap system with a leather chin cup.

right A pair of high-sided airborne forces boots. As with many such items, they were also worn by other soldiers who thought some "airborne glamour" might rub off on them too.

RANGERS

The Rangers were formed in early 1942 and saw their first action in the Torch landings in November of that year, going on to participate in the Anzio landings and in actions in Northwest Europe. The man who raised them was Colonel William Orlando Darby and they were usually known in the European Theater as "Darby's Rangers" although he was, in fact, only the senior battalion commander. At Cisterna in Italy, and after a most determined stand, the 2nd and 4th Ranger Battalions were overwhelmed by German armed forces and all but seven of the 767 men involved were either killed or captured. In January 1945 the 6th Ranger Battalion conducted a highly successful raid in the Philippines, attacking a Japanese prisoner-of-war-camp and freeing 511 US and Allied inmates at a cost of 2 Rangers killed and 523 Japanese killed or wounded.

above and below A fierce-looking wide-bladed knife with "D"-shaped knuckle-duster handle and scabbard as used by Ranger units.

left Originally made in France for the previous war, the M1917 combat knife and knuckle-duster was carried by many US soldiers in World War II.

RANGER BATTALION

The highest wartime command level was battalion and there was no overall Ranger force HQ as such. One result was that higher command usually had little understanding of Ranger capabilities, strengths and limitations which led, not infrequently, to them being misemployed as conventional infantry, a role for which they were not equipped. In mid-1944 a Ranger Battalion had an authorized strength of 26 Officers and 478 enlisted men, divided into a Headquarters Company and six Ranger companies. Despite their name, these subunits were very much smaller than a conventional rifle company.

BATTALION HEADQUARTERS

A large battalion headquarters (5 officers, 35 enlisted men) was needed to cope, not only with conducting operations, but also with the planning and coordination needed to set them up. The

above Rangers embark for the short journey over the English Channel and the D-Day assault. One man is carrying sections of explosive "Bangalore Torpedo". Note also the load-carrying assault vest and inflatable life-preserver around the waist.

commanding officer, executive officer, adjutant and intelligence officer were tasked as in a conventional battalion; the other officers and most of the enlisted men were involved in planning and coordination.

HEADQUARTERS COMPANY

A large Headquarters Company (3 officers, 53 enlisted men) was responsible for communications (22 men) and also fulfilled the supplies and transportation functions. An unusual feature was that it maintained a pool of weapons which could be drawn upon by the Ranger companies. These included 81 mm mortars, 60 mm mortars, sub-machine guns and Bazookas. Curiously, this pool did not include any heavy machine guns.

FIRST SPECIAL SERVICE FORCE

right The "Spearhead" shoulder flash of the US/Canadian Special Service Force.

below A Special Service Force soldier in US uniform with the small M1936 "Musette" bag on his back.

A suggestion was made by Vice-Admiral Lord Louis Mountbatten, the Chief of (British) Combined Operations to General George C. Marshall for a combined US/Canadian special forces unit to undertake a specific mission – to attack hydroelectric facilities in German-occupied Norway. The unit was duly raised by Colonel (later Major-General) Robert T. Frederick, and was found from volunteers from both the US and Canadian Armies. Designated the First Special Service Force (FSSF), its authorized strength was just short of 2,200 men, with its main strength in the 1st, 2nd and 3rd Special Service Regiments, each 600 strong.

Each of these regiments was divided into two battalions, each of three companies, with three platoons to a company, two squads to a platoon. Squads were commanded by a sergeant and, apart from rifles, were armed with a BAR, a Johnson M1941 LMG and a 2.36in bazooka. The FSSF Service Battalion included an HQ Company, a Service Company, a Maintenance Company and a Medical Unit.

The FSSF was raised in 1942 at Fort Harrison in Montana, with every man being required to be physically fit and able to ski, climb mountains, and live, move and fight in conditions of extreme cold. The Norwegian operation was canceled in late 1942, so the FSSF deployed first to the Aleutian Islands (1943) before moving to Europe where it operated in Italy and Southern France. It had reached the Rhineland by December 1944, but by then the need for a small, independent special operations unit had passed and it was disbanded.

Reversible winter coat with white-colored lining and fur-edged hood.

M1928 Thompson sub-machine gun.

Pouch for 20-round Thompson magazines.

M1936 "Musette" bag, a handy and popular sack for carrying essential supplies.

Standard officers' belt with dressing pouch and leather holster for M1911A1 pistol.

Airborne forces high-sided boots.

M1943-pattern combat trousers.

above and left Front and rear views of a Special Service soldier dressed for Norwegian winter conditions.

UNITED STATES MARINE CORPS

The United States Marine Corps fought with great determination and distinction from Wake Island in 1941 to Okinawa in 1945, conducting many amphibious landings in the process and repeatedly fighting the much-vaunted Japanese to a standstill. The Marines had two basic missions: to seize or defend advanced naval bases and to conduct such land operations as were considered essential to the prosecution of a naval campaign; and to provide detachments and organizations for service in armed vessels of the Navy or for protection of naval property on naval stations and bases. The Corps was just under 20,000 strong in 1939, but had increased to some 66,000 in December 1941 and to over 450,000 in August 1945 – larger than most national armies. Total losses in the war were 15,161 killed in action, with another 4,322 lost due to other causes.

Marine Corps' organization and equipment were oriented totally towards the mission of an island-hopping campaign across the Pacific, in which each objective could only be reached by sea,

below A Coy, 2nd Bn, 5th Marines on Okinawa in May 45. They have a mixture of rifles and carbines, and a Bangalore Torpedo ready to use against obstacles and fixed defenses.

and all logistic support was by means of ships from distant bases. Heavy firepower was almost always available from warships offshore as was dedicated air support from carrier-based Marine Corps and naval aircraft. The Marines relied almost entirely on the US Army for the provision of ground weapons such as rifles, machine guns, artillery and tanks, and the unpalatable fact was that until mid-1944 the Corps was often last in line for the issue of new equipment. To achieve the Corps mission there were no infantry, armored or mountain divisions, but only one type – the Marine Division.

above An impractical pre-war sun helmet with the Marine Corps badge.

below A soft peaked cap in Herring-Bone Twill (HBT) material.

left HBT was originally designed for fatigues and general work clothes, but proved to be lightweight, hard-wearing and comfortable in tropical conditions. The fatigue dress became the basis of Marine Corps combat uniform in the early months of the Pacific War. As well as his personal ammunition this figure is carrying extra pouches of equipment and ammunition for the squad.

MARINE DIVISION

Between 1941 and 1945, many Marine Corps field formations and units were in a state of almost constant flux, influenced in part by the lessons of the most recent operations, but also by new equipment arriving from the factories in the United States. However, the overall organization of a Marine Division remained the same throughout, with a divisional headquarters and three infantry regiments, an artillery regiment, as well as engineers, pioneers, tanks, and the usual communications, medical and logistic support.

The Artillery Regiment originally consisted of three Light Artillery Battalions, each with twelve 75 mm pack howitzers, and one Medium Artillery Battalion with twelve 105 mm guns. The first major change was to convert one Light Battalion to Medium, thus giving two Light and Two Medium Battalions, all with the same number of weapons as before. By early 1945 this was changing yet again: the light battalions disappearing completely, and there were now three Medium Artillery Battalions plus one Heavy Artillery Battalion with twelve 155 mm guns. All guns and howitzers were towed.

The story was similar with tanks. In 1941

right The Marine Corps made extensive use of camouflage uniforms once production got up to speed. This figure wears the 1944-style clothing and is carrying light combat order.

left On parade and barrack dress Marine NCO rank badges had a red background, as seen here.

through 1944 the division had a Light Tank Battalion, equipped with eighteen M3 Stuarts, and one Scout Company with fourteen White Scout Cars or Jeeps. By 1944 this had evolved into fifteen M4 Shermans, with the Scout Company transferred to divisional control. By mid-1945 nine flamethrower tanks were also added.

Originally there was an Engineer Regiment, consisting of one Engineer, one Pioneer and one Naval Construction Battalion (CB = "Seebees"). By 1944 the regimental level of command had disappeared and the CB battalion had moved to a separate CB organization, leaving the Engineer and Pioneer Battalions within the division.

left A camouflaged Marine PFC in training in March 1943.

Below Marines come ashore at Bougainville, November 1943.

MARINE BATTALION, 1944

Following repeated reorganizations, by late 1944 the Marine Battalion had reached a strength of 37 Officers and 917 men, probably the largest battalion with the greatest firepower in any army or marine force. One of the main emphases of the reorganizations was to get firepower and its control down to the lowest level; for example, a 1943–44 change led to the end of the Weapons Company when its assets (mainly machine guns) were dispersed to the rifle companies.

BATTALION HEADQUARTERS

A relatively compact battalion headquarters comprised 9 officers and 28 men, plus a twelve-strong Intelligence Section, which nominally belonged to HQ Company.

HEADQUARTERS COMPANY

This group (7 officers and 157 men) comprised the usual headquarters (1 officer, 16 men), a communications platoon (1 officer, 39 men) and a supply section (1 officer, 6 men). It also administered only one heavy weapons sub-unit, the Mortar Platoon (2 officer, 56 men), which was armed with four 81 mm and four 60 mm mortars. Finally, there was a Medical Detachment (2 officers, 40 men) provided by the US Navy.

right HBT material was eventually produced in camouflage patterns, such as with this 1944 combat suit. This man has a bandolier of M1 Carbine ammunition across his chest.

below Most Marine equipment was the same as the army's, such as this M1910 entrenching tool seen here.

below A standard M1910 axe with OD carrier strapped to the soldier's backpack.

US MARINE BATTALION c.1944

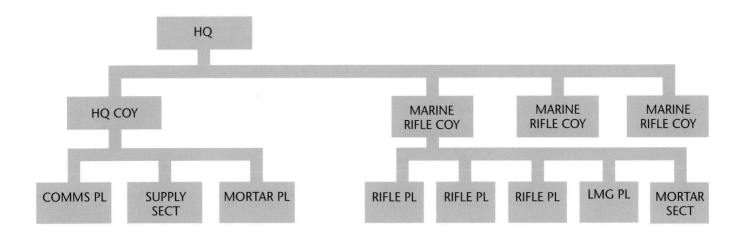

```
                              ┌──────┐
                              │  HQ  │
                              └──────┘
        ┌───────────────────────┴──────────────┬─────────────────┬─────────────────┐
   ┌─────────┐                          ┌─────────────┐   ┌─────────────┐   ┌─────────────┐
   │ HQ COY  │                          │   MARINE    │   │   MARINE    │   │   MARINE    │
   └─────────┘                          │  RIFLE COY  │   │  RIFLE COY  │   │  RIFLE COY  │
        │                               └─────────────┘   └─────────────┘   └─────────────┘
┌───────┼───────┐              ┌──────────┬──────┴───┬──────────┬──────────┐
│COMMS PL│SUPPLY │ MORTAR PL   │RIFLE PL │RIFLE PL │RIFLE PL │ LMG PL  │ MORTAR │
│        │ SECT  │             │         │         │         │         │  SECT  │
```

MARINE RIFLE COMPANY

above Marine Corps sniper version of the M1903A4 rifle with the Unertl scope.

The battalion had three rifle companies, each consisting of 7 officers and 240 men. Each company was divided into a Company HQ, a Mortar Section, a Light Machine Gun (LMG) Platoon and three Rifle Platoons.

The Company HQ comprised 2 officers and 31 men, with a Mortar Section (1 officer and 19 men) armed with three 60 mm mortars under direct command.

The LMG Platoon (1 officer, 56 men) was divided into an HQ (1 officer, 5 men) and three squads, each with two M1919A4 LMGs. There were six M1917 HMGs in reserve, which could either replace or add to the lighter machine guns, as necessary.

Each Rifle Platoon (1 officer, 45 men) consisted of a headquarters (1 officer, 6 men) and three Rifle Squads. Each Squad comprised one sergeant and three four-man Fire Teams armed with one BAR

above Marines on "suicide ridge", Peleliu, in September 1944. One is about to throw an improvised "Molotov cocktail" while another has a grenade launcher attachment on his rifle.

and three rifles, and could also be issued with a flamethrower, if needed. Similarly, a Bazooka was available to the Platoon HQ.

MARINE CORPS SPECIAL FORCES

At the start of World War II there was a tendency in many armed forces to raise brand-new units to take on what appeared to be specialist missions. This process was encouraged by the numbers of volunteers for what appeared to be exciting, novel and daring operations away from the drudgery and routine of conventional units. The US Marine Corps was no exception and spawned two types of what would today be termed special forces – the Marine Paratroopers (or Paramarines) and the Marine Raider Battalions. Neither lasted beyond 1944.

PARAMARINES

Having seen the success of German paratroops and the formation of the British Parachute Regiment, the Marine Corps was quick to identify the possibilities for such units in the Pacific. The first volunteers began jump training in October 1940 and the 1st Paramarine Battalion was formed as soon as enough men had qualified, followed by the 2nd and 3rd Battalions. Despite the knowledge that only 60 per cent of applicants passed the course, there were still plenty of volunteers as, once qualified, the paratroopers received a considerable enhancement in pay.

The three battalions all went to the Pacific in 1942 and operated independently of one another, but always as part of an amphibious force landing from the sea. In 1943 they were concentrated on Bougainville and formed into the 1st Marine Parachute Regiment, which had a total strength of some 3,000 men. This proved to be a short-lived climax as it had become clear that a separate paratroop organization had no real role within the Marine Corps. It was expensive to train and the Corps lacked the necessary resources to support it,

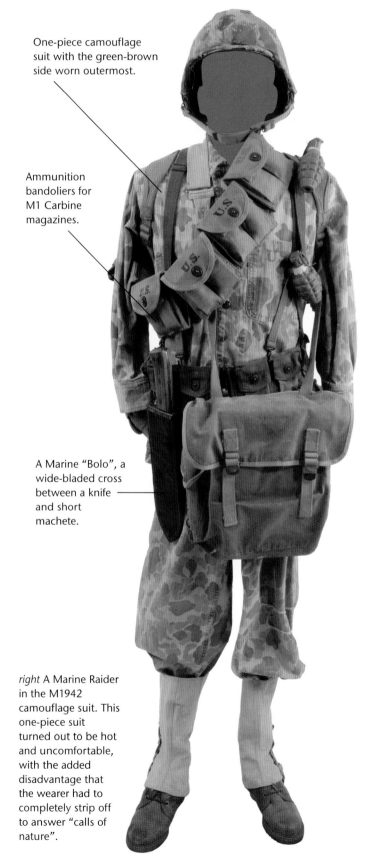

One-piece camouflage suit with the green-brown side worn outermost.

Ammunition bandoliers for M1 Carbine magazines.

A Marine "Bolo", a wide-bladed cross between a knife and short machete.

right A Marine Raider in the M1942 camouflage suit. This one-piece suit turned out to be hot and uncomfortable, with the added disadvantage that the wearer had to completely strip off to answer "calls of nature".

particularly Marine-operated transport aircraft. As a result, the Paramarines were disbanded in February 1944, the officers and men being transferred to line units.

It was through no fault of their own that the Paramarines never carried out an operational jump, but they distinguished themselves both during and after their short existence. Five Paramarines won Medals of Honor, all on Iwo Jima.

MARINE RAIDER BATTALIONS

In the early days of the Pacific campaign it appeared that there would be a role for raiding units conducting 'hit-and-run' operations against the many small, isolated Japanese garrisons, in a similar manner to the recently-formed British Commandos. The first step was to redesignate 1/5th Marines as the 1st Separate Battalion, followed shortly afterwards by a new 2nd Separate Battalion, but with both being redesignated 1st and Second Raider Battalions in mid-February 1942. A further two units were added in August/September 1942: the 3rd Raider Battalion being raised in Samoa and the 4th Raider Battalion in California. All four units fought with distinction but the Marine Corps decided that their role did not require special units and could be adequately performed by standard marine battalions with some extra training. Thus, in February 1944 the four Raider Battalions were disbanded.

right Another Marine Raider in the first pattern M1944 Herring Bone Twill (HBT) two-piece camouflaged combat uniform. Various patterns were made, and unlike army camouflage uniforms, Marine versions were reversible, with a brown scheme on one side and a green-based scheme on the other.

Chest-mounted bandolier with ammunition pouches.

M3 combat knife and scabbard tucked into the front of the combat tunic.

Black leather pistol holster with USMC crest on the cover flap.

M1942 machete, an essential tool for clearing a path through thick tropical forest and jungle.

above Marine Raiders on New Georgia fire a 60 mm mortar at the Japanese. The terrain is relatively open, although the mortar team have set up near the embankment in the background to try and get some protection from incoming fire.

The battalions all took part in amphibious operations, but the only true raid, as such, was that on August 17–18, 1942 when some 200 Marines of 2nd Raider Battalion attacked and annihilated the 73-strong Japanese garrison on Makin Island. The force comprised battalion headquarters plus two companies (each minus one rifle squad) and were carried to and from the objective by two large submarines, USS Argonaut (SS-166) and Nautilus (SS-168). Some 30 men were killed and nine became separated from the others during the evacuation and were later captured and executed by the Japanese.

Not much was really achieved, no prisoners were taken and little intelligence of any value was gained, but the operation had a considerable impact on morale in the United States and also became the subject of a wartime movie.

RAIDER RIFLE COMPANY

The Raiders formed various different organizations in 1942 and early 1943, but by late 1943 had more-or-less standardized on a four rifle company unit with a total strength of 38 officers and 863 enlisted men. The four Rifle Companies (each 5 officers, 130 enlisted men) comprised three Rifle Platoons, each of three 8-man squads, plus a Weapons Platoon, armed with two M1919A4 machine guns, two 60 mm mortars and, uniquely in the US armed forces, two British 0.55 caliber Boys Anti-Tank Rifles. There were fourteen of these weapons in the battalion, and they were quite satisfactory against lightly armored Japanese tanks, although they were eventually replaced (just before the Raiders were disbanded) by the 2.36in bazooka.

WEAPONS COMPANY

The battalion Weapons Company had a mortar platoon with three 60 mm mortars (81 mm mortars were too heavy) and two machine gun platoons, each with four M1919A4 Brownings. There was also a Demolition Platoon of two officers and 74 Marines organized into eight 8-man squads, whose mission, in line with of the unit as a whole was to blow-up enemy installations and facilities.

HEADQUARTERS COMPANY

Headquarters Company comprised a Communications Platoon and a Motor Platoon and nominally also included Battalion Headquarters, which was rather large as it included the usual clerks, stores personnel and so on. Battalion headquarters also included a pool of spare weapons, such as 60 mm mortars and Boys rifles, which could be allocated to companies as required. As was customary in all Marine Corps units, medical staff at battalion and company level were provided by the US Navy.

below Marine Raiders land on the Russell Islands, north of Guadalcanal, in February 1943. The BAR gunner has set up in the bow of the inflatable boat in case the landing is opposed. Note the rough matt texture applied to the outside of their helmets, designed to reduce shine and reflection.

MARINES COMBAT CLOTHING

The Marines wore a combination of Army clothing and equipment and items of their own design. From 1943 all field uniforms were in a sage-green color, unique to the Marines and made from a heavy-duty herringbone twill (HBT) material. The distinctive field cap (cover) had a black stenciled USMC badge and a soft visor, shorter than that on the Army cap, and with several rows of stitching to provide some stiffness. The HBT utility shirt had the corps badge and the letters USMC stenciled on the left breast pocket. During the war the practice of a name embroidered in black cotton on a sage-green backing began with the Marines. Trousers were of the same HBT material.

The M1 steel helmet and liner were the same as the Army's, but the Marines were the first to introduce a camouflage-pattern cover. The HBT field cap was sometimes worn under the helmet but reversed wit the peak pulled down to protect the back of the neck. Both officers and enlisted men wore brown Field Shoes (rough-side out) which were ankle boots with cotton laces. They also wore M1938 canvas leggings which had straps passing under the instep of the field shoes and laced up on the outside of the leg; these were generally unpopular.

right A Marine wearing the first pattern HBT – basically a fatigues and work suit pressed into service as a combat uniform. He also has a lightweight sun helmet bearing the USMC crest.

above The HBT jacket has the USMC label and crest printed in black on the breast pocket.

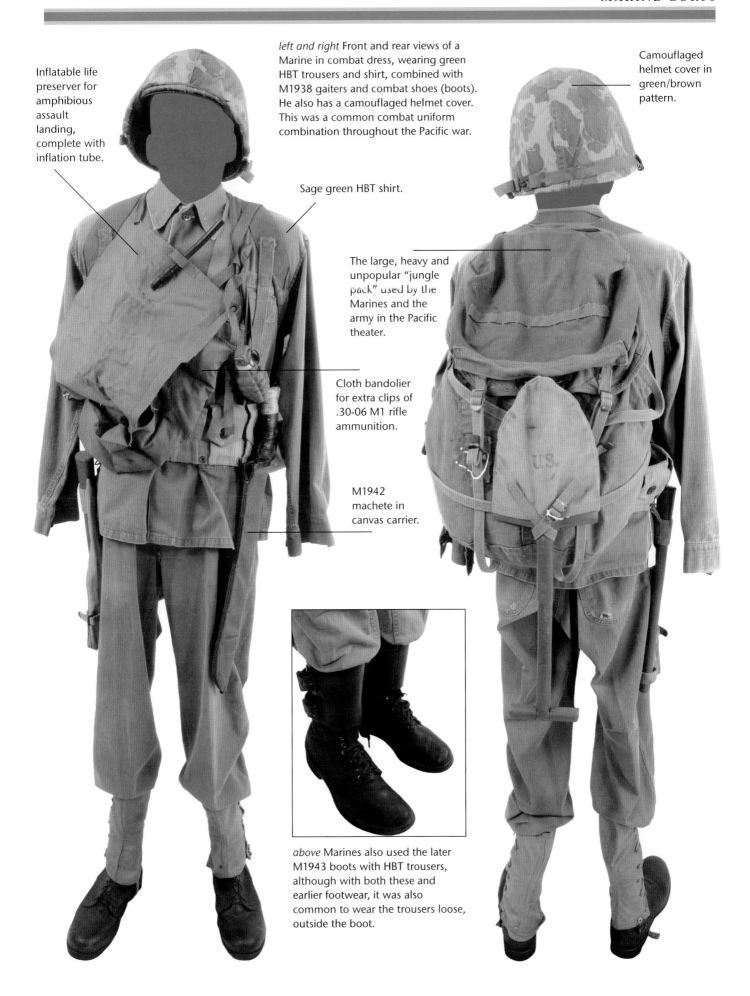

Inflatable life preserver for amphibious assault landing, complete with inflation tube.

left and right Front and rear views of a Marine in combat dress, wearing green HBT trousers and shirt, combined with M1938 gaiters and combat shoes (boots). He also has a camouflaged helmet cover. This was a common combat uniform combination throughout the Pacific war.

Camouflaged helmet cover in green/brown pattern.

Sage green HBT shirt.

The large, heavy and unpopular "jungle pack" used by the Marines and the army in the Pacific theater.

Cloth bandolier for extra clips of .30-06 M1 rifle ammunition.

M1942 machete in canvas carrier.

above Marines also used the later M1943 boots with HBT trousers, although with both these and earlier footwear, it was also common to wear the trousers loose, outside the boot.

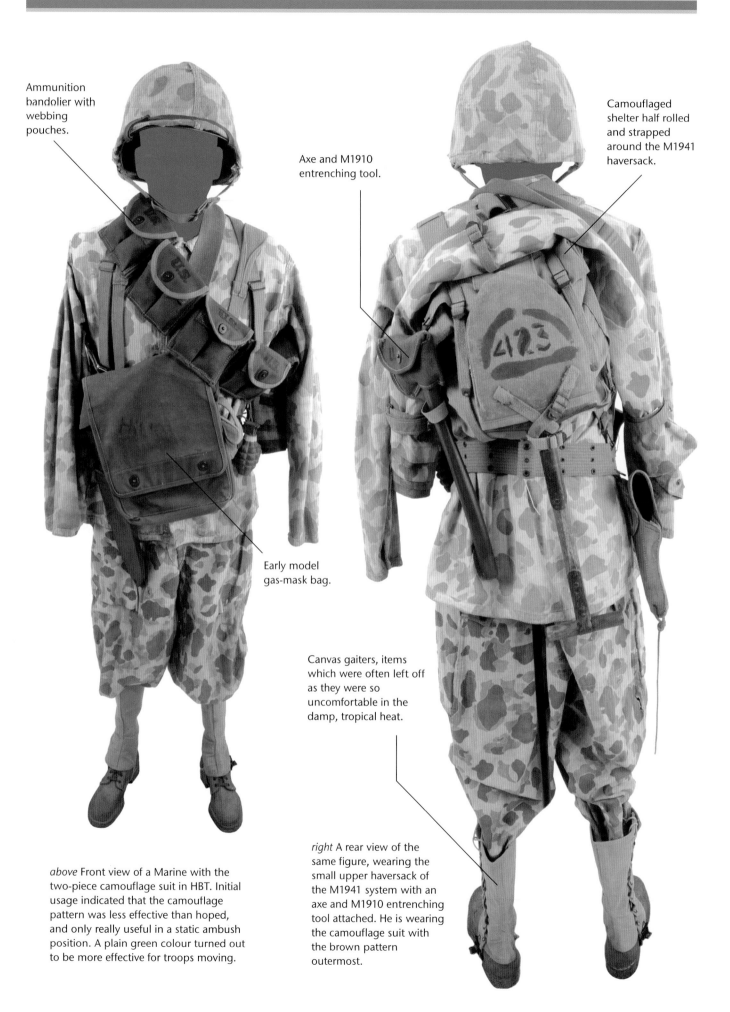

Ammunition bandolier with webbing pouches.

Axe and M1910 entrenching tool.

Camouflaged shelter half rolled and strapped around the M1941 haversack.

Early model gas-mask bag.

Canvas gaiters, items which were often left off as they were so uncomfortable in the damp, tropical heat.

above Front view of a Marine with the two-piece camouflage suit in HBT. Initial usage indicated that the camouflage pattern was less effective than hoped, and only really useful in a static ambush position. A plain green colour turned out to be more effective for troops moving.

right A rear view of the same figure, wearing the small upper haversack of the M1941 system with an axe and M1910 entrenching tool attached. He is wearing the camouflage suit with the brown pattern outermost.

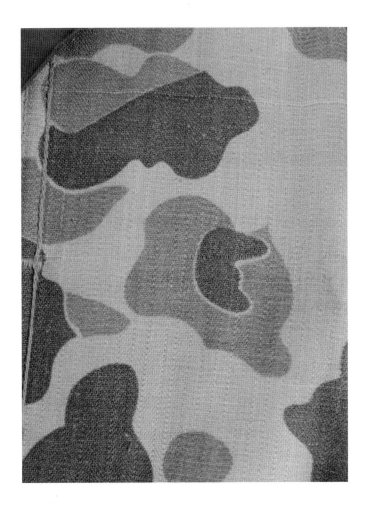

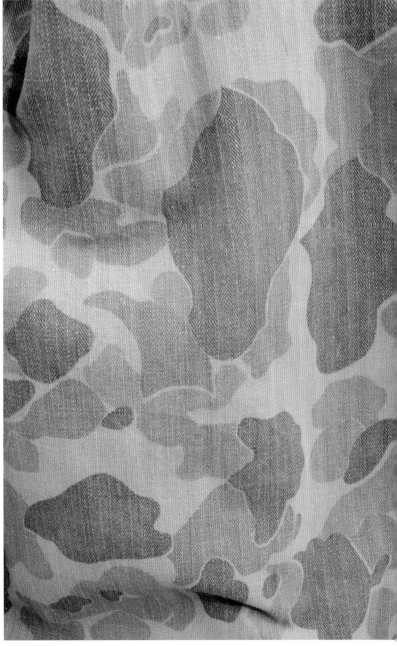

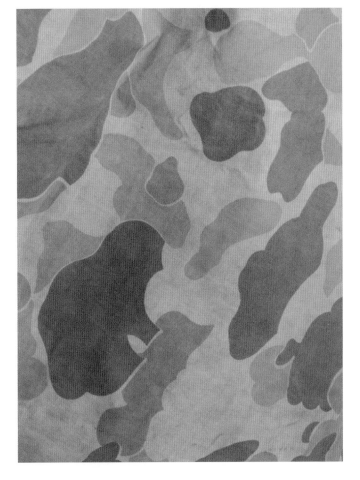

above The green-brown pattern on one side of a Marine camouflage tunic. The other side of the material has the brown pattern.

left and top left Two variants of the brown pattern of USMC camouflage uniforms. There were many variations of color and style in use.

The Marines were among the first to introduce camouflage-pattern clothing and equipment, now adopted by virtually every force involved in land combat. First was the M1942 helmet cover and this was followed by a two-piece camouflage suit in 1943.

MARINES EQUIPMENT

The Marine Corps M1941 Pack System was a daring innovation – it was actually designed by a three-strong team of real soldiers, a team of senior NCOs from 5th Marines, led by Master Gunnery Sergeant Diamond. These three designed and tested the outfit which, not surprisingly, proved a great success and remained in service for many years. The basic components were a haversack, knapsack, blanket roll and suspenders, which could be assembled in numerous configurations. The most basic, the Light Marching Pack consisted of the haversack only, while the Marching Pack consisted of the haversack plus suspenders. The Field Marching Pack consisted of the Marching Pack, plus the short blanket roll, which was the blanket, tent-pole, pins and cords, wrapped in the Shelter-Half. The Transport Pack increased load-carrying capacity, with the knapsack strapped on below the haversack. This was used when traveling by rail or ship when the blanket roll was not required. Finally, the most comprehensive – and heaviest – of all, was the Field Transport Pack which consisted of the Transport Pack plus the long Blanket Roll

strapped horseshoe fashion around three sides of the haversack/knapsack combination.

The M1910 canteen (water-bottle) had a distinctive Marine Corps carrier which hung from the belt and all ranks also carried either a Marine Corps stiletto or a Marine Corps fighting/utility knife, usually in a leather sheath.

right A Marine wearing his camouflaged shelter-half as a waterproof poncho over the rest of his uniform. He also has chest-mounted pouches for sub-machine gun magazines for either a Thompson or M3 "grease gun".

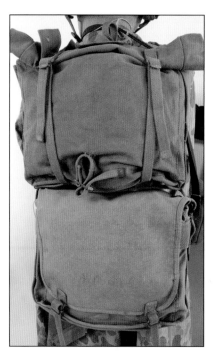

left The full two-piece M1941 system with the haversack on top and the knapsack below.

below USMC black leather pistol holster.

KA-BAR KNIFE

Overall length: 11.88 in (30.2 cm)
Blade length: 7.0 in (17.8 cm)
Weight - complete: 4.0 lb (1.8 kg)
Weight blade: 0.68 lb (0.3 kg)

One of the best-known emblems of the Marine Corps in World War II was the famous KA-BAR knife, which was carried by every Marine. In the early months of the war Marines were issued with M1917 Stilettos or the so-called Mark 1 Dagger, but these were not satisfactory and a traditional hunting knife was selected, with minor modifications to suit military requirements, including: a slightly longer blade but with a small fuller, a stacked leather handle for a good grip, and a non-reflective finish. These were essentially fighting knives but were also used for more routine tasks such as hammering tent stakes, driving nails, opening ration cans and even digging foxholes.

below A neat "Bolo" knife in a leather scabbard attached to the webbing pistol belt.

above An iconic photograph of a Marine running with a message for his platoon in May 1945, in "Death Valley", Okinawa.

below A close-up of ammunition belt, grenade and machete worn over the green HBT uniform.

right Two Marine fighting knives, the top one being made by Pal and the lower by Cataraugus.

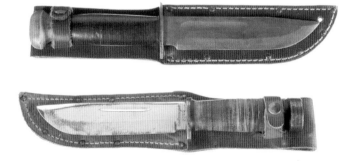

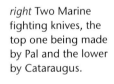

left A wide-bladed "Bolo" knife often carried by Marines in jungle conditions. This one was made in 1945.

USMC MARINE'S BASIC WEAPONS AND EQUIPMENT

Total Weight between 65–70 lb (30–32 kg)

left An M1941 haversack assembly, this time with the shelter half rolled with the green/brown pattern outermost. The entrenching tool is the M1943 folding-head type.

above The black-enamelled M1942 canteen and cup used widely by Marines in the Pacific theater.

	Item	Number	Where
Clothing Worn	Field utility cover (cap)	1	One worn,
	M1 steel helmet and liner	1	one carried
	Shirt	1	
	Drawers	1	
	Socks	1 pair	
	Jacket	1	
	Trousers	1	
	Field shoes, rough-side out	1 pair	
	Leggings, canvas	1 pair	
Weaponry	Rifle M1 (Garand)	1	Carried
	Sling	1	Carried
	Ka-Bar knife with sheath	1	On belt
	M1942 bayonet with scabbard	1	Knapsack
	Rifle cleaning kit	1	Knapsack
	M1 cleaning rod with case	1	Knapsack
	M1 combination tool	1	Knapsack
	Cleaning patches	Several	Knapsack
Personal Equipment	M1941 haversack	1	M1941 Field
	M 1941 knapsack	1	Transport Pack
	M1941 belt suspenders	2	Assembly
	M1923 cartridge belt	1	
	M1910 Entrenching tool with cover	1	

Clothing, Spare	Socks	3 pairs	Knapsack
	Shirt, dungaree	1	Knapsack
	Trousers, dungaree	1	Knapsack
	USMC undershirt and undershorts	1	Knapsack
	USMC Boondockers (boots)	1 pair	Knapsack
	Spare laces for shoes and leggings	Several	Knapsack
	Sewing kit	1	Knapsack
Sustenance	Mess tin, two-piece with lid	1	Haversack
	Canteen, aluminum with cup & carrier	1	Belt
	K-ration meals	2	Haversack
	D-ration bars	2	Haversack
	Chocolate bars	2	Haversack
	Food bag, waterproof	1	Haversack
	Knife, fork, spoon	1 set	Haversack
First-aid	Battle dressing and pouch	1	Belt
	Jungle first aid pouch	1	Belt
Washing/shaving	Mirror, metal	1	Knapsack
	Razor, blades	Several	Knapsack
	Towel	1	Knapsack
	Soap	1	Knapsack
Miscellaneous	Blanket	1	Rolled together
	Shelter half	1	wrapped in
	Pole and tent cords	1	horseshoe around
	Mosquito head net (camouflaged)	1	knap/haversack
	Tent pegs	5	
Personal	Bible, cigarettes, Zippo lighter, book, letters, etc		At personal discretion

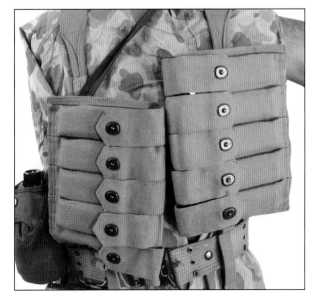

left Typical light combat order, with weapons, grenades and ammunition being carried – and not much else.

right Sub-machine guns could burn up ammunition very quickly so the extra magazines carried in these pouches would be welcome.

AIR DEFENSE

The Artillery branch was responsible for the US Army's ground-based air defense, with the Anti-Aircraft Artillery becoming an arm of service in its own right in 1942. Weapons ranged from .30 in Browning M1917 machine guns on pedestal mounts up to 120 mm guns. The infantry could also use their machine guns, BARs and even rifles for air defense on an ad-hoc basis, although for most of the war they fought under the umbrella of US air superiority.

Some light anti-aircraft weapons were found to be effective in a ground role, especially the quad Browning M2 heavy machine gun mounts,

whether carried by truck, trailer or half-track. These could provide devastating fire support to infantry in combat.

M51 MAXSON MOUNT

The vast majority of infantry M2s were single weapons on tripods or vehicle mounts, but there was also the Maxson Mount (more properly, the Multiple Caliber .50 Machine Gun Carriage M51) with four M2s controlled by a single gunner, which entered service in 1943. The mount was

above A Maxson mount on the back of a vehicle with its four M2 .50 cal heavy machine guns. This setup was also sometimes used in the ground fire role where it could produce withering amounts of fire.

heavy – well over lb (1,000 kg) – and included not only the four M2s, but the pedestal, seat, batteries, battery charger and 200 rounds of ammunition per gun. As a result, it was usually found mounted on either a truck or a trailer. Combined firing rate was some 2,300 rpm. These weapons were normally held at regimental level, but deployed forward into battalion areas.

40 mm Automatic Gun M1

The 40mm Automatic Gun M1 was an Americanized version of the Bofors 40 mm L60, the most successful light anti-aircraft gun ever. Originally a Swedish design, the Bofors was sold around the world and was adopted by many armies. Variants of it are still in service in the 21st century, deployed on land, on armored vehicles and on ships.

In US Army service the 40 mm replaced the less successful 37 mm anti-aircraft gun and became the link between machine guns and heavier AA artillery. It fired short bursts of 2 lb (900 g) explosive shells at 2,800 ft/s (850 m/s), the shells exploding to create a spray of fragments after a fixed time controlled by the fuse.

One gun wouldn't have much of a chance of a hit, but a battery could put enough lethal fragments into the air to discourage an aircraft from flying through, and damage or destroy those that did.

Various sights were used, the most common being the British "Stiffkey" system, where a standing operator adjusted the whole sight framework to account for target speed. All the two gunlayers then needed to do was keep the target in the center of their sights.

UNITED KINGDOM

Following World War I the British Army was quickly reduced to a small colonial force, with the infantry concentrating on imperial policing and small campaigns in Iraq and the North-West Frontier. In the 1930s some experiments were conducted into armored warfare but progress was slow and money was very tight.

During World War I, British infantrymen proved themselves to be dogged, loyal, capable of enduring hardships and, in the years 1939–42, able to recover from defeat. Once they had held the Italian, German and Japanese advances they retrained and then went over to the offensive, steadily pushing their enemies back to their homelands and defeat.

There were numerous special units, such as the commandos, paratroops, Special Air Service and the Long Range Desert Group, all of which had some major successes, but, in the end, it was the infantry of the line that bore the brunt, although without their comrades from the Dominions, the United States, the Soviet Union and the armies of the German-occupied countries, such as Poland and France, final victory would have been infinitely more difficult.

BRITISH INFANTRY

At the start of the war the British infantry was split between two major elements: the pre-war professional Regular Army and the Territorial Army (TA), made up of civilians who voluntarily undertook part-time training and were called-up for fulltime service in war or national emergency. But, no matter whether an infantry soldier was a regular or a territorial the highest realities in his military life were the battalion and the "regiment".

THE REGIMENTAL SYSTEM

The British infantry was organized into administrative units designated as regiments, each of which had its own headquarters, title, cap-badge, customs and, in many cases, variations in

below A neat Bren gunner in an early-war exercise. He has the 37-pattern small pack on his back and a gas mask case on his chest. A The 1939-pattern entrenching tool hangs from his belt, a design which was withdrawn in 1941 in favor of the earlier and more compact 1908-pattern pick/mattock.

above As the war progressed a whole range of colored shoulder flashes appeared, denoting regimental or corps affiliation.

dress. The function of these regimental headquarters was, however, confined to recruiting, some personnel management functions, welfare, training and the maintenance of traditions. (These regiments are not to be confused with armored, cavalry and artillery regiments, which were the battalion-sized operational units of those arms.)

Within this structure there were four types of designation. First in order of precedence came the Guards, considered the elite of the infantry, of which there were five regiments: Grenadier,

Coldstream, Scots, Irish and Welsh.

"County Regiments" bore the names of the counties to which they were affiliated and which were the primary source of their recruits: e.g., Devonshire Regiment, Yorkshire Regiment, Royal Sussex, and so on. Nine of these county regiments had been given the additional title "fusiliers" in the 18th and early 19th centuries as a collective reward for good service; e.g., Northumberland Fusiliers, Royal Inniskilling Fusiliers, etc.

A third group were the seven regiments classified as "light infantry," essentially an honor conferred during the Peninsular War (1808–1814): e.g., Durham Light Infantry, Highland Light Infantry. Apart from minor differences in uniform and a faster rate of marching, these were no different from normal infantry units.

The four "rifle" regiments, collectively known as the "Greenjackets" comprised: Rifle Brigade,

King's Royal Rifle Corps, Cameronians (Scottish Rifles), and Royal Irish Rifles. These had been raised as sharpshooters armed with rifles in the late 18th century, at a time when the rest of the infantry was armed with muskets.

INFANTRY BATTALION

Infantry regiments didn't fight as regiments. Their operational strength lay in their battalions, of which most regiments had more than one. While these battalions may have worn the same cap-badge, for all operational purposes they were deployed around the world, tasked and organized as independent units by the War Office in London.

Each was organized and manned according to their tactical role, which varied from a standard infantry battalion, through motor battalion, parachute battalion and air-landed battalion to commando.

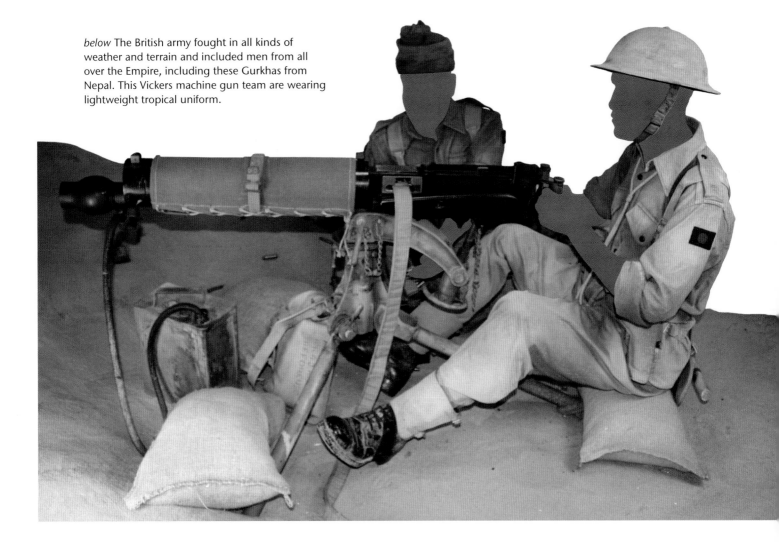

below The British army fought in all kinds of weather and terrain and included men from all over the Empire, including these Gurkhas from Nepal. This Vickers machine gun team are wearing lightweight tropical uniform.

RANKS

As a general rule, an officer's rank was displayed on the shoulder, warrant officer's on the cuff and senior and junior NCO's on the upper arm. On both Service Dress jackets and Battle Dress blouses, officers' badges of rank were worn on the epaulette and were in either metal or embroidered. The metal badges had pins which passed through the epaulette and were secured underneath by a split-pin, while embroidered badges were sewn on. When in shirtsleeves the badges were placed on a slide made from the same material as the shirt and slid over the epaulette, being held in place by the button. A similar arrangement was made for pullover order, except that the epaulette passed through a slit in the pullover.

For warrant officers in shirtsleeve order the badges were worn on a brown leather wristlet, but in pullover order were attached directly to the sleeve. NCOs wore their chevrons on the upper shirtsleeve, the main difference being that instead of embroidered material they were made of narrow white tape, as was the crown for color sergeants.

Certain badges were allowed in the field, including divisional badges and combined operations and paratroop flashes. Qualified pilots wore their wings on the left breast. Some proficiency badges, such as for marksman and drivers, were also worn on the lower sleeve. Medal ribbons and neck insignia were never worn in the field.

left NCOs wore their stripes high on the sleeve while officers put their rank badges on their shoulder straps. This image shows a close-up of the brown woolen material of the British battle dress jacket and the shoulder flash of the Royal Engineers.

Group	Rank	Badge	Where Worn	Remarks	Typical appointment
Field marshal	Field marshal	Crown above crossed Batons within laurel wreath	Shoulders	Red collar patch with gold oak leaves	Theater commander
General officers	General	Crown above Star above crossed Sword/Baton			Army commander
	Lieutenant General	Crown above crossed Sword/Baton			Corps commander
	Major General	Star above crossed Sword/Baton			Divisional commander
Field officers	Brigadier	Crown above three stars	Shoulders	Red collar patch with dark red cord	Brigade commander
	Colonel	Crown above two stars			Staff only
	Lieutenant Colonel	Crown above one stars			Battalion commander
	Major	Crown			Company commander
Junior	Captain	Three stars	Shoulders		Company 2IC
Officers	Lieutenant	Two stars			Platoon commander
	Second Lieutenant	One stars			
Quartermaster	Major Captain Lieutenant	As above		Commisioned from ranks, usually after long service	Unit quatermaster appointments
Warrant Officers	Warrant Officer 1st Class	Royal coat of arms (embroidered)	Above cuff		Regimental sergeant-major
	Warrant Officer 2nd Class	Crown in laurel wreath (brass)	Above cuff	After 1942 badge was a single crown	Company sergeant-major

	Warrant Officer 3rd Class	Crown (brass)	Above cuff		Platoon commander
Senior NCOs	Color sergeant	Crown above three chevrons	Upper sleeve	Known as 'staff sergeant' outside the infantry	Company quartermaster-sergeant
	Sergeant/ Lance-Sergeant	Three chevrons			Platoon sergeant
Junior NCOs	Corporal	Two chevrons			Section commander
	Lance-Corporal	One chevrons			Section 2IC
Privates	Private	None			

BRITISH INFANTRY RANK BADGES

Shoulder (Officers)

left British rank badges. The red background to the officers' stars denotes the infantry, although rifle regiments had a black background.

2nd Lieutenant	Lieutenant	Captain	Major	Lieutenant-Colonel	Colonel

Arm (NCOs)

Lance-Corporal	Corporal	Sergeant	Staff-Sergeant	Warrant Officer 3rd Class	Warrant Officer 2nd Class	Warrant Officer 1st Class

THE INFANTRY BATTALION

The infantry battalion had a strength of some 800–1,000 all ranks and was the basic tactical unit throughout the war. Occasionally a battalion would function independently, but more often combined with two other battalions to form an infantry brigade. As with other types of brigade, this had integral artillery, engineers and signals, as well as logistics units.

The battalion went through two major reorganizations. The Type 1939 battalion was the organization with which the infantry went to war, but this was superseded by the Type 1941 which incorporated the costly lessons of the early campaigns, particularly the debacle at Dunkirk. Then came the Type 1943 which not only incorporated the lessons of the war to date as well as incorporating various new weapons, but also anticipated the invasion of Europe and advance into Germany, and it is this which is outlined here. The strength climbed steadily during this process: 688 all ranks (Type 1939); 806 (Type 1941); 844 (Type 1943). These organizations were laid down in a document known as an "Establishment Table" which told the personnel managers how many officers and men, and of what ranks and skills, and the quartermasters how much equipment and of what types to supply them with. It should, however, be noted that within a unit the commanding officer was able to move people around and to change the organization to suit the situation.

Infantry battalions were always commanded by a lieutenant-colonel and were organized into four Rifle Companies. Initially, the fifth sub-unit was Headquarters Company, which included not only logistical and administrative elements, but also the support weapons. In the Type 1943, however, these were hived off into a separate Support Company. All these companies were commanded by majors. It should be noted that unlike the German infantry battalion there was not, even in the British Type 1939 battalion, a single horse; all transport being mechanized.

left A soldier in the 1940 campaign in newly issued battle dress. His webbing equipment has the small Double Cartridge Carrier pouches issued for a while to signallers, weapons crews and those who were not part of an infantry section.

above Infantry cautiously moving out of the Rhine bridgehead in 1945, past German dead. They wear the popular sleeveless leather jerkin over their battle dress and carry the No. 4 rifle, an updated Lee-Enfield.

BATTALION HEADQUARTERS

The command group comprised 4 officers, namely the commanding officer, second-in-command, adjutant, and intelligence officer. There were also 25 men, who included the Regimental Sergeant-Major (RSM), clerks, drivers and orderlies. The fifth officer was the doctor, a member of the Royal Army Medical Corps who headed the Regimental Aid Post, which was manned by 20 stretcher-bearers, who, in peacetime, formed the battalion band. In the Type 1943 battalion there were initially two snipers in each rifle company, but in 1944 these were centralized, becoming part of Battalion HQ, under the command of a sergeant.

HEADQUARTERS COMPANY

The HQ Company had a strength of 4 officers and 91 men. One component was the Signals Platoon (1 officer, 35 men), responsible for radio, wire and telephone communications within the battalion, and to the next unit on the right, while the rear link to brigade was the responsibility of a Royal Signals wireless detachment. The Administrative Platoon (2 officers, 51 men) provided the majority of vehicles and drivers, maintenance men (fitters), cooks and storemen. Company HQ comprised 1 officer and 5 men.

SUPPORT COMPANY

Formed in 1943, the Support Company comprised 7 officers and 185 men, grouped into Company HQ and mortar, carrier and assault pioneer platoons, plus the newly-formed anti-tank platoon. At this time the earlier anti-aircraft platoon was disbanded.

MORTAR PLATOON

A vital element of the battalion's firepower, the Mortar Platoon (1 officer, 42 men) was formed of three sections, each of two detachments. A detachment comprised one 3-inch mortar and 4-man crew, mounted in a Universal Carrier, plus its own ammunition truck, while platoon headquarters had one carrier, one truck and one motorcycle. Unlike some other armies, the mortar could not be fired from the carrier but had to be dismounted. Each section included a Mortar Fire Controller (MFC) who was usually located at a Rifle Company headquarters from where he directed and corrected fire.

CARRIER PLATOON

Carriers (Bren, Universal and Lloyd and others) were a series of small, lightly armored tracked vehicles which were used to carry small groups of infantry, mortars, machine guns and other loads. The battalion's Carrier Platoon (2 officers, 61 men) was a source of mobile firepower which could be deployed and redeployed rapidly, exploiting an advance or plugging a gap in the defense. It was not suitable, however, for holding

below Simple and lightly armored carriers acted as transport for weapons and personnel. They were perhaps not the most effective fighting vehicle but they were cheap, reliable and available.

ground. The platoon was equipped with thirteen carriers, two trucks and fifteen motorcycles. These were divided into four sections, each with three carriers, with a 4-man crew (commander, driver, two privates), plus a motorcyclist. Each carrier was armed with a Bren, PIAT and 2-inch mortar. Platoon HQ included one carrier, two trucks and two motorcycles.

ANTI-TANK PLATOON

Added to the battalion in the 1943 reorganization, this group of 2 officers and 53 men was equipped with 6-pounder guns. The platoon was divided into six detachments, each consisting of one gun towed by a carrier, with a second carrier for ammunition. Platoon HQ fielded a Universal Carrier, plus the usual trucks and motorcycles.

above A hasty discussion in a Dutch town. One man has a No. 4 rifle while the other two have Sten sub-machine guns. The man in the center has a PIAT anti-tank weapon over his shoulder.

ASSAULT PIONEER PLATOON

This platoon had a complement of 1 officer and 21 men. One element was the Pioneer Section which performed light engineering tasks and whose specialists included carpenters, masons, bricklayers, and a metal smith. It was commanded by the Pioneer Sergeant, who, in one of those idiosyncrasies so beloved of the British Army, was allowed to grow a beard and, on peacetime parades, to wear a white apron and carry a silver-plated axe. There were also two Assault Sections, each of a corporal and four privates, responsible for mine clearance and demolition work.

FIRE SUPPORT

left A Bren gunner from the Durham Light Infantry. The Bren provided most of the firepower for a British rifle section (squad).

The battalion was thus able to bring to bear the fire of some 700 rifles, 100 LMGs, six 6-pounder anti-tank guns and six 3-inch mortars. It did not have its own medium machine guns, as these were centralized in a machine gun battalion under divisional control, although a platoon of four would normally be allocated.

In addition, a battery of the brigade artillery regiment would normally be allocated, as well as at least one section of 4.2-inch mortars. So flexible was the British artillery fire control system, however, that any forward observer could quickly bring down the fire of every weapon within range, whether allocated to the battalion or not.

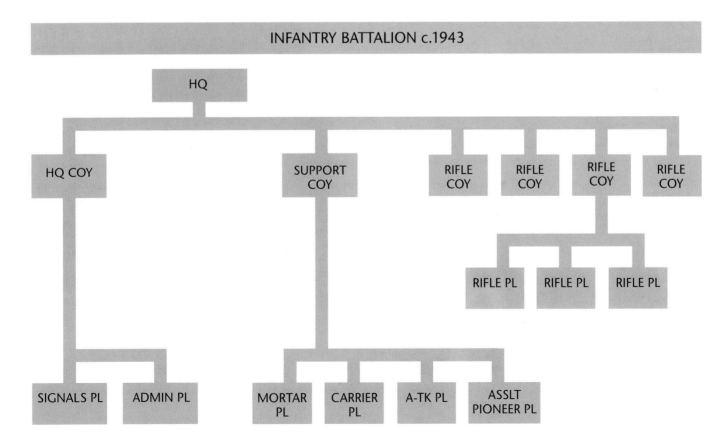

INFANTRY BATTALION c.1943

HQ

HQ COY — SUPPORT COY — RIFLE COY — RIFLE COY — RIFLE COY — RIFLE COY

RIFLE PL — RIFLE PL — RIFLE PL

SIGNALS PL — ADMIN PL

MORTAR PL — CARRIER PL — A-TK PL — ASSLT PIONEER PL

THE RIFLE COMPANY

The primary fighting strength of the rifle battalion lay in the four Rifle Companies, each of 5 officers and 122 men. There were 2 officers and 14 men in company HQ, and 3 officers and 108 men in the three Rifle Platoons.

The Rifle Platoon divided into three Rifle Sections (1 corporal plus 6 men in a rifle group and a lance-corporal and 2 men in a Bren group, a 2-inch mortar team (one mortar, 3 men) and an HQ (1 officer, 1 sergeant, 1 officer's orderly and 1 runner). Previously, each platoon had its own truck but these were now centralized under company control, which thus had one Jeep, three 15-cwt trucks and a Universal Carrier.

left An officer with drawn revolver leads his men (with fixed bayonets) through a smoke screen into the attack.

above In the Bois de Bavent in 1944. The man on the right with the Sten gun is wearing a woolen sweater under his jacket.

above Produced from mid-1942 onwards, "utility" battle dress had unpleated pockets and exposed buttons. This man also has circular pouches for Thompson drum magazines.

THE MOTOR BATTALION

The motor battalion was a mobile infantry unit which was an integral part of an armored brigade. As such, it trained with the tanks it would support in battle, while its vehicles enabled it to travel at the same speed and over the same terrain. By D-Day the Type 43 Motor Battalion was mounted in US-supplied half tracks (known as Carrier, Personnel, Half-Track M3) and the four-wheeled White Scout Car M3 in both reconnaissance and command vehicle versions, both of which had a degree of armored protection for their occupants. There were also numerous British vehicles such as Universal Carriers and 15-cwt and 3-ton trucks. Total strength was 854 all ranks (37 officers and 817 men) but its organization and weapons differed from that of the conventional infantry battalion. Two examples were that, in this case, the Vickers machine guns were part of the battalion while the 3-inch mortars were permanently dispersed in pairs to the companies, rather than held centrally. The significant features are described below.

BATTALION HEADQUARTERS

The command group (5 officers, 27 men) was almost identical to that in the Infantry Battalion, with the addition of two scout cars.

below For much of the war Motor Battalions had to make do with unprotected trucks for mobility. As demonstrated in this 1940 exercise in southern England they invariably dismounted to fight on foot.

left The Vickers medium machine gun fitted to a carrier. The vehicle provided mobility and some protection to the gun and crew, while the belt-fed gun could also be dismounted and placed on its normal tripod.

THE MOTOR COMPANY

There were only three Motor Companies, each of 7 officers and 168 men, compared to four rifle companies in the infantry battalion.

Each company had three Motor Platoons, consisting of three 8-man Motor Sections, each in a half-track, while Platoon HQ (1 officer, 6 men) consisted of an officer, sergeant, signaler, two-man 2-inch mortar team, and a driver, all mounted in a half-track. There was also a single motorcyclist.

Company HQ (2 officers, 37 men) was mounted in scout cars or half-tracks and had two 3-inch mortars, which were carried in Universal Carriers (but dismounted for firing).

The Scout Platoon (2 officers, 41 men) had no equivalent in the Infantry Battalion, and comprised three sections, each of 10 men, who were mounted in three carriers (4+3+3). Each section also carried a PIAT and a 2-inch mortar. Scout Platoon HQ deployed two carriers, a scout car, a 15-cwt truck and two motorcycles.

SUPPORT COMPANY

Although very similar in size to that in an infantry battalion, this company (7 officers, 191 men) had a totally different organization. There were three Anti-tank Platoons, each with 1 officer and 37 men. The platoons had four 6-pounder guns, each of which required two Lloyd carriers, while Platoon HQ had a Universal Carrier, several trucks and a number of motorcyclists. There were also two Machine Gun Platoons, each with 1 officer and 28 men, and each with four Vickers machine guns and eight Universal Carriers. Unusually for British support weapons of this period, the Vickers could be fired from the vehicle if required. Company HQ comprised 2 officers and 25 men.

HEADQUARTERS COMPANY

With a total of 5 officers and 94 men this consisted of the Signals Platoon (1 officer, 16 men), the Administrative Platoon (2 officers, 71 men) and Company HQ (1 officer, 8 men). On paper both these platoons included two and four 20 mm anti-aircraft guns respectively, but how these were to be deployed while the platoons carried out their other tasks was not made clear and may explain why, as far as is known, they were never issued.

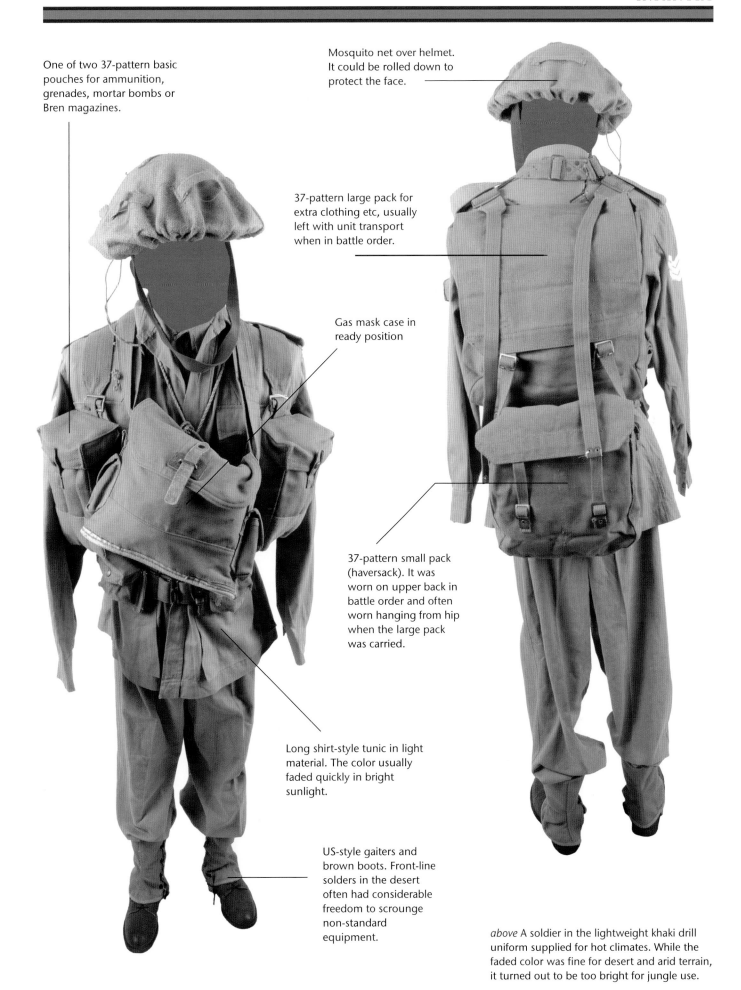

One of two 37-pattern basic pouches for ammunition, grenades, mortar bombs or Bren magazines.

Mosquito net over helmet. It could be rolled down to protect the face.

37-pattern large pack for extra clothing etc, usually left with unit transport when in battle order.

Gas mask case in ready position

37-pattern small pack (haversack). It was worn on upper back in battle order and often worn hanging from hip when the large pack was carried.

Long shirt-style tunic in light material. The color usually faded quickly in bright sunlight.

US-style gaiters and brown boots. Front-line solders in the desert often had considerable freedom to scrounge non-standard equipment.

above A soldier in the lightweight khaki drill uniform supplied for hot climates. While the faded color was fine for desert and arid terrain, it turned out to be too bright for jungle use.

FIELD UNIFORM

Most of the British infantry went to war in 1939–40 wearing the same service dress that their fathers had worn in World War I, consisting of a jacket and knickerbockers in a khaki serge material. The jacket had a high collar, brass buttons and a short skirt. Khaki-colored puttees some 9 ft (2.8 m) long were rolled around the leg from below the boot tops upwards to just below the knee and secured with a tape. A heavy woolen shirt was worn under the jacket, but without a tie, and was not visible.

This was progressively replaced by "battle dress," usually spoken of as "BD," which was first issued in 1937, spreading relatively slowly until the outbreak of war when deliveries increased rapidly. This consisted of a waist-length blouse with a wide waist band, buttoned cuffs, two patch pockets, two shoulder straps, and a high collar secured by two hooks-and-eyes, although officers tended to leave this open to expose a collar and tie being worn underneath. The trousers were deliberately baggy for easy wear in combat and had two side pockets, two rear pockets, a small pocket on the front right for the Field Dressing and a large map-pocket on the left thigh. The leg ends were secured by 37 Pattern web anklets, although a surprising number of officers and soldiers insisted on continuing to wear the less

left A recruit to a Scottish regiment being kitted out in new battle dress. The short blouse jacket buttoned to the top of the trousers to form a neat, economical, combat and barracks uniform. The cut allowed free movement and looked smart enough on young soldiers, although it was perhaps less flattering on those older officers and senior NCOs who had more "robust" waistlines.

above Apart from on the wartime "utility" version, the battle dress jacket had its front and pocket buttons hidden behind covering flaps.

above and top Issue braces for general use and the "tam o' shanter" bonnet worn by Scottish regiments.

practical puttees; these were, however, much shorter, being required only to close the gap between boots and trousers.

Throughout the war, some Highland regiments continued to wear the kilt, even in action, which was in the appropriate regimental tartan. This was combined with a variation of the service dress jacket with a cut-away front, known as a doublet. On their legs they wore khaki-colored knitted hose-tops, which were not, as appeared, a continuation of the socks, but a separate item some 16 in (40 cm) long. The hose tops were turned over at the top and held in place by garters, which sometimes also had flashes in regimental colors. A short puttee closed the gap between the top of the boots and the bottom of the hose-top. For headdress Scottish soldiers wore the "tam o'shanter" bonnet made of a soft khaki material, with a woolen pompom in the center (also in khaki) and a broad headband. The capbadge was worn above the left ear, except in the case of the Black Watch, who wore a red hackle but no badge.

left An early-war photo of a Highland soldier in kilt guarding the English coastline. Most kilts were eventually withdrawn from battlefield wear.

Mk II helmet with elasticated strap and netting cover to allow camouflage and foliage to be applied.

Utility battle dress was an attempt to cut costs with a simpler unconcealed front button arrangement.

Front pocket of Assault Jerkin. This was intended to take a similar load to the 37-pattern Basic Pouch, such as ammunition clips, Bren magazines, grenades or mortar bombs.

Battle dress trousers had two rear pockets, a small field dressing pocket on the right leg and this large map pocket on the left leg.

A very pale 37-pattern web belt over the Assault Jerkin.

above and opposite An infantry soldier at the time of D-Day in June 1944. As well as his battle dress uniform he wears the short-lived Assault Jerkin, a canvas jacket designed to replace the 37-pattern webbing system in some circumstances. It had less flexibility than the webbing, while the wearer couldn't get to the rear pockets without taking the whole thing off. It was issued for D-Day but disappeared from use soon after.

above One reason for the unpopularity of the Assault Jerkin was the pouch fasteners. They were apt to pop open when the wearer was moving about, allowing the contents to fall out.

The jerkin was supposed to make the infantryman's load easier to carry with its wide shoulder straps and even distribution of weight.

The jerkin rear upper pouch carried the same contents as the 37-pattern small pack. The smaller pouch below it was for the folding entrenching tool.

The right side pocket was intended for the water bottle or for slabs of guncotton demolition explosive.

The left hand side pocket was normally used for grenades or more ammunition.

below The Assault Jerkin had a tab to allow a pistol holster to be attached.

Webbing anklets wrapped the top of the boots and the bottom of the battle dress trousers. Anklets were also made from leather.

Known as the ammunition boot, this was a short, black boot with leather uppers and a leather sole with studs driven into it.

HEADGEAR

The combat headdress in the early part of the war was the sidecap, known as a "fore-and-aft" with a metal regimental cap-badge above the left eye. This cap was made so that it could be opened out to form a balaclava-type cold weather hat, although this was seldom done. During the war this was progressively replaced by the beret, initially a rather baggy khaki affair, but gradually becoming smaller and smarter.

Unlike the US and German armies where the steel helmet was routinely worn, British officers and soldiers tended to wear their helmets only when forced to do so. Named after its designer, the Brodie helmet was worn throughout the war. It was stamped out of steel sheet with a broad rim designed to prevent shrapnel from bursting artillery shells falling onto the wearer's shoulders. The outside was painted a matt green (khaki matt in the Middle East) and in most units it was covered with a layer of sacking and a camouflage net into which small pieces of foliage could be stuffed. In snow, the helmet was either painted white or covered with white cloth. There was an internal frame with various adjustments for size and comfort, and a chin strap. Some soldiers wore a cap comforter or a knitted balaclava under the helmet for both comfort and warmth. The Brodie was not universally popular particularly because it used to bounce when running and, under certain conditions, could strangle the wearer.

A new 1944-pattern helmet came into service towards the end of the war. There was no reduction in weight but it was of an improved ballistic shape and more comfortable to wear.

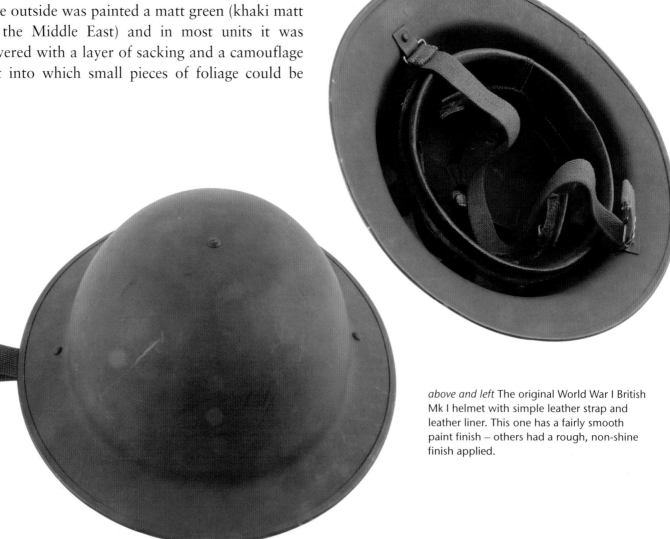

above and left The original World War I British Mk I helmet with simple leather strap and leather liner. This one has a fairly smooth paint finish – others had a rough, non-shine finish applied.

right The General Service (GS) cap was introduced in 1943 to replace the sidecap or Field Service (FS) cap.

above and right The Mk II version of the steel helmet, this time in a sand finish. The Mk II had an improved liner with a top pad and an elasticated strap. Most frontline units had Mk II helmets.

above and right The Mk III "turtle" helmet had a deeper shape to give more protection to the neck and side of the head. They were worn by units of 30 Division on D-Day.

COLD WEATHER

The British tend to adopt the attitude that cold weather will eventually go away, so that preparations for protracted wintry periods were poor or non-existent and, if absolutely necessary, a special – and rushed – purchase would be made. This certainly applied in 1939–40 when snow oversuits and rubber Wellington boots were issued. One item that was widely available throughout the war was a brown leather sleeveless jerkin which was worn over the battledress blouse. There were also special outfits for motorcyclists, particularly dispatch riders, for whom there were reinforced cord breeches and knee-length leather boots. Every officer and soldier had a greatcoat.

left A woolen jumper for cold weather use, often worn under the battle dress jacket.

below A mortar loader wearing the sleeveless leather jerkin over his battle dress. A World War I design, the leather jerkin helped the wearer keep warm in cold weather while leaving his arms unencumbered.

below Winter issue knitted woolen gloves.

below Gloves made from serge material with a leather palm.

MIDDLE EAST

The British infantry took part in many campaigns in hot climates stretching from North Africa to Northwest India. At the start of the war the basic uniform in these areas was a sand-colored equivalent to temperate dress, but made from a cotton material known as "khaki drill," which, in peacetime was heavily starched to give a smarter appearance. The jacket was similar to the temperate Service Dress and was worn with either slacks or short trousers, the legs of the latter being rather long and particularly widely cut. In combat long trousers were worn with short puttees or web anklets, but it was by no means unknown for troops to fight in short trousers with hosetops. In the very early days solar topees were sometimes worn, but these quickly abandoned and thereafter there was no specific headgear for wear in the desert, as there was, for example in the Afrika Korps.

above Men from the Indian Brigade in Eritrea, wearing sand-colored khaki drill tunic and shorts, with puttees around the ankles.

Once the desert war had been going for a short period, dress standards began, of necessity to be relaxed. Starching was clearly out of the question, but men of the same unit could be seen together in a wide variety of styles, including long and short trousers, slacks with and without puttees, sleeves rolled up and down and various forms of headgear.

One item that seems to have started in the Middle East and then spread across the British Army and beyond was the woolen pullover. This was originally in khaki with reinforced sections at the elbow and shoulder, the latter incorporating a slit through which the shirt epaulette was pulled and, in the case of officers, used for rank slides. Warrant officers wore their badges either metal on a wrist strap, or embroidered on the short/pullover. NCOs wore their stripes but in white or khaki-colored tape.

left This man is dressed for desert warfare, in khaki drill uniform, shorts and 37-pattern webbing, with the large pack and entrenching tool carrier at the back. He also has a veil to keep mosquitoes and flies away from his face.

TROPICAL

Until 1942, the army in India and the Far East wore the same uniform as in the Middle East; i.e., khaki drill. However, the early campaigns in Malaya and Burma showed that this was highly unsuitable for jungle warfare for many reasons: the color stood out against the green undergrowth, the material did little to keep down body temperature, and it ripped easily. This led to the introduction of a new uniform, manufactured in India, in "jungle green" color. This consisted of either a shirt or bush jacket, made out of a cellular material known as aertex that was designed to enable sweat to evaporate quickly, thus cooling the skin underneath.

above Troops in India and the far east wore a slouch hat, often with the side of the rim pinned up.

above Khaki drill shorts may not have been fashionable but they were comfortable in hot conditions.

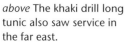
above The khaki drill long tunic also saw service in the far east.

left Long trousers in tropical green drill cotton.

BOOTS

right The standard black leather ammunition boot and anklet. This anklet is made from webbing material with leather straps; others were made from leather throughout.

left As an alternative to anklets, puttees could be wound around the ankle and tied with fabric tapes.

below Issue woolen socks. Soldiers had to darn and repair their socks themselves.

right A pair of webbing anklets opened out.

Standard combat footwear was the "Ammunition Boot." This had strong black, dimpled leather uppers, large tongue, a substantial toecap, and a reinforced section at the heel. The brown leather sole was protected by a semi-circular steel toe-plate at the front while the heel was protected by a horseshoe-shaped steel heel-plate. A pattern of steel hobnails, usually between eleven and thirteen, was hammered into the flat bottom of the sole to protect it and to give added grip; these had to be regularly renewed. These boots weighed about 4 lb (1.8 kg) and once properly worn-in were comfortable and long-lasting.

The front was secured by two rows of eyelets and a square-profile leather lace, which was usually tied in an unusual manner, but always horizontally between opposite eyelets. One end was knotted and the lace then threaded through either of the lowest eyelets, from the inside out, with the knot inside. The lace was then threaded, from one side to another until the top was reached, carefully tightened and the loose end passed around the ankle and tied back on itself. The top of the boot and the lace was then covered by either web anklets or puttees.

PERSONAL EQUIPMENT

After his rifle, nothing was more important to an infantry soldier than his personal equipment, which he wore every day in combat and in which he carried his military belongings. For the vast majority of British and Commonwealth soldiers in World War II, this was the Pattern 1937 Web Equipment, known universally as '37 Pattern' which had been developed from the World War I-vintage Pattern 1908, but adapted to make it lighter, easier to wear, simpler to adjust, and to carry new items, such as magazines for the Bren and Boys anti-tank rifle.

37 PATTERN

The new webbing outfit was made of a stout woven cotton material, which was dyed, pre-shrunk and waterproofed to ensure durability, while strap ends and buckles were made of brass. The basic outfit consisted of belt, two basic pouches, cross straps and bayonet frog. Marching

order was the same, but with addition of a haversack, carried high on the back, and an entrenching tool and carrier suspended from the rear center of the belt. In field service marching order (FSMO) the 1908 pattern large pack was added, which was worn on the back, displacing the haversack, which was suspended from the belt on the left buttock, with the waterbottle suspended on the right buttock.

There were also two additional "utility pouches" which were carried in combat. The tops were connected by a wide strap which either passed over the left shoulder with one pouch in front and one behind, or passed around the back of the neck with one pouch on each side of the wearer's chest. A second, narrower strap passed around the upper body to prevent the pouches from bouncing. Each pouch could contain either: three Bren magazines, two anti-tank rifle magazines, three 2-inch mortar bombs, or a number of grenades.

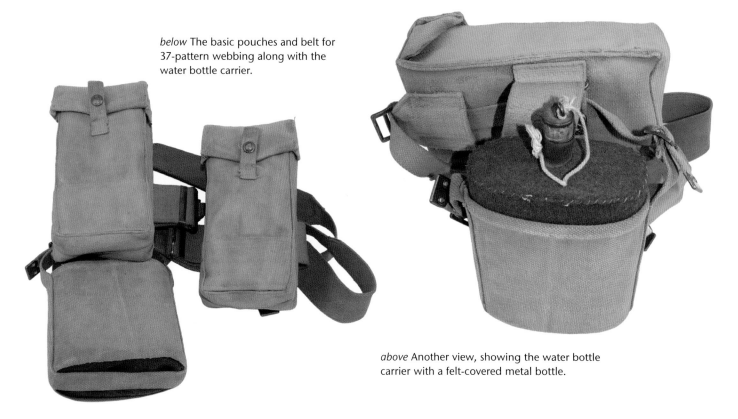

below The basic pouches and belt for 37-pattern webbing along with the water bottle carrier.

above Another view, showing the water bottle carrier with a felt-covered metal bottle.

left The small pouch intended to hold binoculars but also used as a general pouch.

below and right The large pack was carried during administrative moves but left behind with unit transport before going into battle.

right The 37-pattern web carrier for the water bottle.

below The Suffolk Regiment training in beach assault tactics in preparation for the D-Day landings. Note the use of the small assault ladder to cross the barbed wire.

BASIC WEAPONS AND EQUIPMENT OF THE BRITISH INFANTRYMAN

	Item	Number	Weight oz (g)†	Where
Clothing	Cap	1	4 oz (113 g)	Worn or carried
	Steel helmet	1	35 oz (.99 kg)	
	Shirt	1	15 oz (.43 kg)	
	Drawers	1	12 oz (.34 kg)	
	Socks	1 pair	4 oz (113 g)	
	Jacket	1	32 oz (.91 kg)	
	Trousers	1	33 oz (.94 kg)	
	Boots	1 pair	65 oz (1.84 kg)	Ammunition-type
	Web anklets*	1 pair	8 oz (226 g)	
Weaponry	Rifle	1	8.2 lb (3.7 kg)	Carried
	Sling*	1	6 oz (170 g)	On rifle
	Oil bottle	1	2 oz (57 g)	In butt trap
	Pullthrough	1	2 oz (57 g)	In butt trap
	Bayonet and scabbard	1	24 oz (.68 kg)	In frog
	Bayonet frog*	1	2 oz (57 g)	On belt
	303 ammunition (5-round clips)	10 clips	50 oz (1.42 kg)	In basic pouches
	Strip Flannelette	Strip	1 oz (28 g)	Pouch (four-by-two)
	Gauze	1	1 oz (28 g)	Pouch
37 Pattern web equipment	Waistbelt*	1	10 oz (280 g)	
	Braces*	2	6 oz (170 g)	Over shoulders
	Basic pouches*	2	22 oz (.62 kg)	Front of belt
	Entrenching tool carrier*	1	10 oz (280 g)	Suspended at back
	Haversack, with 2 straps*	1	28 oz (.79 kg)	11 x 9.5 x 4 in. On back or from belt
	Large pack, with 2 straps**	1	27 oz (.76 kg)	15 x 13 x 41in. Usually in vehicle.
Equipment	Entrenching tool		80 oz (2.27 kg)	In carrier
Spare Clothing	Cardigan	1	15 oz (.43 kg)	Haversack
	Ground sheet	1	48 oz (1.36 kg)	Haversack
	Cap comforter	1	3 oz (.85 kg)	Haversack
	Great coat	1	91 oz (2.58 kg)	Large pack
	Socks	1 pair	4 oz (114 g)	Large pack
	Laces	1 pair	1 oz (28 g)	
Sustenance	Emergency ration	1	6 oz (170 g)	Haversack
	Knife, fork, spoon (KFS)	1 set	8 oz (227 g)	Haversack
	Mug, brown enamel	1	6 oz (170 g)	Haversack

	Waterbottle carrier**	1	4 oz (114 g)	On belt
	Water bottles** (filled)	2	40 oz (1.13 kg)	One in carrier One in haversack
Gas	Service Respirator Mark IV (in bag)	1	48 oz (1.36 kg)	Worn around neck (incl anti-dimming cream)
	Anti-gas cape	1	39 oz (1.11 kg)	Haversack
Miscellaneous	Field dressing	1	6 oz (170 g)	Jacket pocket
	Clasp knife	1	5 oz (142 g)	Pocket
	Paybook (AB 64 Pt 2)	1	2 oz (56 g)	Jacket pocket
	Identity discs	2	1 oz (28 g)	Round neck
	Holdall containing boot laces, comb, tooth brush, tooth paste, cased razor, shaving brush	1	8 oz (227 g)	Large pack
	Housewife	1	3 oz (85 g)	Large pack
	Soap	1	3 oz (85 g)	Large pack
	Towel	1	12 oz (340 g)	Large pack
Personal	Cigarettes, book, matches, letters, etc			At individual discretion, subject to security rules

*   Part of 37 Pattern, made of canvas webbing with brass attachments
** These were carried forward unchanged from 1908 Pattern
† Where items varied in size, figures given here are for an average man.

The table shows the official "loadout" of the infantryman, although many variations occurred due to the tactical situation, terrain, climate and unit custom. Also, wherever possible, large packs were carried in unit transport.

Those chosen to be Bren gunners did not carry a rifle, saving 9 lb (4.1 kg), although their LMG with sling weighted 22 lb (10 kg). In addition, the spare parts wallet and holdall had to be carried, which included, most importantly, the spare barrel.

In addition to the items listed in the table there were others to be shared around, which might include wireless batteries, flare pistol and cartridges, grenades, pick axe and handle, and yet more ammunition, usually in cloth bandoliers slung around the neck. In the worst case the infantryman could be wearing and carrying between 50–60 lb (23–27 kg), no mean load when he also had to move across country, negotiate obstacles and fight.

right British water bottle in a US-style carrier.

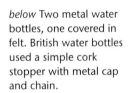

below Two metal water bottles, one covered in felt. British water bottles used a simple cork stopper with metal cap and chain.

OFFICERS

Infantry company officers wore the same basic 37 Pattern, but did not carry a rifle, extra .303 ammunition, basic pouches or entrenching tool. Instead, the pouches were replaced by two "brace attachments" to connect the braces to the belt at the front. Cases (holsters) for the pistol, .38 ammunition, binoculars and compass fitted on the belt or brace attachments. Officers had at least four lanyards around their neck for pistol, binoculars, compass and the map case.

The map case consisted of a bakelite board for stiffness and as a backing to write on, metal clips to hold the map in place, clear plastic overlay, canvas cover, which included pockets for pencils, chinagraphs and a protractor, and canvas carrying sling.

Binoculars, Prismatic No2 Mark III were light and handy, with a magnification of 6 x 30. They were made by a number of companies in the UK and Australia.

The Prismatic Compass, Oil-Filled Mark III remains one of the finest and most accurate military compasses ever made. It had a black-lacquered brass body 2.4 in (60 mm) in diameter with a hinged lid and a small hinged prismatic viewer. The compass card floated in a bath of purified kerosene and was accurate to 0.5 degrees.

left A selection of pistol and revolver holsters for use with 37-pattern webbing. The furthest left is made from leather while the other three are webbing. Note the extra cartridge holder on one and a cleaning tool with another.

below A light valise pouch used by officers.

left Binoculars case with compass carrier above, as worn by officers and NCOs. Pistol ammunition was carried in a similar case to that for the compass.

below Various designs of binocular were issued, some having been in service since World War I. This pair has a 1940 date stamp.

It was an extraordinarily adaptable instrument, usable by day and night and very rugged; it weighed 10.6 oz (300 g).

In the days when the platoon commander had no wireless communication to his sections many commands were given by whistle, which was usually a silver-plated brass model with a "pea" known as the "Acme Thunderer" although many other models were used.

OFFICERS' EQUIPMENT

	Item	Number	Weight (oz)	Where
37 Pattern web equipment	Brace attachments*	2	5 oz (142 g)	Replaced basic pouches
Weapon	Pistol case*	1	8 oz (226 g)	Belt, left
	.38in revolver	1	32 oz (.91 kg)	Smith & Wesson/Webley
	Lanyard	1	3 oz (85 g)	On revolver
	Ammunition pouch*	1	4 oz (113 g)	Over brace attachment
	.38in ammo	12rds	7 oz (198 g)	In pouch
	Cleaning rod		1 oz (28 g)	Haversack
Observation/ navigation	Binocular case*	1	16 oz (.45 kg)	On belt
	Binoculars, prismatic, No 2	1	48 oz (1.36 kg)	
	Compass pocket*	1	5 oz (142 g)	Over brace attachment
	Compass prismatic	1	6 oz (170 g)	
	Lanyard	1	3 oz (85 g)	
	Map case	1	12 oz (340 g)	Slung on shoulder
	Whistle	1	2 oz (57 g)	

*   Part of 37 Pattern, made of canvas webbing with brass attachments

PATTERN 1944 WEBBING

Pattern 1944 Web Equipment was intended to overcome the generally acknowledged shortcomings of 37 Pattern, particularly those relating to jungle warfare. The webbing itself was lighter in weight, dark green in color, better waterproofed and more resistant to rotting. In addition the buckles, hooks and connectors were made of a light alloy, rather than brass. The basic yoke was more complicated than that for 37 Pattern but was far easier to adjust and distributed the weight better. There were two ammunition pouches which were identical except that on its left-hand side the left pouch had two webbing loops for the bayonet. The small pack was larger than that for 37 Pattern, but much better laid out, with separate compartments for the mess tins. The waterbottle was also slightly larger and made of aluminum, as was its screwcap, although opening/closing the bottle could be noisy unless great care was taken. The waterbottle sat inside a metal drinking utensil/kettle and both were carried in a special webbing carrier which hung from the belt. Universally known as "44 Pattern," the new webbing was only beginning to reach units, especially in the Far East, in early 1945.

GAS PROTECTION

above A training exercise for the Irish Guards, with the men wearing their Mk IV gas masks and carrying Thompson sub-machine guns. Note the gas capes still rolled up on their backs.

British soldiers entered the war with the Service Respirator Mark IV. Introduced in the late 1920s and developed from the World War I-era Mark III, this outfit consisted of four elements: face mask, a metal box containing the filter, a hose connecting the two, and a haversack in which to carry it all. The filter was permanently connected to the facepiece by a length of corrugated hose made from molded rubber and covered in a stockinette material.

The complete outfit was carried in a khaki-colored canvas haversack, which in the "ready" position was worn on the soldier's chest suspended from a strap passing around his neck

and prevented from bouncing by a thin cord passed around his back. On a gas alert being given the soldier doffed his steel helmet, opened the haversack, donned the respirator, replaced his helmet and closed the bag. The filter canister remained in the haversack on the wearer's chest.

In addition to the respirator soldiers carried a set of anti-gas clothing, including an Anti-Gas Cape made of treated cotton and worn over the battledress uniform, webbing and haversack. There was also a pair of large mittens and a separate head cover made out of the same material. The cape was usually rolled into a neat cylinder, containing the mittens and head cover, and carried at the top of the haversack.

The Mark IV design was progressively improved during its service, and the Mark V was introduced with a new molded facepiece, made from black rubber.

A totally new respirator began to enter service in 1943. The Light Anti-Gas Respirator Mark 1 had a fully shaped rubber facepiece with two circular glass eyepieces. On the left side was a 2.4 in (60 mm) diameter threaded inlet into which was screwed a removable drum-shaped filter. This enabled a larger and improved exhalation valve to be positioned in front of the wearer's mouth. This was a most satisfactory design and set the style for respirators for the following half-century.

right A Mk V gas mask with molded rubber facepiece, showing the connecting hose to the filter inside the carrying case.

below A close-up of the rubber facepiece and exhalation valve of the Mk V.

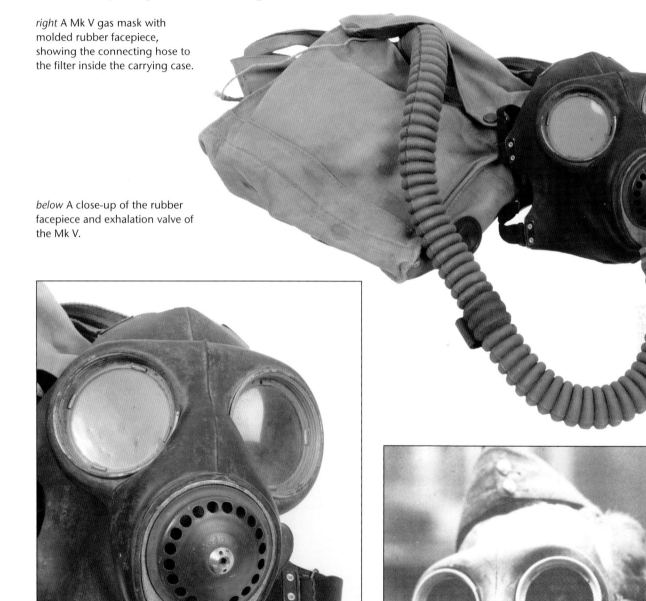

right The 1943 model gas mask brought the filter up to the cheek, removing the need for the cumbersome hose and separate filter.

161

MAKING LIFE EASIER

MESS TINS

Every soldier carried two rectangular mess tins; the inner measured 6.3 x 4.7 x 2.2 in (16 x 12 x 5.5 cm) and fitted inside the outer, which measured 7.0 x 5.1 x 2.4 in (18 x 13 x 6 cm). Together the pair weighed 15 oz (420 g). Both were fitted with folding wire handles and could be used for cooking, tea-making, as well as for eating. They were made of aluminum, one unfortunate consequence being that if they hit each other or were hit with cutlery they emitted a drumming noise that traveled over considerable distances.

For personal cooking, soldiers carried a small stove, known as either a "Tommy cooker" or "Hexi burner." This was rectangular in shape – 5 x 4 x 1 in (13 x 10 x 0.4 cm) – and made of very thin metal. When closed it contained a packet of eight blocks of Hexamine, a compound of formaldehyde and ammonia, which burned easily, with a minimum of smoke and left no residue. To use, it was opened out, forming a simple stove, on which rested a single mess-tin.

RATIONS

The British infantry spent a lot of effort making sure that its men be properly fed, with the general principle that all soldiers would receive one properly cooked hot meal every night, which would be prepared in the logistic echelon.

Where tactical considerations made this impossible, 14-man composite rations packs (always known as "Compo") were issued for the

below Cpl Albert Burton displays the mess tin filled with cigarettes which absorbed a bullet and saved his life. Note how the wartime censor has erased the unit flashes on his shoulder.

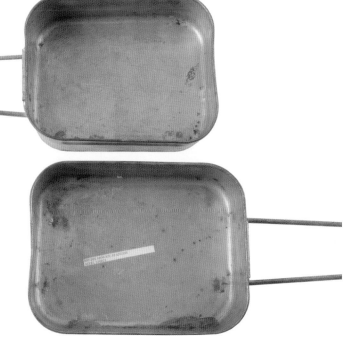

right Mess tins came as a pair, each with folding handles. The smaller mess tin fits neatly inside the larger to make a compact package. Other personal items could be carried inside the smaller tin.

riflemen to cook themselves. There were seven different combinations in boxes labeled "A" to "G" to provide some variety, but all contained not only meat and vegetables, but also items such as coffee, tea, cigarettes, toilet paper and sweets.

Starting in early 1944 soldiers were issued with 24-hour ration packs, which came in a light cardboard box and contained a carefully balanced selection of small tins and packets, which could be stowed in the haversack or pouches.

OTHER EQUIPMENT

Soldiers were also issued with a canvas roll containing pockets for washing kit and knife fork and spoon.

Other equipment included weapons cleaning kits and, as this was the British Army, brushes and blacking for keeping boots neat and clean.

below A soldier's personal kit, including: the canvas roll with shaving equipment and knife, fork and spoon; metal shaving mirror; boot and clothing brushes; foot powder and two enamelled mugs.

left Improvisation is a key skill for a soldier. Here, Cpl Noble takes a bath in a slit trench lined with a canvas tarpaulin.

above A "housewife" clothing repair kit with needles and thread.

left Folding map case with transparent overlay and pocket for pens etc.

above A pair of issue metal soap dishes.

left and below Cigarettes such as these were a vital factor in preserving morale.

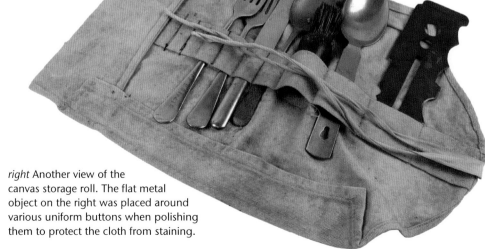

right Another view of the canvas storage roll. The flat metal object on the right was placed around various uniform buttons when polishing them to protect the cloth from staining.

MEDICAL EQUIPMENT

British soldiers were luckier than those of many other armies, in that their medical services were effective and robust, with front-line dressing stations feeding casualties back through an efficient system of higher-level stations and hospitals, and finally, in severe cases, back to the UK.

The first line of medical defense was the individual soldier and his personal field dressing (for use on himself). There was also a selection of other field and shell dressings available to the frontline units.

above the First Field Dressing was carried by every man, usually in a special pocket in their battle dress trousers.

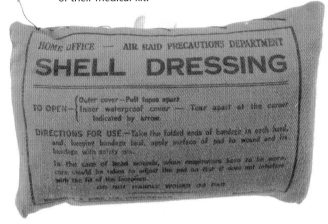

below A shell dressing, normally carried by platoon medics as part of their medical kit.

below Stretcher bearers from a Highland regiment in 1940. Note the drab protective and cover over their kilts. Stretcher bearers often came from the regimental band.

below Another field dressing. Wise infantry soldiers would carry more than one.

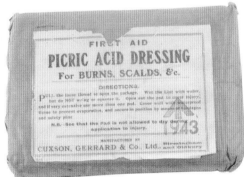

above A dressing impregnated with picric acid for use on burns and scalds.

COMMUNICATIONS

The basic principle was that all communications within a battalion were manned by unit specialists, but that the rear-link from battalion HQ to brigade HQ was provided and manned by operators from the Royal Corps of Signals. The primary means of battlefield communications was by radio ("Wireless" in British terminology). In line with the technology of the time, virtually all sets worked in the high frequency (HF) band, i.e. between 3 and 30 MHz. They also used a processing system known as "amplitude modulation" (AM).

Radios were used to establish networks (nets) and the battalion command net, for example, included "control" at battalion HQ and "outstations" at each company headquarters, as well as at specialist sub-units such as the mortar platoon, and supporting arms, such as the Royal Artillery.

The great majority of sets were free-tuning, which meant that they could not be set up on a precise frequency and had to be lined up by the operators. So, at the time for opening communications, the control station transmitted a steady tuning signal, enabling outstation operators to align their frequency with that of control, following which a netting call was made in which control confirmed contact with each outstation in turn. It was a cumbersome procedure which was only overcome when crystal control came into use.

In general, wireless communications worked well, but suffered some unavoidable problems. The HF band was both noisy and crowded with other users, range was limited and all communications were liable to be overheard by the enemy. Even at battalion level Morse had to be used when voice could not get through. Power supply was a particular problem. Wet batteries could be used in vehicles and kept charged by the engine, but dry batteries for manpack sets were heavy and had limited life.

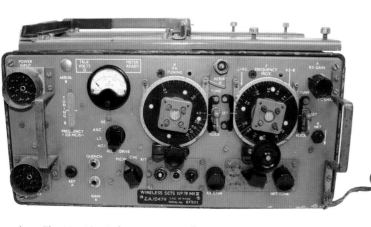

above The No. 19 wireless was normally used for communications from the battalion to higher formations.

right No. 18 manpack sets were used for signals between battalion and company HQs.

MAIN INFANTRY WIRELESS SETS 1939–1945

Set	Type	Role	In svc	Freq range	Power	Mode	Range	Remarks
No 8	Manpack	Battalion/company HQ	1940	6–9 MHz	0.25 W	Voice	5 miles (8 km)	Replaced by 18 set
No 18	Manpack	Battalion/company HQ	1941	6–9 MHz	0.25 W	Voice Morse	10 miles (16km)	Widely used
No 19	Vehicle or dismounted	Rear link to brigade HQ	1941	2–8 MHz	2.5–9 W	Voice Morse	15 miles (24km)	Widely used
No 22	Vehicle or dismounted	Rear link to brigade HQ	1942	2–8 MHz	1.5 W	Voice Morse	20 miles (32km)	Widely used. Looked like WS19
No 28	Manpack	Battalion/company HQ	1941	6-9 MHz	.25 W	Voice Morse	3–5 miles (5-8km)	Limited production
No 37	Manpack	Paratroops	1941	340–385 MHz	.5 W	Voice Morse	1* miles (1.6km)	Limited production
No 38 Mk2	Manpack	Company/platoon HQ	1942	7.4–9.2 MHz	.2 W	Voice	1 miles (1.6 km)	Mk 3 was tropical version
No 46	Manpack	Paratroops and Commandoes	1942	3–9.1 MHz		Voice Morse	10 miles (16 km)	Crystal control. Fully waterproof
No 48	Manpack	Battalion/company HQ	1942	6–9 MHz	.25 W	Voice Morse	10 miles (16 km)	Developed in USA
No 58	Manpack HQ	Battalion/company	1943	6–9 MHz	.3 W	Voice	5 miles (8 km)	Developed in Canada
No 68	Manpack	Battalion/company HQ	1943	1.75–2.9 or 3–5.2 MHz	.25 W	Voice Morse	10 miles (16 km)	Similar to 18 set but different frequencies

* 15 miles (24 km) in ground-air role

The table shows the main sets to be found in an infantry battalion during the war.

Cable (line) was also used but primarily in static positions. The cable was heavy and had to be laid from machines which were either back-packed, on wheeled trolleys, or in vehicles. Networks were formed by using either the 10-Line Concentrator or the antiquated 24-line Field and Fortress (F&F) exchange mounted in a wooden box. Subscribers used either Telephone Set F, a bulky and heavy bakelite instrument in a wooden box, or Telephone J, a more modern unit in a metal box. One-to-one links were sometimes laid in the forward areas, for example, to a listening or observation posts.

As in other armies, flags were sometimes used, as were whistles and pyrotechnics.

All the equipment in use was heavy, unwieldy and unreliable, but was still a major step forward compared to previous wars. But, despite all this, recourse had to be made at battalion level to dispatch riders and at company and platoon level to runners.

left and below The No. 38 was used between company HQ and the platoons.

above Very flare pistols were a quick and cheap method of transmitting simple signals.

above The "Fullerphone" allowed morse to be sent over the same lines and at the same time as voice.

right The "F-type" field phone was widely used between static positions.

right The Swedish-designed Hagelin cipher machine used a similar rotor system to the German Enigma.

below Signal lamps had some uses at night, although they were fragile and cumbersome.

below Hagelin designs were used by the British, German, United States and French armies.

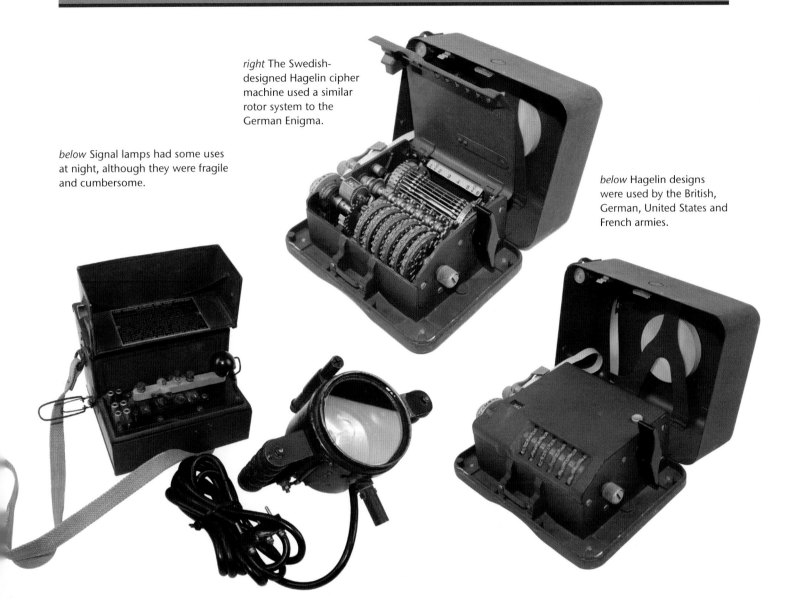

right Whistles were useful for simple messages and sounding the alert, as demonstrated by this corporal on the lookout for enemy aircraft.

INFANTRY WEAPONS

Britсh infantry weapons were, on the whole, conservative in design, mostly based on those used in World War I.

Some were excellent examples of their class, such as the SMLE and No.4 rifles and the (Swiss-designed) Bren LMG. Others were adequate, such as the No.2 revolver, while others were hastily-designed and manufactured responses to early war experience. Often crudely made and lacking in finesse, these wartime designs, such as the Sten and PIAT, were effective enough though, and enabled the infantry to go head-to-head with their enemies.

A British infantry platoon tended to have fewer automatic weapons under its direct control than a US or German equivalent, especially as the war progressed. Medium machine guns were held centrally, leaving the platoon to manage with a box-fed LMG, bolt-action rifles and sometimes a few SMGs as its firepower.

below Men from the 2nd Seaforth Highlanders advance behind a "Crocodile" flamethrower tank in the Reichswald in February 1945. They are in light fighting order, although still weighed down with extra ammunition and shovels.

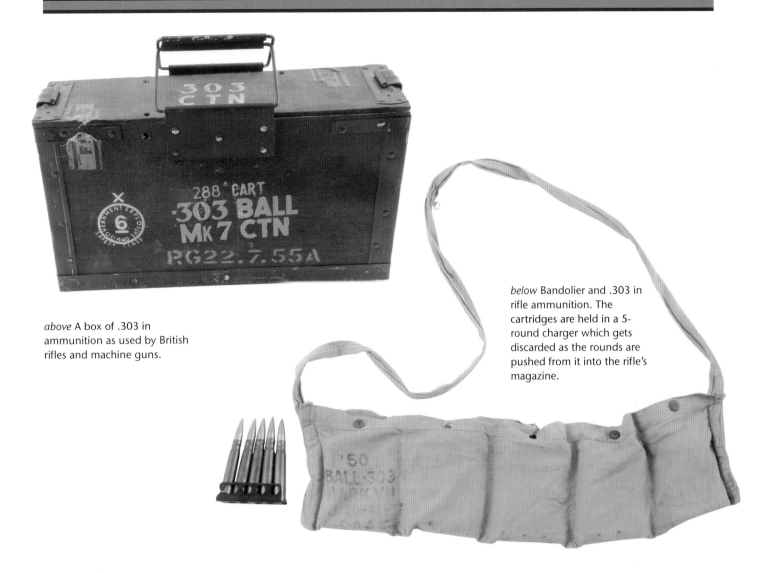

above A box of .303 in ammunition as used by British rifles and machine guns.

below Bandolier and .303 in rifle ammunition. The cartridges are held in a 5-round charger which gets discarded as the rounds are pushed from it into the rifle's magazine.

left An infantry section moving cautiously through a jungle village. SMLEs, a Bren gun and a Sten are all in evidence.

RIFLES

SHORT MAGAZINE LEE-ENFIELD MARK III AND V

Type: bolt-operated rifle
Origin: UK
Caliber: .303 in
Weight (empty): 8.2 lb (3.7 kg)
Barrel length: 25 in (635 mm)
Feed: bolt-operated, 10-round box magazine

below An SMLE Mk III with the action cocked, and showing the leather sling and very substantial sword bayonet.

The British Army fought World War I with the Short Magazine Lee-Enfield Mark III and Mark III* rifles, which were strong, easy to fire and maintain, and thoroughly reliable. The Mk III came with a fearsome 18-inch (46 cm) sword bayonet and could fire various types of grenade. In the early 1920s the army began the search for a new rifle, incorporating all the good points of its predecessor, but which would be easier to manufacture by modern mass-production methods. This led to the SMLE Mark V which had an additional

barrel band in front of the forward sling swivel and an aperture backsight, graduated up to 1,400 yd (1,280 m), which was relocated from atop the barrel to the bridge above the bolt. After trials with the Mk V it was decided that conversion of the large existing stocks of rifles would be too expensive and although the development of a new rifle was continued (which led eventually to the Number 4 Rifle) large numbers of Short Magazine Lee-Enfields remained in service well into World War II.

below Another Mk III, this time with the bayonet in its metal scabbard.

NUMBER 4 .303 IN RIFLE

Type: bolt-operated rifle
Origin: UK
Caliber: .303 in
Weight (empty): 9.1 lb (4.1 kg)
Barrel length: 25.2 in (640 mm)
Feed: bolt-operated, 10-round box magazine

below The No. 4 was a simplified SMLE but with the same superb action.

Prototypes of the new rifle appeared in 1928, which was similar in general appearance, operation and capabilities to the SMLE, but much easier to produce in quantity. Designated No. 4, it proved to be a very reliable and capable weapon and was placed in large-scale production from 1941 onwards, mainly in factories in the United States and Canada. One of the

changes was in the bayonet attachment which was placed over the muzzle and turned to lock, as opposed to the boss on the SMLE. Various types of bayonet were produced, some with blades, other of the "screwdriver" type. Selected specimens were adapted for use by snipers, with a No. 32 telescopic sight, detachable cheek rests and a special leather sling.

above The No. 4 Mk 1* was further modified to make the bolt easier to remove.

above The No. 4 Mk I(T) was the sniper version, seen here both inside and outside its case.

right As well as an extra cheekpiece the sniper rifle came with the No. 32 telescopic sight.

above Sniper's kit, comprising a No. 4 Mk I (T) rifle and scope, No. 4 "spike" bayonet and scope carrying case.

left Close-up of a fabric case for the No. 32 sight. Metal cases were also widely used.

NUMBER 5 .303 IN RIFLE

Type: bolt-operated rifle
Origin: UK
Caliber: .303 in
Weight (empty): 7.2 lb (3.3 kg)
Barrel length: 18.8 in (475 mm)
Feed: bolt-operated, 10-round box magazine

After some serious setbacks in the 1941–42 campaigns in Malaya and Burma British Empire forces took to jungle warfare with a will. One of the first lessons was that the standard infantry rifles – the SMLE and Rifle No 4 – were too long and heavy for a very short-range war in which he who fired first usually survived. These longer rifles were also easily snagged on jungle undergrowth. To overcome these problems the Rifle, Number 5 was developed from the No. 4. It had identical working parts but was 5 inches (127 mm) shorter and 1.9 lb (0.85 kg) lighter than the Number 4. The shorter barrel required a flash suppressor, which, in turn, necessitated a new type of bayonet. In addition, the fore-end stock was cut back and a rubber butt-pad fitted to protect the firer's shoulder from the increased recoil, and the rear sling swivel was replaced by a different type of hook. The weapon was criticized for having a heavy recoil and large muzzle flash, but as far as the users were concerned it was an excellent, reliable and popular weapon. The No. 5 was only used in the Far Eastern theater.

below The No. 5 Rifle was a shortened variant for jungle warfare.

below P17s had been made in the US to a British design in World War I and many were issued to second-line formations in 1939 and 1940.

right Moving though jungle terrain, these men wear tropical uniform, including long shorts. They are still carrying gas masks at the ready position, a practice that stopped as the war progressed.

right Men from the 3rd Division firing at snipers in Lingen. Some have leather jerkins while there is a mixture of the Mk III "turtle" helmet and the Mk II.

TRAINING RIFLES

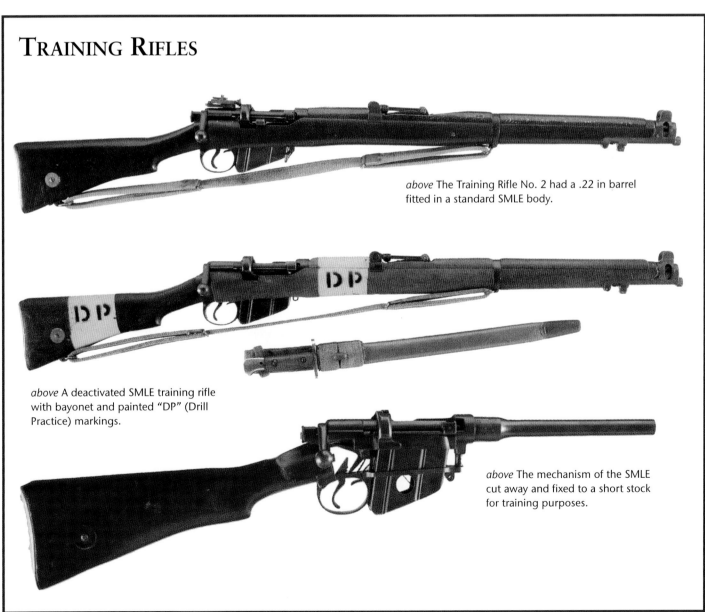

above The Training Rifle No. 2 had a .22 in barrel fitted in a standard SMLE body.

above A deactivated SMLE training rifle with bayonet and painted "DP" (Drill Practice) markings.

above The mechanism of the SMLE cut away and fixed to a short stock for training purposes.

REVOLVERS

The British infantry tends to be conservative, particularly where small-arms are concerned, and long after most major armies had moved on to the automatic the army retained the revolver, which was considered stronger, easier to fire accurately and simpler to maintain. There was also a need for a really powerful bullet with good stopping power for use in colonial wars, resulting in the retention for many years of the .455 in round. Nevertheless, there were some developments in the inter-war years, including a move from .455 in to .38 in 200 grain cartridge, while during World War II special forces took the lead in adopting self-loading pistols such as the Colt M1911A1 and Browning GP35, which are described in the US and Belgian sections, respectively.

WEBLEY & SCOTT MARK VI

Type: revolver
Origin: Webley & Scott, UK
Caliber: .455 in
Weight (empty): 37 oz (1.05 kg)
Barrel length: 6 in (15.2 cm)
Feed: six-round revolving cylinder

The Mark VI, introduced in 1915, was intended to provide officers leading attacks on enemy trenches with a powerful and reliable weapon; there was even a bayonet for use when all else had failed. It was popular, but its powerful.455 in round caused a strong recoil and made training difficult, which led to the adoption of a less powerful .38 in weapon in the 1930s. Nevertheless, the Mark VI remained in use among reserve officers well into the war, although obtaining the superseded .455 in round became increasingly difficult.

above The heavy and powerful Webley and Scott Mark VI.

ENFIELD NO. 2 AND NO. 2 MK1

Type: revolver
Origin: Royal Small Arms Factory, Enfield
Caliber: .38 in
Weight (empty): 27 oz (770 g)
Barrel length: 5 in (127 mm)
Feed: six-round revolving cylinder

below The No. 2 Mk I* with no hammer spur.

above An Enfield No. 2 Mk 1* made by Albion Motors.

In the 1920s the British Army concluded that .455 in caliber resulted in too large a weapon and that a new weapon of .38 in caliber was required. This resulted in the Enfield No. 2 revolver, which was very similar to, but smaller and lighter than its predecessor. The original No. 2 Mk 1 production version had a hammer spur to allow it to be cocked by hand, but it was replaced in the late 1930s by the No. 2 Mk 1* ("Mark 1 star") without the spur. This modification was originally introduced at the request of tank crews as the original spur could catch on clothing and fittings inside the cramped confines of an armored

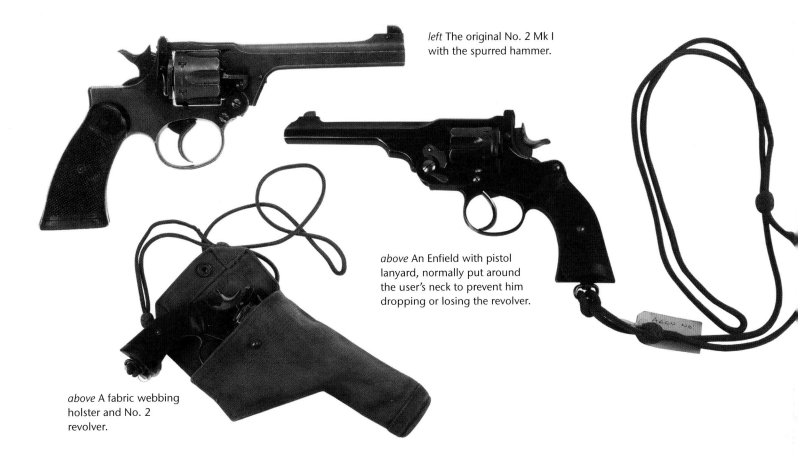

left The original No. 2 Mk I with the spurred hammer.

above An Enfield with pistol lanyard, normally put around the user's neck to prevent him dropping or losing the revolver.

above A fabric webbing holster and No. 2 revolver.

SMITH & WESSON BRITISH SERVICE REVOLVER

Type: revolver
Origin: Smith & Wesson, USA
Caliber: .38 in
Weight (empty): 29 oz (800 g)
Barrel length: 5 in (127 mm)
Feed: six-round revolving cylinder

In reply to an urgent request from the British Government, Smith & Wesson began production in 1940 of a revolver adapted for the British .38/200 cartridge. Known variously as the British Service Revolver and the Pistol No. 2 it was of orthodox, double-action design and, as did all Smith & Wesson products, proved sturdy and reliable in service.

below A Smith and Wesson revolver, complete with the leather holster and Sam Browne belt usually worn by officers in Service Dress.

above Many Colt revolvers were bought by the British in 1940.

SUB-MACHINE GUNS

The British required sub-machine guns for a variety of uses, including personal weapons for infantry section commanders. In the early years of the war, considerable numbers of Thompson ("Tommy") guns were imported from the United States, but main production was devoted to the homegrown Sten. A direct copy of the German MP 28 was also produced, which was named after the factory that produced it as the "Lanchester" but virtually all of these went to the Royal Navy, the remainder to the RAF. Silenced SMGs were developed for use by special forces.

Sten 9 mm Sub-machine gun

(Figures for Sten Mk 2)
Type: sub-machine gun
Origin: UK
Caliber: 9 mm Parabellum
Weight (empty): 6.7 lb (3.0 kg)
Barrel length: 7.8 in (197 mm)
Feed: 32-round box

The Sten took its name from the first letters of the names of its two designers – Shepherd and Turpin – coupled with the first two letters of the factory where they worked, the Enfield Royal Small Arms Factory. Developed in a hurry in 1941 to meet a requirement for a simple, effective and reliable SMG, which could be manufactured in large numbers in British factories, the Sten used a blowback system with a heavy return spring, and was chambered for the widely available 9 mm Parabellum round. The Mark 1 was quickly in service but it was soon replaced by the Mark 2, which was even simpler and cheaper, and did away with such "refinements" as the wooden stock and pistol grip, and rudimentary flash hider. This was followed by the generally similar Mark 3, which was manufactured in huge numbers, following which production switched to the Mark 5, which was more robust and even had a wooden butt, pistol grip and bayonet fittings. The Sten had some weaknesses, but nevertheless was very effective and issued in vast numbers to the British infantry. The Sten was also produced in Canada.

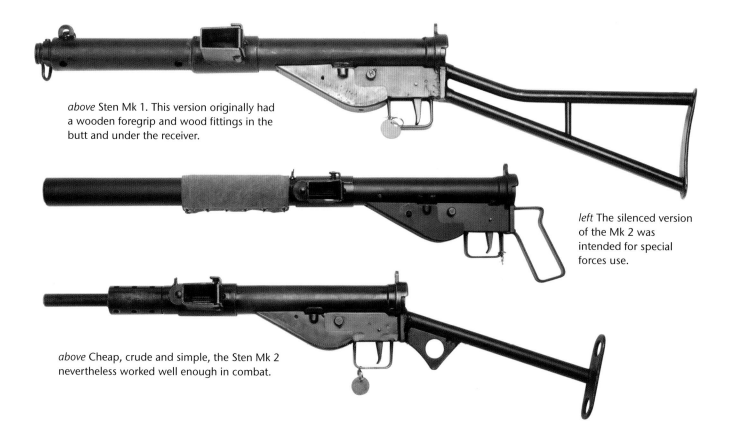

above Sten Mk 1. This version originally had a wooden foregrip and wood fittings in the butt and under the receiver.

left The silenced version of the Mk 2 was intended for special forces use.

above Cheap, crude and simple, the Sten Mk 2 nevertheless worked well enough in combat.

Sten 9 mm Sub-machine gun Mark 6(S)

Type: silenced sub-machine gun
Origin: UK
Caliber: 9 mm Parabellum
Weight (empty): 9.8 lb (4.5 kg)
Barrel length: 3.75 in (196 mm)
Overall length: 35 in (908 mm)
Feed: 32-round box

The Sten Mark 6(S) was developed to meet a special forces requirement for a silenced automatic weapon. This consisted of a Mark 5 Sten fitted with a Mark 2 silencer and, since the silencer tended to heat up rapidly, a canvas lace-up cover on the handguard. The main problem was that the 9 mm round normally traveled at supersonic speed (1,250 ft/sec, 381 m/s), which caused very undesirable "sonic booms," so gas escape holes were drilled into the barrel to bring the muzzle velocity down to the required subsonic figure of 1,000 ft/sec (305 m/s).

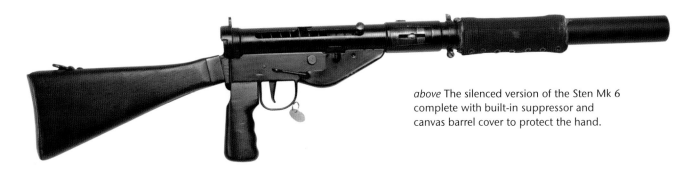

above The silenced version of the Sten Mk 6 complete with built-in suppressor and canvas barrel cover to protect the hand.

De Lisle Silenced Carbine

Type: bolt-action silenced carbine
Origin: UK
Caliber: .45 in ACP
Weight (empty): 7 lb (3.2 kg)
Barrel length: 9 in (228 mm)
Feed: 10-round box

The De Lisle silent carbine was a curious hybrid which did not fit neatly into any category so is placed here for convenience. It consisted of a Short Magazine Lee-Enfield mechanism converted to take a .45 in rimless cartridge, with a short bolt, extended chamber, and new magazine and magazine opening. The major feature was the new .45 in barrel surrounded by a 15 in (38 cm) long, 1.75 in (4.4 cm) diameter sheet metal casing. The casing housed ten metal discs, each with a 0.5 in (12.7 mm) central hole, two smaller holes and a radial slit. The discs, separated by spacers, were then placed on two rods and the pieces on either side of the cut were pulled apart and joined, thus creating a continuous Archimedes screw. This, combined with the subsonic bullet resulted in a truly silent weapon, which could be fired accurately to a range of about 300 yd (274 m). There were minor variations: some were produced with solid wooden butts, others with folding skeleton butts, some had pistol grips, others did not, and so on.

above The unusual silenced De Lisle carbine fired the .45 in Colt cartridge.

MACHINE GUNS

Worrld War I saw the wide scale adoption of automatic weapons, with the British infantry being equipped with the Lewis light machine gun (LMG) and the Vickers-Maxim medium machine gun (MMG). Both fired the standard .303 British cartridge, which they shared with the standard rifle. The Lewis was complicated and prone to a wide variety of stoppages, so that a search for a replacement began almost as soon as the war had ended. But, the army had to contend with rapid development in armored warfare techniques and tank technology, which meant that the infantry's role was constantly changing. Secondly, constant financial crises meant that little money was available for defense, and major programs, such as the complete replacement of all LMGs, were viewed with great suspicion.

LEWIS MACHINE GUN

Type: light machine gun
Origin: USA
Caliber: .303 in
Weight (empty): 27 lb (12.25 kg)
Barrel length: 26 in (660 mm)
Feed: 47-round, circular drum
Cyclic rate: 550 rpm

The Lewis gun was designed by Colonel Lewis of the United States Coastal Artillery. Prototypes appeared in 1912, but although greatly admired few orders were forthcoming until early 1915 when the British Army decided to arm every infantry battalion with four, later increased to 36. The gun was instantly recognizable by its flat cylindrical magazine and the jacket which surrounded the cooling fins. The weapon fired on automatic only, but was very accurate. In the ground role it used a lightweight bipod clamped around the jacket. As the Bren entered service in the late 1930s Lewis guns were progressively withdrawn, but were still in store when the BEF lost huge numbers of Brens in the Dunkirk campaign so were hastily reissued, mainly for use in the anti-aircraft role.

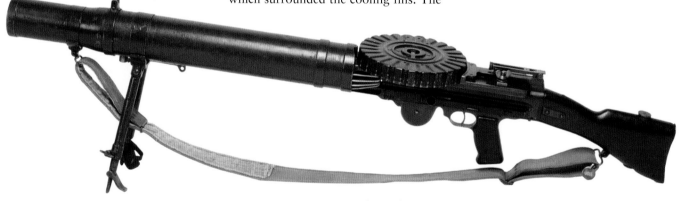

above Obsolescent when the war began, the venerable Lewis was pressed into service, mainly in the anti-aircraft role.

BREN LIGHT MACHINE GUN

Type: light machine gun
Origin: UK
Caliber: .303 in
Weight (empty): 22.5 lb (12 kg)
Barrel length: 25 in (635 mm)
Feed: 30-round box
Cyclic rate: 500 rpm

The Czech 7.92 mm ZB26 LMG had a major impact in the late 1920s and a version rechambered for the .303 round won the competition for a new LMG for the British Army in 1934. It was quickly placed in production and began to reach infantry battalions in mid-1938. It proved to be a winner from the start, being reliable, tough, very accurate and easy to maintain. Its cyclic rate of 500 rounds per minute was much slower than the German MG34 and MG42 but the Bren would go on firing long after other LMGs had overheated and seized up. All wartime modifications were minor, generally intended to reduce weight and make manufacturing easier. One development was in the backsight, which in the Mark 1 was controlled by a drum, but on subsequent marks was an adjustable leaf. The gun was given its name by combining the first two letters of its place of origin – Brno – and of its place of manufacture in the UK – Enfield. It was also produced by Inglis in Canada.

The Bren was issued on a scale of one per section and required a crew of two, although spare loaded magazines had to be dispersed around most of the rest of the section. There was also a simple tripod, weighing 26.5 lb (12 kg) for use in the sustained fire role. Stoppages were few and quickly dealt with and barrel-changing was very straightforward. With a weight of 22.5 lb (12 kg) the Bren was light enough to be fired from the hip by most soldiers and in the hands of a strong man could be used for anti-aircraft fire without the need for a special mounting.

left A superb Czech design, the Bren LMG served the army well throughout the war and beyond.

right Bren teams would normally carry a spare quick-change barrel.

below A tripod mounted Bren. For this sustained fire role the gunner would need lots of ammunition, as shown by the box which holds 12 magazines.

VICKERS .303 MACHINE GUN

Type: medium machine gun
Origin: UK
Caliber: .303 in
Weight (empty): 40 lb (11.55 kg)
Barrel length: 28.5 in (723 mm)
Feed: 250-round cloth belt
Cyclic rate: 500 rpm

The original British medium machine gun was the Maxim, which entered service in the 1880s. It was followed by the Vickers-Maxim and then by the definitive 1912 Vickers Mark 1 gun, which remained in army service until the 1960s. The gun was heavy and could not be used without either its tripod (50 lb/22.7 kg) or its water-cooling system, which meant that it was invariably carried in a truck and dismounted for firing. It was originally issued to infantry battalions, but in 1915 all medium machine guns were transferred to the Machine Gun Corps. That corps lasted until 1922 when it was disbanded and the Vickers were

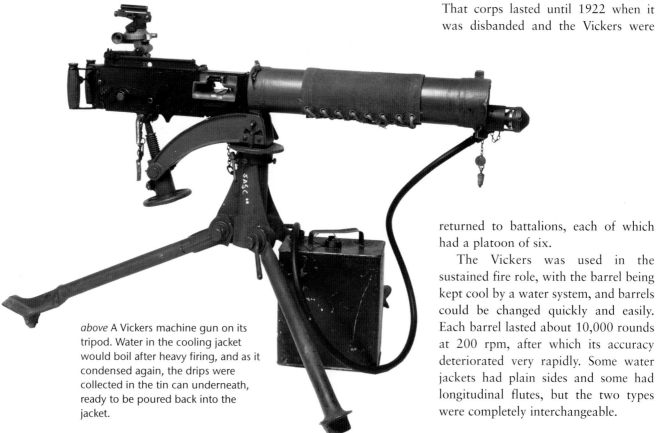

above A Vickers machine gun on its tripod. Water in the cooling jacket would boil after heavy firing, and as it condensed again, the drips were collected in the tin can underneath, ready to be poured back into the jacket.

returned to battalions, each of which had a platoon of six.

The Vickers was used in the sustained fire role, with the barrel being kept cool by a water system, and barrels could be changed quickly and easily. Each barrel lasted about 10,000 rounds at 200 rpm, after which its accuracy deteriorated very rapidly. Some water jackets had plain sides and some had longitudinal flutes, but the two types were completely interchangeable.

left The pile of used fabric belts next to this gunpit of the 1st Middlesex Regiment indicates the ability of the Vickers to provide long periods of sustained supporting fire.

VICKERS K-GUN

Type: light machine gun
Origin: UK
Caliber: .303 in
Weight (empty): 21 lb (9.4 kg)
Barrel length: 20 in (508 mm)
Feed: 100-round flat box
Cyclic rate: 1,050 rpm

below A famous photograph of an SAS patrol in the western desert with fast-firing Vickers K guns mounted on their jeeps. Note the drum magazines, flash eliminators and under-barrel gas tubes on the guns.

The Vickers Type K, also known as the Vickers G.O. (Gas-operated) was designed in the 1930s for use in aircraft. It employed an action developed from the Vickers-Berthier and had a high cyclic rate of fire (1,050 rpm versus 500 rpm for the Bren) which was intended to take advantage of the brief opportunities presented in aerial warfare. It was deployed in a variety of RAF aircraft on the late 1930s but was quickly superseded by the Browning M1919, whose main advantage was the use of chain-link ammunition feed, as opposed to the K-Gun's 100-round drum.

It was, however, adapted for ground use and was very popular with the SAS who mounted it in pairs on their jeeps, where the combined rate-of-fire was ideal for their hit-and-run tactics. Some jeeps had a single fixed, forward-firing K-gun operated by the driver and two paired-K-guns in flexible mounts. It was also used as a single weapon on a bipod mount by Army and Royal Marine Commandos.

It had a single; spade grip and trigger behind the receiver and an unusual spoon type flash climinator. The 100-round magazine fitted on top of the weapon, but its very high rate-of-fire meant that a magazine could be emptied in about 6 seconds, making ammunition carriage and resupply a major headache.

GRENADES & FLAMETHROWERS

The British Army made widespread use of grenades in World War II, mainly as an offensive weapon against enemy who were sheltering in trenches, with the intention of killing them where they were or of driving them out into the open where they could be attacked by rifle or machine gun fire. The British set great store by throwing grenades like a cricket-ball but also introduced cup launchers to fit on rifles.

No. 36 Grenade

The "Mills Bomb" was a classic design which remained in production and front-line use from 1915 to well into the 1980s. Designed by a golf-club designer, it consisted of a pineapple-shaped, cast-iron outer casing which contained the explosive and a central cylindrical passage for the fuse and detonator (which was closed by a base-plug) and a safety lever. The outside of the casing had a pattern of deep grooves, intended by the designer to enable the thrower to grip it more securely, but which had a secondary effect of causing the casing to break up, so that the danger area was filled with flying iron segments, plus, most lethal of all, the base plug. The grenade was gripped in one hand with the fingers firmly over the safety lever, a finger of the other hand placed through the ring on the safety pin. The grenade was then pulled away from the pin and all the soldier then had to do was to throw it, the safety lever flying off as it left his hand.

The base-plug could be removed and replaced by a plate for use with a rifle-launcher, which gave a range of some 150 yd (137 m). The lethal radius was some 20 yd (18 m), although some fragments such as the baseplate could fly up to 100 yd (91 m), which made it essential that the thrower took cover immediately he had thrown it. The standard delay fuse was 7 seconds, but in 1940 this was reduced to 4 seconds.

The Mills Bomb entered service in 1915 as the No. 5 Grenade and underwent numerous developments and versions, such as the Number

left The No. 36 Mills Bomb (grenade) with firing pin in place but the striker missing. The holes indicate this one has been deactivated after the war.

above An SMLE with grenade cup attached. Rifles allocated as grenade launchers usually had metal or wire bands around their barrels to strengthen them and protect the firer from a possible burst barrel.

23, before the Number 36, which entered service in the 1930s. Over 30 million examples were produced during World War II.

OTHER BRITISH GRENADES

The only known British stick grenade on the German pattern was the No 74, also known as the "sticky bomb" from its adhesive coating intended to fix it to the armored vehicle target and improve its explosive effect.

The British also introduced a range of anti-tank grenades, although their effectiveness against ever-improving German armor was strictly limited, as was their use.

One oddity was the No. 82 Grenade designed for special forces, which comprised a metal cap, a fuze and a bag made of stockinette, whose contents could be selected by the user to suit the target. Combinations of explosive and small projectiles such as nails, screws or stones could be used, depending on the circumstances.

above and right Another grenade-launching SMLE, this time with copper wire wound round the barrel. The close-up shows the launching cup which would take a standard No.36 grenade.

FLAMETHROWERS

The main British infantry model was the Flamethrower, Portable, No. 2 Mark 2 (the Mark 1 was only used for training), the main component of which was a doughnut-shaped fuel pack worn on the back; when loaded, this weighed no less than 64 lb (29 kg). This was connected by an armored hose which ran under the operator's armpit to an aiming/igniting nozzle, which was held in both hands. The inner sphere on the back pack contained an inflammable gas at high pressure (140 Bar/2,000 psi) while the outer ring contained 4 gallons (18 liters) of fuel. The nozzle unit had two pistol grips each with a trigger, one of which released the fuel, the other activating a magnesium igniter. There were ten igniters and the operator could either launch a jet of flame or could spray raw fuel (known as a "wet shot") to douse a target before firing a flame to ignite it.Maximum range was about 110 ft (36 m) and the normal drill was to fire 10 one-second bursts. The device was nicknamed "Lifebuoy" due to the shape of the ring-shaped fuel tank.

It was never popular with the infantry and the British had much more success with vehicle-mounted flamethrowers on coverted carriers and tanks.

BAYONETS

The British Army had long laid great emphasis on the value of bayonets in close-quarter fighting and during World War I established a well-known school in France where the art of "applying cold steel" was taught with considerable enthusiasm. British bayonets usually consisted of a blade, crosspiece and handle and were carried in easily accessible frogs which either hung from the belt or were attached to a pouch. In most cases the blades were between 9 and 12 inches (23–31 cm) long although the Pattern 1907 was 17 inches (43 cm). They usually had a longitudinal fuller, one on each side; these were grooves which added strength and stiffness. The exception was the World War I "spike" bayonet.

British pattern bayonets were manufactured in the UK, Australia, Canada, India and South Africa as well as in the United States. Until 1927, bayonets were designated by a "Pattern" number, indicating the year in which they were introduced to service. Thereafter, they were numbered, starting with the Pattern 1907 which was redesignated Bayonet No. 1.

BAYONET PATTERN 1903

The oldest British bayonet in use in World War II, the Pattern 1903 was a development of the earlier Pattern 1888 with a 12-inch, double-edged blade, which was not fullered. The crosspiece had a ring which fitted over the muzzle of the rifle and the handle incorporated a catch which engaged on a lug below the barrel.

BAYONET PATTERN 1907

The Bayonet Pattern 1907 was introduced to fit the Short Magazine Lee-Enfield rifle, and had a

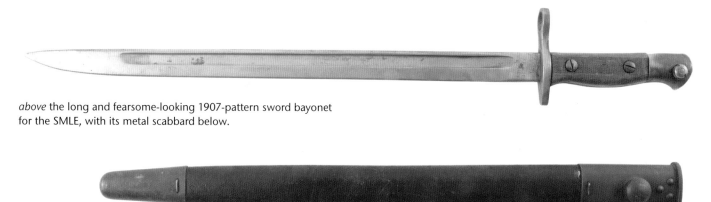

above the long and fearsome-looking 1907-pattern sword bayonet for the SMLE, with its metal scabbard below.

below A close-up of the hilt, crosspiece (quillion) and release catch of the 1907 bayonet.

below The opening and catch of the metal scabbard for the 1907 bayonet.

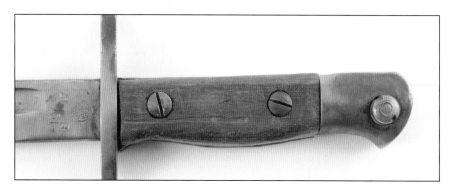

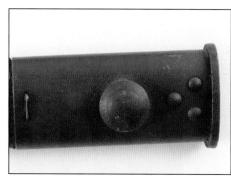

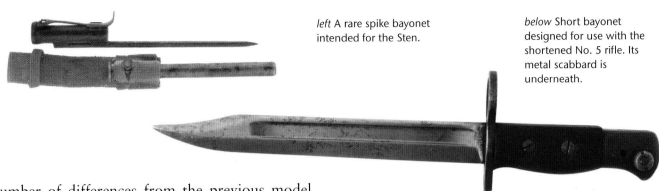

left A rare spike bayonet intended for the Sten.

below Short bayonet designed for use with the shortened No. 5 rifle. Its metal scabbard is underneath.

number of differences from the previous model. The blade was 5 inches (12.7 cm) longer, fullered and had a single-edge. The quillion had a forward curve, which was intended to trap and break an opponent's bayonet, but this was abandoned in 1913 in favor of a very short crosspiece. New bayonets were manufactured without the curve and existing bayonets had it removed in workshops. The scabbard was made of leather, with steel mounts. In 1927 this was redesignated the Bayonet Number 1 Mark 1. A similar design, the No.3, was made for the P14 rifle.

No. 4 Spike Bayonet

The British first introduced a spike bayonet in the 1780s. The No. 4 Bayonet, introduced in 1939, was one of the simplest ever made, consisting of a socket which fitted over the muzzle and then twisted to enable a sliding-catch to engage on a lug. The spike, which was integral with the socket, was 8 inches (203 mm) long and 0.5 inch (1.3 cm) in diameter, tapering to a point. In its original Mark 1 form the spike had milled flutes, giving a cruciform cross-section, intended to make wounds more difficult to treat. In the Mark 2, introduced in 1940, the flutes were omitted to make manufacture easier, resulting in a circular cross-section. The Mark 2* had the blade produced separately then pinned and welded to the socket. The Mark 3 had a socket manufactured from sheet steel and its overall looks are much cruder. These spike bayonets were not popular with infantry battalions, who considered them far inferior to the blade type, even though the spike was useful for punching holes in condensed milk tins.

Bayonet No. 5

The Bayonet No 5, introduced in 1944, was designed specifically for the No. 5 Rifle for jungle use. It had a 7.75 inch (20 cm) fullered blade with a "bowie-knife" tip. The crosspiece had a large muzzle ring to fit over the No. 5 Rifle's flash suppressor. There were two marks of the No. 5 Bayonet, but these differed in only very minor detail.

below House-clearing in Normandy, 1944. The kneeling man is actually a dispatch rider, but he has a No. 4 rifle with the spike bayonet. The standing man has a captured MP 40 sub-machine gun.

KNIVES

FAIRBAIRN-SYKES

Most knives are designed to be multi-purpose, capable of cutting, hewing and even opening cans as well as for combat; the Fairbairn-Sykes knife, however, has but one purpose – killing by stabbing or slashing. It was designed by Fairbairn and Sykes, British officers in the Shanghai Municipal Police, and was one of a number of self-defense weapons for use by the force's officers in fights in a city rated as one of the toughest in the world. The knife was designed in the 1930s but became famous when it was adopted by British and then by other special forces, including many in the US, and is still widely used today.

The straight, double-edged blade, normally some 6.6 in (16.8 cm) long (lengths vary slightly) has prominent risers to give it rigidity. The hilt (grip) is an extended vase-shaped in profile with maximum girth near the guard, and is circular in cross-section; it is usually made of brass, but hard wood versions are also found. The tang extends from the rear of the blade through the guard and handle and is secured by a nut. The guard, made

of steel or cast-iron, is usually 2 in (5.1 cm) long, 0.6 in (1.6 cm) wide and 0.13 in (0.3 cm) thick. A typical knife less scabbard weighs 8 oz (227 g).

The double-sided blade is designed to penetrate any clothing, including thick cold-climate wear, and then slide between the victim's ribs. It is of sufficient length to penetrate the vital organs. Alternatively, it is used from the rear to penetrate upwards through the base of the skull, when the victim dies so quickly that he has no time to utter any sound. Both edges are finely honed in order to sever any arteries. The knife is carefully balanced to enable it to be thrown accurately and the handle is so shaped as to enable it to be gripped firmly and not be pulled from the user's hand.

GOLOK

The Golok, or Jungle Knife, was introduced in the Far East as experience of jungle warfare grew. Based on an Indonesian design, but made by Martindale in England, it was used to cut a path through dense undergrowth and to cut down

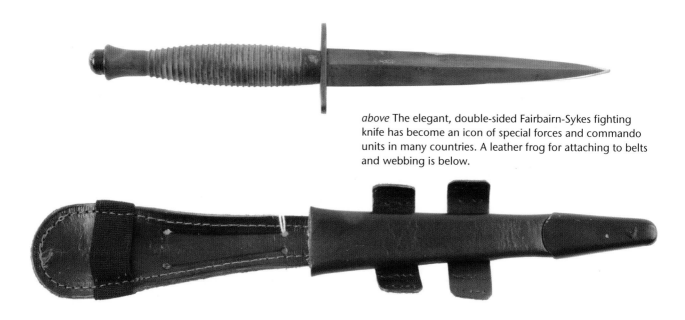

above The elegant, double-sided Fairbairn-Sykes fighting knife has become an icon of special forces and commando units in many countries. A leather frog for attaching to belts and webbing is below.

small trees, saplings and undergrowth to make overnight bivouacs. It had a full tang with the two-piece wooden grip attached by two rivets. The blade was 13.8 in (35 cm) long and made of a soft steel, which required frequent sharpening but did not get stuck in green timber. The Golok weighed 18.3 oz (520 g). It was issued with a green webbing sheath with a metal mouth and hooks for attaching to the 1944 Pattern belt. There was a webbing reinforcing strip around the bottom end of the scabbard and soldiers opened the upper seam on the outer side, which formed a convenient pocket for the sharpening stone.

BRITISH ARMY POCKET KNIFE

In use since the early 1900s, the issue pocket knife was an essential part of every infantryman's personal equipment. Made of high quality Sheffield steel it housed a blade, a can-opener, a marlin spike, all of which were retractable, and a fixed screwdriver blade at the opposite end to the shackle. The knife was 4.5 in (114 mm) long when closed (including the shackle) and the blade was 2.5 in (64 mm) long. Total weight was a mere 4.8 oz (136 g).

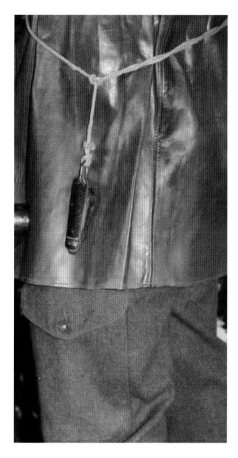

above The pocket knife was a useful tool for general field life. This man has his hanging from a piece of string tied around the waist of his leather jerkin.

below Machetes were essential for clearing a route through undergrowth in jungle warfare but were also used in other theaters as a general tool for cutting down branches and foliage.

MORTARS

The British infantry greatly valued the use of mortars and the battalion commander had direct control of two types, the 3-inch (76.2 mm) and 2-inch (51 mm). There was also a heavier weapon, the 4.2-inch (107 mm), but this was operated by divisional artillery regiments.

LIGHT MORTAR

The British Army's 2-inch (51 mm) mortar was the platoon commander's own fire support weapon. It was probably one of the simplest weapons ever conceived, consisting of a steel tube, trigger group and spade. The barrel was 21 inches (533 mm) long and so short that the normal method of dropping the bomb down onto a fixed firing-pin would not work; hence the trigger which was operated by a lever with a short lanyard attached.

Unlike the German Granatwerfer 36 the British weapon had neither baseplate, sights nor carrying handle. The base was a simple spade. The firer ("Number 1 on the mortar") held the tube with one hand and the trigger lever with the other, while his loader ("Number 2") placed the bombs in the muzzle and allowed them to drop under gravity. The Number I then aligned the mortar on the target, using a white line painted along the barrel, setting the angle by hand based on his calculation of the range combined with experience. It was very basic but worked well. There were three main rounds: high-explosive (2.25 lb / 1 kg); smoke (2.25 lb / 1 kg) and illuminating (1 lb / .45 kg), the maximum range with HE being 500 yd (457 m).

There were a number of developments during the war, including several for vehicle installations, and the Mk VII* and Mk VIII which had shorter barrels for use by airborne forces.

above An immaculate 3-in mortar team on exercise. They still wear the pre-war puttees around their ankles rather than anklets.

left The 2-in light mortar was about as light and simple as a mortar could be. It was a handy source of firepower for the platoon, and especially of smoke and illumination rounds.

MEDIUM MORTAR

The infantry has always needed close support firepower under its own control and in the 1920s the British allocated 3.7-inch howitzers to this role. These were large, expensive and unpopular, so in 1932 it was decided to replace them with a new 3.2-inch (81 mm) caliber mortar, although for ease of reference it was always known as the 3-inch mortar. This was manufactured in large numbers and used by British and Commonwealth infantry throughout the war. The original barrel gave a range of only 1,600 yd (1,463 m) so in 1942 this was replaced by a new longer (8.4 ft (2.56 m) long barrel, increasing range to 2,750 yd (2,515 m). The weapon weighed 126 lb (57 kg), comprising: the barrel at 44 lb (20 kg); the 45 lb (20 kg) baseplate; the tripod at 37 lb (17 kg). The most commonly used bombs were HE (10 lb/4.5 kg) and smoke, although other payloads such as illuminating were also available. Unlike the 2-inch mortar, the 3-inch was fitted with proper sights and could be fired at angles between 45 and 80 degrees and traversed 11 degrees without moving the baseplate. The Australian Army developed a version for use in the jungle with a genuine 3-inch (76.2 cm) barrel, which saw service in the Far East campaigns.

left A Gurkha 3-in mortar crew in Italy in 1943. The kneeling man has a cotton bandolier around his back as well as a Kukri knife hanging from his belt. A dismantled entrenching tool can also be clearly seen below his belt.

ANTI-TANK WEAPONS

BOYS ANTI-TANK RIFLE

Specifications: See separate box

As did many other armies, the British infantry entered World War II with a large caliber anti-tank rifle, in this case a .55 in (13.9 mm) weapon, named after its designer, Captain Boys, although it was also known for security purposes as Project Stanchion. It fired as large a bullet using as powerful a charge as a rifleman could reasonably be expected to fire. It used bolt action with a five-round box magazine and the recoil was attenuated by a muzzle brake, a spring-operated shock-absorber and a large rubber shoulder pad. The first version had a monopod, the second a bipod. Once war started and German tank armor began to increase the Boys was quickly outclassed and, despite having a variety of rounds, it could no longer cope. From 1943 onwards was replaced by the PIAT. A special version was developed for airborne forces featuring a shorter barrel without a muzzle brake but the recoil proved to be more than even the paratroops could handle.

above Boys rifle with ammunition clip underneath. Typical of 1930s-vintage infantry anti-tank weapons, the Boys turned out to be completely outclassed by most armor once the war began. But until the PIAT arrived it was pretty much all the infantry had.

PROJECTOR INFANTRY ANTI-TANK (PIAT)

Specifications: See separate box

In the 1930s a British Army officer named Blacker invented a spigot mortar – the Blacker Bombard. This consisted of a thin metal barrel containing a powerful spring which acted against a cylinder and spigot, ramming them forward, inside the rear of the projectile, thus igniting a small propulsive charge. The charge not only propelled the bomb but also acted rearwards to reset the spring. As the detonation of the propellant was inside the tail tube of the projectile the short-range Bombard didn't need the weight and complexity of a high-strength gun barrel.

The Bombard saw very limited wartime service, mostly with the Home Guard, although some regular infantry battalions received them and one is known to have been deployed at Tobruk in 1942.

The PIAT used the same principle, but was much smaller and lighter, propelling a 2.5 lb (1.13 kg) projectile

below The PIAT was an effective anti-tank weapon, if almost as frightening to its user as to its target.

above PIAT bomb with shaped-charge warhead.

to a maximum range of 115 yards (105 m), although much shorter ranges were the norm. The weapon was made from low-grade materials and consisted of a cylinder, which housed the spigot and spring, a cup in which the bomb was placed, a trigger group, butt and a monopod. In order to launch the first round in an engagement the weapon had to be cocked, requiring considerable physical strength and ideally done standing up, which was not recommended in close-combat with tanks. Once in use, however – and provided the weapon was being held correctly – each round automatically caused the action to be recocked.

The PIAT had a reputation for being a fearsome weapon to use, difficult to cock and with a vicious recoil, but it was the British infantry's first effective man-portable anti-tank weapon and its HEAT warhead claimed many tanks.

Two advantages of the PIAT over rocket launchers were that it emitted no tell-tale smoke on firing, nor was there a danger area behind the weapon. When the US M1A1 Rocket launcher (Bazooka) was offered to the British Army it was refused on the (mistaken) grounds that the PIAT was the superior weapon.

below A PIAT team guarding a crossroads with a projectile loaded in the bomb "tray".

2-POUNDER ANTI-TANK GUN

Specifications: See separate box

The 2-pounder (40 mm) gun was developed in the early 1930s for use by tanks as a main armament and in a towed version as an anti-tank gun. In the latter role it was initially operated by the Royal Artillery, but was later handed over to the infantry, which formed one six-gun anti-tank platoon per battalion.

The weapon was accepted in 1934 as the Ordnance QF 2-pounder Mark IX (QF = quick-firing) and in the ground role was mounted on the Carriage Mark II. This was an ingenious three-legged affair in which one leg served as the trail and when in action the two wheels were removed, resulting in a low profile and a 360 degree traverse. The 2-pounder tended to be criticised by the British Army, but its 40 mm round was very effective against early-war tanks, and against Italian and Japanese tanks throughout the war and it had a better range and terminal effect than the German 3.7 cm Pak 36.

An excellent gun in the late 1930s,

it's reputation suffered by being kept in production for too long.

The 2-pounder fired various types of ammunition, including armor-piercing; Armour-Piercing, High Velocity (APHV); Armour Piercing, Capped (APC); Armour Piercing Capped, Ballistic Capped (APCBC); and in 1944 an Armour Piercing Discarding Sabot (APDS) round fired through a Littlejohn adapter fitted to the muzzle.

Curiously, although an HE shell was developed it was never issued, even though it would have been helpful against soft targets.

Maxumium effective range was 1,000 yd (914 m) and a typical round, the APCBC, weighed 4.9 lb (2.22 kg) of which 2.6 lb (1.2 kg) was the projectile and would penetrate 2.26 in (57.5 mm) armor plate at a range of 500 yd (457 m).

left The 2-pounder was an excellent gun in 1939 and 1940, but became much less useful as newer tanks with increased armor entered service.

6-POUNDER ANTI-TANK GUN

Specifications: See separate box

Even in the late 1930s the British realised that armour thickness would quickly outstrip the capabilities of the 2-pounder and started to develop the more capable 6-pounder (57 mm). This weapon was ready by 1940 but following the Dunkirk debacle it was considered militarily essential to continue proudction of the 2-pounder to make good the losses and to rapidly strengthen anti-tank defences on mainland UK. As a result, introduction of the 6-pounder was delayed until April 1942, but it proved to be a successfull design and apart from serving with British and Commonwealth forces it was also adopted by the US Army as the 57 mm Gun M1.

The 6-pounder equipped infantry battalion anti-tank platoons from 1943 through to 1945 and proved more than adequate against German tanks up to and including PzKpfw IV and any Italian or Japanese tank. It was not always successful against Panther and Tiger, although from the right angle and range it could deal with those as well. Early ammunition was a straightforward solid Armour Piercing (AP) anti-tank round which was followed by Armour Piercing, Capped (APC), and Amour-Piercing, Capped, Ballistically Capped (APCBC), and, in 1944, by Armour Piercing Discarding Sabot (APDS). Unlike the 20-pounder, an HE round was also issued.

The replacement for the 6-pounder was the 17-pounder (76.2 mm), but although this was an excellent weapon it was simply too heavy and bulky for infantry use

right Emplacing a 6-pounder. A capable anti-tank gun of low silhouette and light weight, it served with distinction from 1943 to the end of the war.

BRITISH INFANTRY ANTI-TANK WEAPONS

Weapon	Country of Origin	Projectile	Length	Barrel	Weight	Muzzle Velocity	Feed
Boys Rifle	UK	.55in (14 mm)	63.5 in (1.61 m)	36 in (914 mm	36 lb (16.33 kg)	3,250 ft/s (990 m/s)	5 round box; bolt action
PIAT	UK	3.5 in (89 mm)	39 in (.99 m)	10 in (.25 mm)	34.5 lb (15.7 kg)	450 ft/sec (137 m/s)	Manual
2.36in RCL	USA	2.36 in (60 mm)	61 in (1.55 m)	61 in (1.55 m)	13.3 lb (6 kg)	265 ft/sec (81 m/s)	Manual
2pdr	UK	1.56 in (40 mm)	135.5 in (3.44 m)	83 in (.21 m)	1,794 lb (814 kg)	2,600 ft/s (792 m/s)	Semi-automatic vertical breech
6pdr	UK	2.2 in (57 mm)	110 in (2.82 m)	96 in (2.45 m)	2,520 lb (1,140 kg)	2,800 ft/s (853 m/s)	Vertical block

AIR DEFENSE

Air defense in British infantry battalions never seemed to receive the same priority as other requirements. At the start of the war each infantry battalion had an anti-aircraft platoon commanded by a Warrant Officer Class 3 (WO3), which comprised fifteen men and four 15cwt trucks (15 hundredweight = 762 kg) each fitted with a single Bren .303 LMG on a Motley-mounting. In addition, when attacked by relatively slow-moving aircraft such as the Ju-87 Stuka, almost every man with a weapon blazed away in the hope – all too seldom fulfilled – that a round would hit home. Following experience in North Africa and the Dunkirk campaign, these platoon were re-equipped with twin Brens in a new mounting, thus doubling the firepower at minimal cost. Some battalions did not have enough Brens in the early days of the war, particularly after the heavy losses in the Dunkirk campaign, and used Lewis Guns, instead.

There were several proposals to re-equip battalion anti-aircraft platoons with 20 mm cannon, and Hispanos, Polstens and Oerlikons were all considered, but were always eventually deployed elsewhere, usually within the divisional anti-aircraft regiment of the Royal Artillery. The heaviest air defense weapons ever actually fielded with the infantry were Vickers machine guns, with airlanding battalions having two platoons of eight guns each. By this time – mid-1944 – the Luftwaffe was no longer a serious threat to forward ground units and these guns were more often used in the ground as opposed to the anti-aircraft role.

above A Bren gun on an anti-aircraft mount. With no deflection sight and with only a 30-round magazine, a single Bren's effectiveness in this sole was marginal.

left Brens in the anti-aircraft role mounted on carriers during an exercise in England.

PARATROOPS

The early German paratroop successes in the attack on Belgium and the Netherlands in 1940 resulted in an order from British Prime Minister Winston Churchill that similar forces be urgently developed in the United Kingdom. The first unit was formed in 1940, the requirement being for a force which could be delivered to the battlefield by air, hold ground for a period of several days and then be relieved by advancing ground forces. This meant that the units had to be lightly but effectively armed, that all kit and equipment had to be deliverable by air, and that individuals had to be as self-sustaining as possible. After various organizations had been tried, the Type 1944 parachute battalion evolved, although the organization was flexible, sometimes deliberately so, but at other times because commanding officers simply reorganized matters to suit the situation or to match the resources available. Individual soldiers were well armed, but the battalion as a whole was lacking in heavy support weapons.

above Glider-borne troops assembling after landing. They wear airborne smocks and helmets and carry No. 4 rifles, Stens and a US-made SCR 536 radio.

UNIFORMS

right A British airborne soldier in combat gear. Non-paratrooper infantry battalions trained for glider operations were also regarded as airborne soldiers and equipped accordingly.

Paratrooper's rimless helmet with leather chinstrap, netting and hessian strips for camouflage.

Mk 2 Sten with simple welded metal butt.

The camouflaged Dennison smock was popular with snipers and other specialized troops as well as airborne soldiers.

Standard 37-pattern webbing system.

General issue battle dress trousers. There was also an airborne version with strengthened and expandable thigh pockets.

Standard boots. Some airborne soldiers had boots with crepe rubber soles.

Paratroops wore a modified version of battledress. They wore one of the first-ever camouflage jackets, known as the Dennison smock, which was weatherproof, and had a crotchstrap to prevent it riding up during the descent. The trousers were made of the same material as other BD items but had larger pockets, and the boots had rubber soles, as opposed to leather with hobnails, which damaged aircraft. The headgear was the most distinctive, being either the famous red beret or a "para helmet" which was rimless and had a leather chincup. The smock bore the para wings. There was also a camouflage-pattern face veil, which served as quick personal camouflage, scarf, sweatrag or towel.

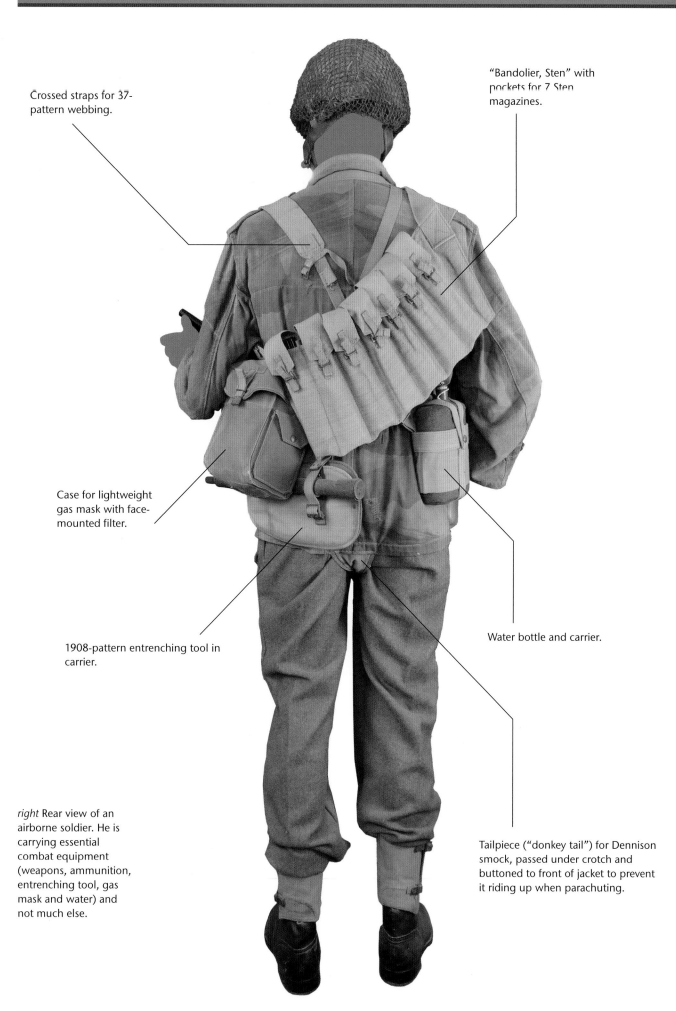

Crossed straps for 37-pattern webbing.

"Bandolier, Sten" with pockets for 7 Sten magazines.

Case for lightweight gas mask with face-mounted filter.

1908-pattern entrenching tool in carrier.

Water bottle and carrier.

right Rear view of an airborne soldier. He is carrying essential combat equipment (weapons, ammunition, entrenching tool, gas mask and water) and not much else.

Tailpiece ("donkey tail") for Dennison smock, passed under crotch and buttoned to front of jacket to prevent it riding up when parachuting.

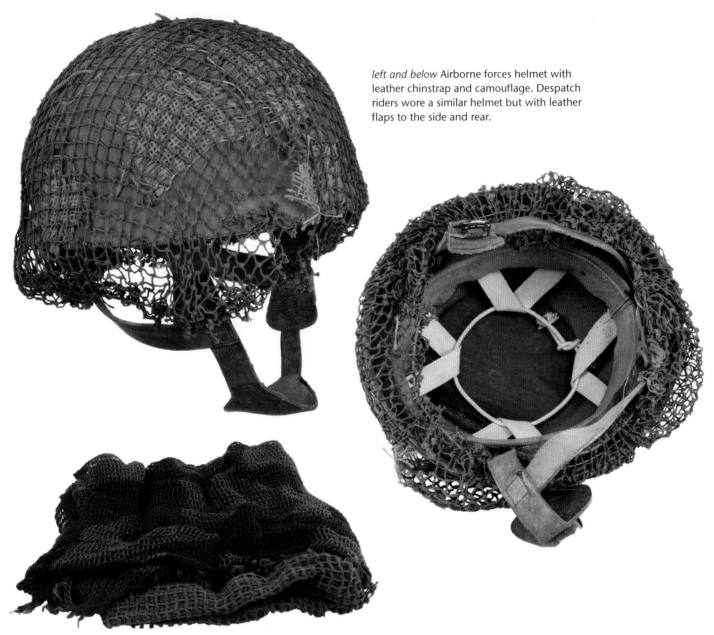

left and below Airborne forces helmet with leather chinstrap and camouflage. Despatch riders wore a similar helmet but with leather flaps to the side and rear.

above Face veil used to camouflage face and head, but more often worn as a simple scarf.

PARACHUTES

British paratroops used the PX Mk 5 parachute. This was a radial canopy, 28ft (8.5 m) in diameter with 32 gores and four sets of annular, zig-zag seams. The canopy and rigging lines were carried in a backpack and were tugged out automatically as the men jumped by a static line attached to the aircraft. There were four lift webs, each with eight rigging lines, and the harness had quick-release levers to free these lift webs if the canopy dragged the jumper along the ground on landing.

EQUIPMENT

The amount of kit a parachutist can carry is limited by the potential for injury on landing to about 50 lb (22.7 kg) so the British paratrooper used a kitbag and valise on a 20 ft (6 m) strop. He held these clasped to his chest while jumping and then released them during the descent. Heavier equipment was either pushed out the back of the transport aircraft or dropped by converted bombers in containers carried either in the bomb-bay or from underwing strong points. These included folding bicycles, lightweight motorcycles, wireless sets and batteries, 3-in mortars, and all types of ammunition. The British gunners also had a US-supplied 75 mm pack-howitzer, which broke town into nine loads for parachuting.

THE PARACHUTE BATTALION

The "paper strength" of a Type 1944 Parachute Battalion as employed at D-Day, Arnhem and the Rhine Crossing was 613 all ranks (29 officers and 584 men).

left Kitting up before the Arnhem operation. The soldier with the parachute also has a large bag containing ammunition, grenades and equipment. The others have very full pockets on their Dennison smocks.

BATTALION HEADQUARTERS

As in a conventional infantry unit, battalion headquarters (each 5 officers, 22 men) comprised the commanding officer (lieutenant-colonel) second-in-command (major), adjutant (captain) and intelligence officer (lieutenant), plus his associated intelligence section. There was also a medical officer to run the regimental aid post.

RIFLE COMPANY

The fighting strength of the battalion was its three Rifle Companies (5 officers, 112 men), each with three rifle platoons (1 officer plus 33 men). In addition to their normal scale of personal weapons, platoons had an extra Bren LMG and PIAT, plus one sniper rifle per section. Company HQ comprised 2 officers and 13 men.

right Airborne soldiers firing a 3-in mortar during the Arnhem battles.

above Airborne troops pick their way through the ruins of Oosterbeck. Note the larger map pocket on the thigh of the man in front, typical of the airborne version of battle dress trousers.

HEADQUARTERS COMPANY

Combining both support weapons and administrative functions, the Headquarters Company comprised 9 officers and 226 men in total. Company headquarters comprised 1 officer and 10 men. The Company had four sub-units:

above A lightweight folding bicycle used by airborne forces and commandos.

SIGNALS PLATOON

One officer and 27 men with the usual radio and line equipment but including a number of airborne bicycles for dispatch riders.

ANTI-TANK PLATOON

One officer and 39 men carried ten PIATs.

MORTAR PLATOON

The Headquarters Company had two Mortar Platoons, each of 1 officer and 40 men, with four 3-inch mortars per platoon. There were also four Vickers MMGs, but these could only be taken in place of a similar number of mortars.

ADMINISTRATIVE PLATOON

As with the infantry battalion, there was an Administrative Platoon (3 officers and 62 men), comprising clerks, drivers, storemen, armorers, etc. Not all would be taken into battle.

COMMANDOS

Another Churchillian initiative designed to take the war to the Germans on continental Europe, the Commandos started as raiding parties and were formed from volunteers looking for excitement and danger. Since the British Isles were separated from Europe by water it was inevitable that the major requirements were the ability to cross the sea barrier and to land on a defended shore. The early Commando units were found from the Army, but the Royal Marines also adopted the commando role, ethos and organization, although they still retained their traditional shipboard role aboard warships.

Part of the Commando requirement was the ability to be unconventional in the planning and conduct of operations and this led to a more flexible approach to organization. This can be seen by the choice of titles, which need to be explained as they were, in some instances, identical to those in a conventional infantry battalion, but denoted a sub-unit of considerably different size.

Commando was the title of the fighting unit, which was commanded by a lieutenant-colonel and which approximated in structure to an infantry battalion, although with a strength of between 470–500 all ranks.

The major sub-division of a Commando was a Troop, which was approximately equivalent to a weak company in a conventional battalion, but was commanded by a captain. It did, however, have a sergeant-major.

The sub-division of a Troop was a Section, but although the term was the same as in a conventional battalion, the Commando version was considerably larger, more equivalent to a platoon, while a Commando sub-section was equivalent to a normal rifle section.

above Commandos make their way ashore at Ouistreham during the D-Day operation. They carry bergen rucksacks rather than 37-pattern large packs.

THE TYPE 1944 ARMY COMMANDO

The total strength of the Commando could vary, but was approximately 470 all ranks (24 officers and 464 men).

COMMANDO HQ
This fulfilled the same unit command function as in a battalion, but was somewhat larger (7 officers, 85 men), as it included not only the intelligence officer and his section, but also some of the functions and manpower in a headquarters company, such as the Signal Section and Transport Section.

left The "T" telephone set was completely waterproof and developed for use in amphibious landings.

left The Combined Operations badge, signifying naval, air and land combat, was worn by commandos on their upper arm.

ASSAULT TROOP

Each Commando had five Assault Troops, each of 3 officers and 66 men. The Troop comprised two Sections, each commanded by a lieutenant and sergeant, each section dividing further into two Sub-Sections, each with a Sergeant/Lance-Sergeant in command. The Sub-Sections themselves split into two groups, a rifle group of 6 men led by a corporal and an LMG group of 5 men led by a lance-corporal. Weapons were standard with most men carrying the Rifle No. 4, but there were a larger than usual allocations of Stens, Silenced Stens and Thompson SMGs. Troop HQ consisted of the commander (captain), sergeant-major, batman/runner, two stretcher-bearers and an RAMC nursing orderly (attached). There were two 2-inch mortars and one PIAT.

HEAVY WEAPONS TROOP

The Heavy Weapons Troop (2 officers and 37 men) was split into a 3-in Mortar Section (three mortars, 17 men) and a Machine Gun Section (three Vickers MMG or Vickers K-gun, 16 men).

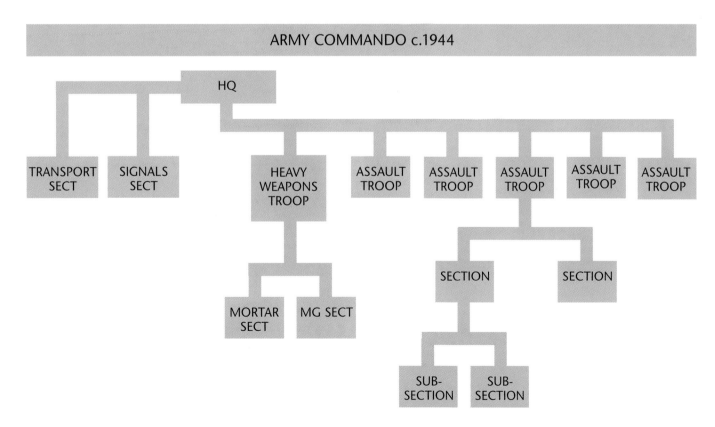

ARMY COMMANDO c.1944

HQ

TRANSPORT SECT — SIGNALS SECT — HEAVY WEAPONS TROOP — ASSAULT TROOP — ASSAULT TROOP — ASSAULT TROOP — ASSAULT TROOP — ASSAULT TROOP

HEAVY WEAPONS TROOP: MORTAR SECT — MG SECT

ASSAULT TROOP: SECTION — SECTION

SECTION: SUB-SECTION — SUB-SECTION

BRITISH DOMINIONS AND COLONIES

During World War II the British Empire and the Commonwealth of Nations consisted of a large number of countries, scattered across the globe. First, there were Dominions, autonomous nation states, defined in the 1926 Balfour Declaration as being equal in status, in no way subordinate one to another but united by common allegiance to the British monarch, who during World War II was King George VI. When Britain declared war in 1939 the Indian Empire and the colonies automatically followed suit, but where the Dominions were concerned, each had to declare war itself, and one, the Irish Free State, chose not to do so. During the 1939–1945 period there were six Dominions: Australia, Canada, Irish Free State, Newfoundland, New Zealand, and the Union of South Africa.

India was officially the Indian Empire, a vast territory which included what is today India and Pakistan, although a number of princely states, such as Hyderabad, were legally independent. Colonies were ruled by governors who reported to the Colonial Office in London and included territories in Africa, Middle East, southern Asia and the Far East. Most of these maintained small military units, predominantly infantry, which were controlled and financed by the colony in peace but came under control of the War Office in London in time of war.

In 1939, all of these forces were organized on British lines and used British weapons and equipment. From about 1943–44 onwards, however, most used increasing amounts of US-supplied weapons and equipment.

CANADA

The Dominion of Canada joined Britain within days of the latter declaring war, even though at that time, September 1939, the Permanent Force (i.e., regular army) numbered a mere 4,261 all ranks, while the reserves consisted of just over 50,000. After a decade of neglect these were neither well-trained nor properly equipped. Nevertheless, 1st Canadian Infantry Division started to arrive in the UK in December 1939 and 1st Canadian Infantry Brigade actually reached France in June 1940, just before it fell, and had no choice but to withdraw to England, where it rejoined the rest of the division. Of the 4,963 Canadians who went to France, 907 were killed, 1,846 were captured and only 2,210 made it back to the UK.

The 3rd Canadian Infantry Division, plus 2nd Canadian Armored Brigade, landed on Juno Beach on D-Day June 6, 1944, and despite heavy losses inflicted by strong opposition, penetrated further than their allies on any of the other four beaches. On the breakout, the Canadians pushed

above A seemingly relaxed tented Orderly Room on exercise. Canada had a number of Highland regiments, originally formed from men who traced their ancestry to Scotland. They wore the same kind of kilts and field dress as their Scottish counterparts.

left Canadian battle dress was usually made from higher-quality material than British uniforms and often had a slightly green cast to the color. This figure has a compass or pistol ammunition pouch attached to the shoulder of one webbing strap and is wearing the Mk III "turtle" helmet. His battle dress jacket is officer's pattern, worn with a shirt and tie.

right A private soldier from The Black Watch of Canada, as indicated by the badge on his beret. The small field dressing pocket is visible on the left side of the battle dress trousers, as is the waist band and buckle arrangement on the jacket. The inset below shows that he has managed to find a pair of brown officer's shoes.

above Canadian sappers checking for mines in the verge alongside the road into Falaise. The man with the mine detector is wearing a sleeveless woolen pullover over his shirt. Canadian forces formed a large component of the Allied armies in Normandy.

through France and Belgium to The Netherlands, clearing the notorious Scheldt Estuary. By this stage, 1st Canadian Army was a huge, multinational force, containing not only 2nd and 3rd Canadian Infantry Divisions and 4th Canadian Armored Division, but two British, one American and one Polish Division, together with Dutch and Czechoslovak brigades.

In the Pacific theater Canada started by sending two battalions to Hong Kong, where they were overwhelmed with the rest of the British garrison on December 25, 1941. The 13th Canadian Brigade took part in operations in the Aleutians, as did members of the US-Canadian First Special Service Force. At the time of the Japanese surrender, the 6th Canadian Infantry Division was undergoing training in preparation for a role in the invasion of Japan.

ORGANIZATION

The Canadians followed a similar organization to the British Army with the infantry based on the "regimental system" where battalions were recruited from the same area and had local titles and capbadges, such as The Loyal Edmonton Regiment. There were also numerous regiments with Scottish traditions, for example The Seaforth Highlanders of Canada, as well as regiments with French Canadian traditions, such as the very highly regarded Royal 22 Regiment, universally known as "The Vandoos" from an anglicised corruption of the French vingt-deux (twenty-two).

left Canadian-pattern Service Cap, with turndown earflaps and regimental badge on the front.

below A 1939 "housewife", a canvas roll used to carry needle, thread and other personal items.

above A simple side cap or garrison cap, in this case with a Royal Engineers badge.

below A neatly packed 24-hour ration pack from 1944. The soldier would break this open so he could distribute the contents around his webbing.

below Macdonald's Gold Standard cigarettes as supplied to the army.

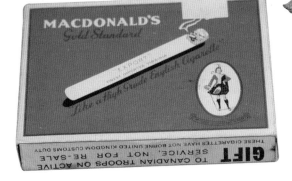

left Sweet Caporal, another brand of cigarettes.

right Regimental flashes were often worn on the upper sleeve of the battle dress.

UNIFORMS AND EQUIPMENT

The uniforms and equipment of the Canadian Army were almost identical with those of the British Army and when in combat there was virtually no visible difference, apart from a shoulder-flash with the word "Canada" and the regimental capbadges. The Canadians wore the same style of battledress as British soldiers but it was made of a better quality material and of a slightly different, but visually detectable, shade of khaki and was much sought after by British troops.

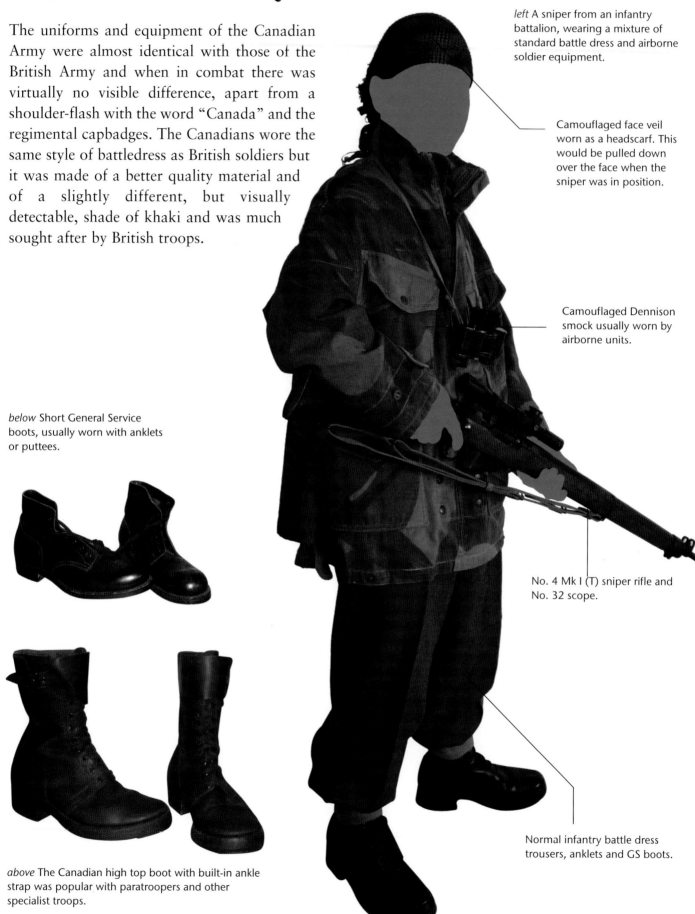

left A sniper from an infantry battalion, wearing a mixture of standard battle dress and airborne soldier equipment.

Camouflaged face veil worn as a headscarf. This would be pulled down over the face when the sniper was in position.

Camouflaged Dennison smock usually worn by airborne units.

No. 4 Mk I (T) sniper rifle and No. 32 scope.

Normal infantry battle dress trousers, anklets and GS boots.

below Short General Service boots, usually worn with anklets or puttees.

above The Canadian high top boot with built-in ankle strap was popular with paratroopers and other specialist troops.

above A Rifle No.4 Mk 1* and No. 4 spike bayonet, made by Long Branch, Canada.

NEW SERVICE 455 ELEY

above A Colt New Service in .455in Eley supplied to Canada for army use.

above Smith and Wesson .38 in revolver as used by the Canadian Army in both world wars.

above When Belgium was overrun the plans for Browning's GP 35 automatic, then being built by FN, were smuggled out to the Allies. Inglis of Canada then began production of this 9 mm pistol for Canadian and British use.

SPECIAL FORCES

The Canadian Army formed two parachute units during the war: 1st and 2nd Canadian Parachute Battalions, although so far as is known the 2nd never deployed. Initial parties were trained in either the British (Ringway) or US (Fort Benning) parachute schools, pending the setting up of Canada's own establishment at Camp Shilo. 1st Canadian Parachute Battalion arrived in England in June 1943 where it immediately became part of the British 6th Airborne Division. The first

paratroops from the 1st Battalion jumped into Normandy at 00.20 hours on June 6, 1944. The battalion remained in Normandy, fighting in a ground role, until August 6 when it returned to the UK. The battalion arrived in Belgium, this time by ship, on December 23, 1944 and marched forward to fight in the Ardennes until February 1945 when it again returned to England. The battalion's final operational drop was in Operation Varsity (Rhine crossing) where it was

right Winter camouflage suits ranged from simple improvised smocks over normal uniform, to substantial jackets and trousers as worn here by men of The Queen's Own Rifles of Canada, near Nijmegen in January 1945.

below Maroon flash worn by airborne units.

left Shoulder flash worn on the battle dress uniform.

involved in very heavy fighting. Eventually successful, the battalion then advanced on foot and reached Wismar on the Baltic coast on May 2, 1945, where it met Soviet forces advancing from the east, the only Canadians to meet the Russians face-to-face.

The First Special Service Force (FSSF) was a joint Canadian/US, all-volunteer unit. Formed July 20, 1942, the FSSF conducted operations in the Aleutians (Kiska), Italy and southern France, before being disbanded December 5, 1944. Most of the Canadians then went to join 1st Canadian Parachute Battalion.

NEWFOUNDLAND

Newfoundland was in a curious position. It had been a self-governing Dominion since 1907 but went into such deep economic crisis in the 1930s that the government was placed in commission, with a British appointed governor and commissioners. This was, in effect, direct rule from Westminster and continued until its people voted to join Canada in 1949. During the war the country supplied many individuals to Canadian and British units and there were two Royal Artillery regiments manned entirely by Newfoundlanders. Newfoundland was also host to numerous Allied facilities, including naval and air bases. The Royal Newfoundland Regiment had established a fine reputation and suffered grievous losses in World War I and although mobilized for home defense it was not sent overseas in World War II.

below Front and rear views of a Canadian parachute soldier, wearing equipment almost indistinguishable from his British counterpart.

Airborne helmet with hessian strips to break up outline.

37-pattern small pack with rolled up gas cape strapped to outside.

Face veil worn as scarf.

Parachute "wings" worn on smock.

Sten Mk 5 with wooden butt.

1908-pattern entrenching tool, with the blade/pick inside the canvas holder.

Dennison smock with four large pockets, partially zippered front, and studs for attaching tailpiece to the lower front.

Airborne pattern battle dress trousers with extendable and strengthened thigh pocket.

Tailpiece for Dennison smock.

AUSTRALIA

In World War II, Australian infantry fought in the Middle East, Mediterranean, Far East and South-West Pacific theaters but, unlike World War I, did not fight in Europe. They were greatly respected by all their enemies, who found them to be doughty, tough and determined fighters, who were never reluctant to find an unconventional solution. Australia was a British colony until 1906 when it became a self-governing dominion, and in 1926 a fully autonomous state, coequal with Great Britain and the other dominions, but still under the constitutional rule of the British monarch. The army had been trained in British methods and fought alongside their British comrades in the Boer War and World War I. Thus, until becoming involved with the US Army from 1942 onwards, the Australians matched the British in almost every way.

On the outbreak of the war in September 1939 the Australian Army numbered some 3,000 regulars and approximately 80,000 in the militia, who were not well trained and who were only committed to homeland defense. British reverses led to a surge in recruiting and within months there were no less than three infantry divisions in the Mediterranean. The 6th took part in the Allied offensive in North Africa in January–February 1941, then went to Greece, where one of its

below Soldiers embarking at Sydney, in December 1939 with full kit. They are wearing World War I-style service dress jackets and 1908-pattern webbing, and are carrying SMLE rifles. Some men have the brim of their slouch hats pinned up.

right A fighting knife typical of those carried by many Australian soldiers.

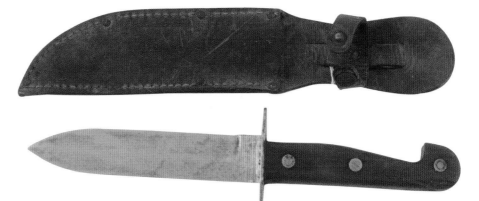

left Canvas sheath for a jungle machete.

above The iconic Australian slouch hat with the left side of the brim pinned to the crown using a stud arrangement.

right A service dress tunic with leather belt and two separate pouches on independent straps. The leather bandolier is from the 1903-pattern equipment originally intended for mounted troops.

brigades was in Crete at the time of the German paratroop landings. The survivors of these two unsuccessful campaigns returned to Australia in December 1941. The 7th Australian Division took part in the attack on the Vichy French in Syria and then it, too, returned to Australia in December 1941. The 9th Division was involved in the defense of Tobruk (February–October 1941) and the battle of Alamein, before returning to the Far East in February 1943.

The 8th Division was virtually destroyed in the Malayan/Singapore campaign, but the remainder of the Australian Army took part in the campaigns in New Guinea and Borneo. By early 1944 there were two corps in the field, each of three infantry divisions and at the time of the Japanese surrender in August 1945 the Australian Army was some 385,000 strong.

above A battalion lines up, with the men all wearing service dress and carrying their large packs. Some men wear puttees wrapped high in the old style while others have neither puttees nor anklets.

ORGANIZATION AND RANKS

Organization, both of the army as a whole and of units, weapons and equipment mirrored that of the British Army, with the basic unit being the battalion, with three or four battalions to a brigade. Ranks for both officers and other ranks were identical with those of the British Army.

UNIFORMS

above Side view of the slouch hat, showing the stud and the large Australian Army badge.

above The cotton beret was an attempt to replace the slouch hat from 1944 but it was never popular with the troops.

above A major wearing service dress with the fabric belt on his jacket and shirt and tie underneath. He has a map case hanging on a leather belt and the 1903 leather bandolier over his shoulder.

Until very late in the war the Australian infantry wore British-style uniforms and web equipment, the only significant exception being the famous "slouch hat." This wide-brimmed felt hat was worn by several armies, but the pinned-up left side, khaki puggaree and leather chin-strap – coupled with the panache with which it is worn – make the Australian version unmistakable. It was worn in all but very close combat, when it was replaced by the British Brodie steel helmet or, from 1944 onwards, by the jungle hat and a soft cotton beret.

Clothing was made in Australia and was cut on British lines, except for brown boots and a unique style of canvas anklet with three buttons instead of straps. Web equipment was initially the somewhat elderly 1908 pattern, but this was quickly replaced by 1937 pattern, and by 1945 miscellaneous items

left Khaki drill uniform was worn in the western desert and the tropics. By now the soldier has 37-pattern webbing although this one has the smaller cartridge pouches instead of the large basic pouches. He also has a water bottle, No. 4 bayonet and light gas mask. Note the identity tags hanging around his neck.

above Rear view showing the 37-pattern large pack.

of US clothing and equipment were also being worn (the British 1944 pattern web equipment did not arrive until after the war had ended).

Experience in the South-West Pacific campaign led to development of Australian combat clothing. This was made of a much tougher material, less likely to tear or rot, and in a "jungle-green" color. Even the beloved slouch hat was replaced by a thin cotton beret, the precursor of the "jungle hat." The jungle environment also had very bad effects on leather boots and these were replaced by the canvas jungle-boot, which was much more suitable, with its high canvas sides keeping leeches and other insects at bay and its soles giving a much better grip on the slippery jungle floor, but these were paid for by a relatively short operational life.

left Australian boots didn't have the same dimpled finish to the leather as did British ammunition boots.

above The large Australian Forces cap badge worn on the slouch hat.

below These large studded plates had to be driven into the sole of the boot.

left As with the British Army, beer was sometimes issued in small quantities in bottles such as these.

left A cigarette lighter carried by an Australian soldier.

WEAPONS

The Australian infantry used almost entirely British weapons, such as Webley and Enfield revolvers, various types of Lee-Enfield rifle, Boy's anti-tank rifle, Bren light machine gun, Vickers heavy machine gun, 2-inch and 3-inch mortars and grenades. A small number of US weapons were also used such as the Colt M1911A1 pistol and the Thompson sub-machine gun. There were, however, a small number of "made-in-Australia" weapons.

right A 1903-pattern bayonet without the fuller (groove) of the later 1917 version. The leather and metal scabbard is underneath.

below SMLEs such as this 1922-made rifle were made at the small arms factory at Lithgow.

below Another Lithgow-made Mk III SMLE complete with 1917-pattern sword bayonet.

OWEN, 9 MM MACHINE CARBINE

Type: machine carbine/ sub-machine gun
Origin: Australia
Caliber: 9 mm Parabellum
Weight (empty): 9.4 lb (4.3 kg)
Barrel length: 9.8 in (250 mm)
Feed: 32-round vertical box
Cyclic rate: 700 rpm

below The Owen's vertical magazine makes it instantly recognizable. Many, like this one, were painted in camouflage colors.

Evelyn Owen, an Australian, designed a sub-machine gun in 1939 which was chambered for the .22 round, but when this was rejected he simply redesigned it around the 9 mm Parabellum round. In this form it became an instant success. Always known as the Owen it was rugged, thoroughly reliable, and easy to carry and use, its only drawback being its weight and a rather high rate-of-fire. It was also easy to manufacture, which was vitally necessary in Australia, cut

off by distance from its allies and with a vast territory to defend. It was accepted in November 1941 and immediately placed in production. It proved very popular with troops.

The gun was instantly recognizable by its vertical magazine, but otherwise it was reasonably conventional with a cylindrical receiver, and a rapidly removable barrel secured by a prominent knurled screw just ahead of the magazine housing. Early barrels had

cooling fins but these were found to be unnecessary, but throughout its life, all barrels had compensators cut into the upper surface of the muzzle. There were two pistol grips and because of the magazine the sights were offset to the right. At the short ranges at which sub-machine guns are used, however, this made little difference. It was fitted with either a skeleton or full butt and from 1943 it was painted in camouflage colors.

AUSTEN 9MM MACHINE CARBINE

Type: machine carbine/
   sub-machine gun
Origin: Australia
Caliber: 9 mm Parabellum
Weight (empty): 8.8 lb (4.0 kg)
Barrel length: 7.8 in (198 mm)
Feed: 28-round box
Cyclic rate: 500 rpm

right Australian fighting men in the western desert, with shorts and slouch hats. These men still have the obsolete 1908-pattern webbing.

This weapon combined many features of the British Sten design, with certain features of the German Erma MP40, its name being derived by combining the first two letters of Australia with Sten. It was produced by two factories, Carmichael and Diecasters, both located in Melbourne, Australia. It had a twin-legged, forward-folding butt, forward pistol grip, with the barrel, retaining collar and trigger mechanism of the Sten. About 20,000 were produced between 1943 and 1945, although with hindsight it seems to have been unnecessary when the excellent Owen was also in production. An unusual 'bunker-busting' device, its full name was "Projector, Motor Rocket, 3-inch, Mark 1" but it was given the more straightforward nickname of "Lilo" (it was not an acronym).

LILO

The Lilo consisted of a motor taken from an air-launched 3-inch rocket, to which was attached one of two warheads; one weighed 21 lb (9.5 kg), the other 60 lb (27 kg), both full of High Explosive (HE). The launcher was, in effect, a short length of large-diameter pipe mounted on four spindly legs. Direction was achieved by aiming the entire launcher, using two iron blades, but elevation could be altered by adjusting the rear legs. The projectile was mounted in the launch-tube, the device was aimed and then fired using a 3.5 volt dry battery. Range was very short and several rounds were usually needed to get the aim right, but a hit was devastating.

left A patrol moving through a jungle swamp in Bougainville, in January 1945. They have Owen sub-machine guns and are wearing the shapeless combat beret.

221

INDIA

left A British officer directing Indian troops. They are shirtless and wearing turbans (puggarees) instead of steel helmets. Camouflage netting or face veils have been put over their turbans to reduce the visibility of the bright cloth.

British India was neither a dominion nor a colony and its huge army – every man a volunteer – occupied a unique position. Its units and soldiers were deployable anywhere in the world although, unlike World War I, only minor units and individuals went to North-West Europe. That apart, the Indian Army played a vital role in the Middle East and Far East campaigns.

Until about 1944 Indian infantry brigades were composed of two Indian infantry battalions and one British infantry battalion, except where Gurkhas were concerned, where no British battalion was considered necessary. A typical organization is shown in the table. The rest of the brigade comprised an artillery regiment, usually all-British; plus engineers, signals and logistics units composed of Indian soldiers, with both British and Indian officers. By mid-1944 British units were becoming harder to find and the need for one in every Indian brigade was quietly dropped without the slightest detrimental effect on fighting efficiency, morale or reliability.

below Men of the 8th Indian Division advance up a hill under cover of smoke alongside a lightly armored carrier.

RANKS

Group	British Rank	Indian Rank
Field Marshal	Field Marshal	
General officers	General	
	Lieutenant-General	
	Major-General	
Field officers	Brigadier	
	Colonel	
	Lieutenant-Colonel	
	Major	Subedar Major
Junior officers	Captain	Subedar
	Lieutenant	Jemadar
Warrant Officers	Warrant Officer 2nd Class	Company Havildar Major
Senior NCOs	Color sergeant	Company Quartermaster Havildar
	Sergeant	Havildar
Junior NCOs	Corporal	Naik
	Lance-Corporal	Lance Naik
Privates	Private	Sepoy

left Shoulder flash of the 19th Indian Division.

right A Gurkha lance corporal in Italy wearing standard British battle dress and with a pistol holster across his chest.

The rank structure of the Indian Army was unique. British officers were commissioned into the Indian Army where they received their commission from the King and were known as King's Commissioned Officers (KCOs). Indian soldiers who had worked their way up through the ranks and who obtained the requisite qualifications and recommendations were commissioned not by the King but by the Viceroy of India. These were known as Viceroy's Commissioned Officers (VCOs) and were, in many respects, equivalent to a warrant officer in the British Army, but were treated in almost the

left Indian troops in a pre-war exercise in Singapore. They are wearing light khaki drill uniform neatly tailored to peacetime standards. The senior NCO is carrying a map case while the men have SMLEs. The Indian Army ended up fighting in tropical jungle, mountains and desert.

same way as British officers, and wore officers' badges of rank on their shoulder straps but backed by a strip of braid running across the strap. They were treated with great respect, especially the Subedar-Major; they were always addressed as "sahib." From the early 20th century there was also an increasing number of King's Commissioned Indian Officers (KCIO) who qualified at the Royal Military Academy Sandhurst, were granted King's Commissions and were equal in every way to British officers.

In an Indian Army infantry battalion, the British commanding officer was supported and advised by the Subedar-Major on all matters pertaining to the Indian soldiers, including religious aspects, customs, diet and soldiers' welfare. At the next level the company commander, a British major or captain, was similarly supported by a Subedar. The great majority of platoons were, however, commanded by VCOs in the rank of Jemadar.

above The light service shirt worn by the Indian Army with epaulettes, attached collar and breast pockets.

above: Slouch hat with cloth "puggaree" wrapped around the brim. Such hats were worn by Gurkhas and other Indian units (and British units within the Indian Army).

above Indian-made webbing used lighter stitching and reinforcement than on British production, while the metal components were of thinner brass.

right Attacking up a rocky escarpment in north Africa with fixed bayonets. The men are in the open, their only cover the smoke screen laid down by mortars or artillery. Note how their helmets have a sand paint scheme.

UNIFORM

above A patrol from the 7th Gurkha Rifles takes a breather. There is a wide variation in uniforms across the group, including woolen pullovers, battle dress jackets and tropical khaki drill. They all have kukris attached to the rear of their belts.

left Sikh troops in Ethiopia before the war. They wear obsolete tropical dress including puttees and "plus four" trousers.

For headdress, many Indian regiments wore the puggaree (turban), a long strip of cloth wound around the head; these were always in regimental colors, and some had embellishments, such as strips of braid and were wound in such a way that those with experience could tell at a glance the

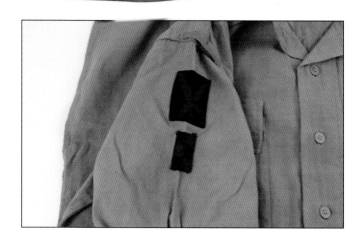

right Short sleeved khaki drill shirt worn both in the tropics and in the western desert. The inset shows that the wearer belonged to a Gurkha regiment.

below A Gurkha soldier in jungle green uniform, introduced when khaki drill was found to be too light-colored to provide camouflage in dark foliage. He has a field dressing taped to his webbing and carries very little equipment apart from ammunition, water and a Thompson M1 sub-machine gun.

wearer's religion, and, in the case of Hindus, the caste. In the combat zone, headdress was a mixture of puggaree and slouch hat, with the British Mark 1 steel helmet worn when under fire. As the wear continued the beret became more frequently worn, as well as a khaki cotton "combat" hat with soft peak and a neck cloth. The combat puggaree was of khaki cloth, and some religious groups refused to wear the steel helmet. Some regiments, such as the Gurkhas and Burma Rifles wore the slouch hat with a khaki puggaree; these hats had a fore-and-aft dent and neither side of the wide brim was turned up.

In the early days in the Mediterranean theater, Indian regiments wore gray woolen shirts, khaki shorts (known as "Bombay bloomers"), hosetops and puttees, even in the combat zone. They were among the first to wear the knitted pullover as a uniform item; originally a standard khaki, regiments soon started having them made in "regimental" colors.

During the war, the Indian Army increasingly adopted the same style of clothing as the British Army, and led the way to "jungle green."

WEAPONS

The Indian Army had its own Ordnance factories, but these produced almost entirely weapons and equipment of British design. There were, however, some exceptions.

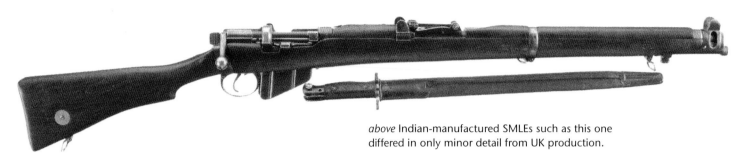

above Indian-manufactured SMLEs such as this one differed in only minor detail from UK production.

VICKERS-BERTHIER MARK 3B

Type: light machine gun
Origin: UK
Caliber: .303 in British
Weight (empty): 20.8 lb (9.4 kg)
Barrel length: 23.9 in (607 mm)
Feed: 30-round box
Cyclic rate: 500 rpm

below An Indian Vickers crew occupy a captured German position in Tunis in May 1943. They are using the long range sight on the gun. Discarded German equipment lies scattered around them.

Designed in 1908 by a French Army officer named Berthier, this weapon failed to gain any orders and was largely forgotten until the early 1920s when the British company, Vickers, saw its potential and bought the manufacturing rights. The British company introduced a few modifications and then placed it in production for various foreign armies. In 1926 it was entered for the British Army competition to replace the Lewis gun, which the Vickers won, with the Czech ZB second, Danish Madsen third and US BAR fourth, but money was short and no orders were placed. A new competition was held in the early 1930s which was eventually won in 1934 by a modified version of the Czech ZB (the Bren). Meanwhile, the Indian Army had lost patience and in 1933 ordered the Vickers-Berthier Mark 3B as its standard LMG, being produced in the Indian Ordnance Factory at Ishapur. The Vickers-Berthier, usually known as the "VB" was perfectly adequate and served Indian Army units well through most of World War II, but was gradually eased out in favor of standardization with the Bren.

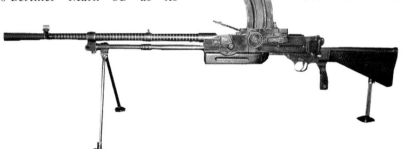

left The Vickers-Berthier resembled the Bren and was an effective light machine gun.

KUKRI

The kukri is the legendary knife carried by all Gurkha soldiers in combat. It has a fearsome reputation, one common misconception being that once drawn it cannot be resheathed without drawing blood, which, if true, would make an overnight jungle camp a blood-spattered place. In reality, in addition to being an excellent weapon in close-quarter combat, the kukri is also a multipurpose tool, being used for tasks varying from chopping small trees and saplings, clearing undergrowth, loosening earth for digging, food preparation (cutting meat and vegetables) and even for opening cans.

Kukris can vary widely in dimensions, but all have the characteristic cranked shape, with the main part of the blade at an angle of some 20 degrees to the upper half of the weapon. The blade has a single cutting edge. It has a full tang, with a wooden or horn handle which is attached by a Nepalese glue, although in some military weapons they are secured by rivets. A typical kukri is about 16–18 in (40–45 cm) long and weighs anywhere between 1–2 lb (450–900 g).

below A Gurkha after despatching a Japanese defender with his kukri. He has cotton bandoliers around his shoulder and is wearing a woolen cap comforter. Gurkhas were especially renowned for their ferocity in close assault.

above Two kukris, one inside its leather scabbard. The characteristic cranked shape is clearly shown.

below A Gurkha patrol cautiously clears a Japanese bunker. Three men cover the entrance with rifle and sub-machine guns while the fourth brandishes his kukri.

PARATROOPS

left Indian paratroops in training. They wear light tropical uniform and the rubber protective headgear used in the early days of British and Indian paratroop operations.

The first Indian parachute formation, 50th Independent Parachute Brigade, was formed in October 1942 from 152 Indian and 153 Gurkha Parachute Battalions, its first action being in Nagaland (Sangshak) where it turned back two reinforced Japanese divisions in a six-day battle which cost the brigade no less than 580 casualties. It then fought its way through Japanese-controlled jungle to the British Indian stronghold at Imphal where it fought on for another three months. Withdrawn to recover it then formed the nucleus of an expanded force, which was originally numbered 9th, then 44th and finally 2nd Indian Airborne Division.

At the same time the units themselves were reorganized; the Indian Parachute Regiment being formed, with 152 Battalion splitting into two to form 1st and 4th Parachute Battalions, made up of Hindus and Muslims respectively, while 153 Gurkha Parachute Battalion became 2nd Parachute and the recently formed 154th Gurkha Battalion being renumbered as the 3rd Parachute Battalion.

A reinforced Gurkha parachute battalion

above Indian paratroopers line up for inspection before boarding their C-47 aircraft.

landed on Elephant Point which controlled the entrance to Rangoon harbor on May 1, 1945. The landing was a complete success.

CHINDITS

The Chindits were a unique type of special force where only a few were volunteers and the vast majority became involved because their units were drafted in. The concept originated with an eccentric British Royal Artillery officer, Brigadier Orde Wingate, who had strongly held ideas about using troops deep behind enemy lines, operating with air support for both ground-attack and resupply. On taking command of 77th (Indian) Infantry Brigade in 1942, Wingate first trained

above Senior Chindit officers shared the same conditions as their men. These filthy, unshaven, scruffy figures are Brigadier Calvert, who took over after Wingate's death, and Colonel Shaw.

left Indian paratroopers deploying by air although not kitted out to drop when they arrive.

them for long-range penetration operations in the jungle and then led them on the first Chindit operation, codenamed Longcloth (February–April 1943). Moving on foot, the force penetrated deep into Japanese-held territory and achieved some successes, including attacks on bridges, railroads and roads, but at a terrible cost, losing approximately 1,000 of the 3,000 men involved and with few of the survivors fit for further service.

The operation was nevertheless regarded as a success and Wingate took command of 11th Indian Infantry Division (Special Force) with dedicated support from the USAAF's 1st Air Commando Group. Wingate was allocated six infantry brigades, of which one was West African, three British and two Indian, although the latter included only Gurkha battalions. Wingate's troops

underwent intensive training in India and the operation, codenamed "Thursday", began on February 5, 1944 with two brigades advancing on foot, while the others, some 9,000 men, flew in. The operation was hindered when Wingate was killed in an air crash, at the same time as critical battles at Imphal and Kohima caused reinforcements to be diverted.

The Chindits undertook heavy fighting which, coupled with marching and surviving in the unforgiving jungle, led to the men being exhausted. The columns were gradually withdrawn until the last left Burma on August 27, 1944. Wingate's men had suffered very heavy casualties – 1,396 killed or missing and 2,434 wounded – and even among those who walked out many needed special medical treatment. The Chindits were disbanded in February 1945.

NEW ZEALAND

above The 14th New Zealand Brigade come ashore at Baka Baka beach, Vella Lavella Island in September 1943. They are relieving the US 35 Infantry Regiment. They are wearing their high-domed, wide-brimmed hats, while there are some US soldiers wearing M1 helmets in their midst.

Despite its remoteness, New Zealand was steadfast in its support of the United Kingdom throughout World War II and proportionally its losses were greater than any other Commonwealth country. On the outbreak of war the New Zealand Army was tiny, comprising approximately 600 regulars, 10,000 volunteers in territorial units, and 400 reservists. On mobilization the country set out to raise the 2nd New Zealand Expeditionary Force (2NZEF) in succession to 1NZEF of World War I fame. Three infantry brigades were sent to Europe. The

4th NZ Infantry Brigade arrived in Egypt in February 1940, while 5th Brigade was originally destined for France. When that country fell the brigade's ships, still on the high seas, were diverted to Scotland. The 6th Brigade arrived in Egypt in late 1940 where 5th Brigade finally joined its compatriots in early 1941 to complete 2nd NZ Division.

The New Zealanders established a reputation second to none, fighting in the Western Desert, Greece, Crete and Italy. In Italy in February 1944 a New Zealand Corps was formed, consisting of

2nd NZ Division, 4th Indian Division and 78th British Division. New Zealanders took part in the long siege of Monte Cassino and as the war in Europe ended they arrived in Triestc.

Even before Japan's entry into the war 8th New Zealand Infantry Brigade was deployed to Fiji in November 1940, followed by a second brigade in mid-1941; this led to the formation of 3rd NZ Division, which was relieved by US forces in June 1942. The division never fought as a whole but its brigades took part in operations in various islands. The main national focus, however, lay in maintaining the strength of 2nd New Zealand Division in Italy.

ORGANIZATION AND RANKS

The organization, uniforms and ranks of the New Zealand Army followed those of the British, except that the vast amount of US clothing and equipment available later in the war resulted in the adoption of some US Army items.

The most famous item of dress for New Zealand troops was the high-domed, wide-brimmed slouch hat made of a khaki felt material. In most units this hat was worn with the "bash" consisting of four deep indentations and four sharp ridges at 90 degrees to each other, the

below A New Zealand soldier wearing battle dress and 37-pattern webbing. The unique wide-brimmed hat was nicknamed the "lemon squeezer" from the shape of the crown.

above View showing the back of the battle dress and the arrangement of the 37-pattern shoulder straps.

forward ridge being straight to the wearer's front. Because of its shape this design was known as the "lemon squeezer." It should, however, be noted that some New Zealand units wore it with a fore-and-aft bash. The hat was fitted with a puggaree whose colors indicated the wearer's arm-of-service; in the case of infantry this was khaki-red-khaki. The cap-badge was worn dead-center.

below Unloading men and supplies at Mono, Treasury Island, in the Solomons in October 1943. The soldiers are wearing tropical uniform and Mk II steel helmets. New Zealand troops fought in the Western Desert, Crete, Greece, Italy and in the island-hopping campaigns in the Pacific.

WEAPONS AND EQUIPMENT

The New Zealand infantry used almost exclusively British equipment, although some US items, such as M1911A1 pistols, were adopted later in the war. Web equipment was initially British 1908 pattern replaced by 37 Pattern mid-war, and, again, some items of US equipment in 1944–45.

SOUTH AFRICA

South Africa occupied a position of the greatest strategic significance in a global conflict and was a valuable source of manpower to the British Empire. However, it had numerous people opposed to becoming involved in a war in far-off Europe, some of whom were so vocal that they were locked up for the duration. In September 1939 the army comprised 3,350 in the Permanent Force (regulars), 14,631 in the Active Citizen Force (equivalent to the US National Guard) and over 100,000 in the Defense Rifle Association (also known as the Commandos). Once Italy entered the war, recruiting picked up but the political situation would never have permitted conscription in the white community. Initially, the Colored (mixed race and Asians) and Black populations were only allowed to fulfill menial roles such as drivers and porters, and were banned from fighting against a European enemy, but this was quietly shelved during the war and some "Native Infantry Battalions" were raised and sent overseas.

South African troops took part with considerable success in operations in Italian East Africa and the invasion of Madagascar. They next took part in the Western Desert campaign where some good service was marred by the fall of Tobruk (June 21, 1942) where 35,000 Allied troops, mainly the South African 2nd Infantry Division, surrendered after only seven days of the second siege. This was through no fault of the troops, but the event remains controversial to this day. Subsequently, the 6th South African Armored Division fought with great success in Italy from April 1944 to May 1945.

Approximately 330,000 men, all volunteers, served in the South African Army during World War II, the racial composition being white – 64 per cent; black – 23 per cent; Colored and Asian – 13 per cent. Of these, nearly 9,000 were killed in action.

WEAPONS AND PERSONAL EQUIPMENT

The South African infantry used almost exclusively British weapons. Individual soldiers wore 1937 Pattern personal equipment, although in the earlier part of the war the anklets, despite being of the same general design as the British, were wider, but the normal narrower type were worn overseas.

The uniforms were generally similar to those of the British Army. The general duty uniform in the 1930s and early 1940s consisted of a gray-green long-sleeved field jacket and shorts, gray woolen long puttees with yellow tying cords, brown boots, and gray polo helmet. On going overseas this was replaced by a khaki drill (KD) uniform with long-sleeved jacket and long trousers. The sun helmet (solar topi) had a noticeably narrower brim than those used in other armies and was based on the design used by contemporary polo players. All ranks wore a square patch in national colors (orange–white–black) on the right side of the polo helmet and all also wore a narrow orange strip at the base of the shoulder straps.

above South African infantry soldiers were equipped with SMLEs, such as this one, made in their own country.

BRITISH COLONIAL FORCES

Throughout their imperial era the British raised local military units, both to save money and to avoid tying down elements of the always overstretched British Army. These units were the responsibility of the Colonial Office and run on a day-to-day basis by the individual colony's government, which also paid for them. This meant that they were not part of the British Army. Varying proportions of officers and senior NCOs were British Army regulars seconded for fixed periods. Such units served in their own colony, being responsible for external defense and supporting the police, but in wartime responsibility for their use was transferred to the War Office, who placed them under the nearest Army commander.

They were invariably armed and equipped by the British and wore British uniforms, although they were allowed considerable freedom in choice of non-combat headdress and cap-badge.

AFRICAN TROOPS

Every empire territory on the African continent supplied units for service. Many of these fought in the East African campaign, in Burma and India and in the Middle East. They included:

- King's African Rifles (KAR), recruited from Kenya, Nyasaland, Tanganyika, Uganda and Zanzibar.
- Royal West African Frontier Force (RWAFF), recruited from British West African territories: Nigeria, Gold Coast, Sierra Leone and Gambia.
- Somaliland Camel Corps, recruited only from British Somaliland.
- Northern Rhodesia Regiment (NRR), which ended up eight full infantry battalions and an independent company.
- Rhodesian African Rifles (RAR) raised in Southern Rhodesia in 1940.

above Cap badge of the Royal Rhodesia Regiment.

left East African soldiers operating a twin Bren anti-aircraft mount. Note the large drum magazines.

MIDDLE AND FAR EAST

Colonial units were also raised in the Middle East and Far East for service in those theaters. They included:

- The Arab Legion, controlled and paid for by the government of Trans-Jordan.
- Trans-Jordanian Frontier Force (TJFF), raised by the British High Commissioner in Palestine.
- Federated Malay States Volunteer Force.
- Unfederated Malay States volunteer forces.
- The Malay Regiment in 1935.
- Straits Settlements Volunteer Force (SSVF) from Singapore, the Straits settlements and nearby colonial outposts.
- Hong Kong Volunteer Defense Corps (HKVDC).

above A British officer and Indian Senior NCO preparing for the defense of Singapore. The officer is wearing tropical dress while the NCO has a woolen pullover. Both men have the early-model gas mask in the ready position.

left The Singapore Volunteer Corps prepares to go to training camp. Wearing solar topees, tropical dress and 1908-pattern webbing, they are carrying machine gun boxes, ammunition drums, a flare pistol, and in the rear, a Boys anti-tank rifle.

THE CARIBBEAN REGIMENT

The Caribbean Regiment was formed in Trinidad in April 1944 and was recruited from volunteers from all over the Caribbean, particularly members of the various island volunteer defense forces.

JEWISH UNITS

Even though they were in conflict with the British over their struggle for an independent state, many Jews volunteered to serve in the British Armed Forces. Numbers were such that a whole brigade was eventually formed, fighting in Italy before being disbanded in 1946.

THE SOVIET UNION

When Russia's Civil War ended in December 1920, economic necessity ensured that the Red Army (including the Border Guards) was reduced from a strength of some 5 million to just over 0.5 million in 1924, its lowest point ever. Thereafter, the perceived threat from capitalist nations resulted in steady growth, reaching 1.5 million by 1938 and well over 30 million by war's end in 1945.

The war against Finland (November 1939–March 1940) showed many shortcomings, while the border war against the Japanese (July 1938–April 1941), although it ended in Soviet success, was by no means an overwhelming victory. Despite these experiences, the German onslaught (June 22, 1941) still caught the Soviet Army by surprise and much ground was surrendered and many troops lost before the front was stabilized.

The army was rebuilt as leaders and men learned how to deal with the German Blitzkrieg. They then went on to master the Soviet version of rapid and overwhelming offensive warfare, and by 1944 the Germans were being driven inexorably back to the final conclusion in the ruins of Berlin.

SOVIET INFANTRY

The Soviet soldier was tough, well used to living under harsh conditions, and remarkably forgiving of a regime that treated him rather badly. They served under officers who were the survivors of the "Great Terror" purges of 1937–38. It was thus fortunate for Stalin and his henchmen that both officers and soldiers hated the Germans even more than they did the Politburo, although for most their loyalty was towards Mother Russia rather than to the Communist regime.

above Instead of ID tags Soviet soldiers carried these containers with a roll of paper inside giving their name and serial number.

above A selection of personal photographs showing training scenes and formal portraits.

left An infantry squad wearing winter greatcoats and M40 helmets, and with a mixture of PPSh sub-machine guns and Mosin-Nagant rifles.

Pre-war collar tabs showing arm of service and rank.

Pre-war M27 *Budionovka* winter hat.

M36 helmet in winter camouflage, a pre-war design that served widely in the early years of the war.

M35 backpack with blanket roll strapped around it and M38 bread bag attached to flap.

Mosin rifle and spike bayonet.

Cotton bandolier for extra ammunition.

Early-war BN gas mask in case.

High leather boots.

left and right An infantry private in the autumn of 1941 in marching order.

below An array of medals and badges, including a badge for guards status. Soviet soldiers usually wore their medals on their combat clothing.

above The Red Star was worn on the front of the service cap and on other headgear.

below Various patterns of military ID document and paybook carried by Soviet soldiers.

THE INFANTRY DIVISION

By 1945 there were over 500 Soviet infantry divisions (*divizeya*), all with their main fighting strength concentrated in three infantry regiments (*polk*), divisional artillery, and an anti-tank battalion, with combat support from engineer battalion, communications company, and combat service support from elements of the medical, transport and supply services, all commanded from a divisional headquarters.

The three infantry regiments each consisted of three infantry battalions (*battalion*) plus an infantry gun company (4 x 76 mm guns), anti-tank gun company (6 x 45 mm guns), anti-tank rifle company (27 x PTRD-41 or PTRS), heavy mortar company (8 x 120 mm mortars), two 100-men sub-machine gun companies and a regimental headquarters.

above After the disasters of the Finnish War the Soviet Army paid much more attention than before to operations in winter conditions. These ski troops are typical of those trained to fight in the north and in Siberia.

right Marshal Zhukov addresses a group during the Khalkin Ghol fighting in 1939, where the Japanese and Soviet Army clashed over the Mongolian border. The men wear summer tunics, M36 helmets and wide-brimmed summer caps.

POLITICAL OFFICERS

A word needs to be said about the political officers. In the German armed forces, the Nazi Party sought to achieve pre-eminence by creating the Waffen-SS, which was a separate force of super-loyal party members, but, generally, left the army to play a non-political role. The Communist Party of the Soviet Union (CPSU) took an opposite course and placed Party activists throughout the chain-of-command right down to company level. It is important to understand that the title generally used in the West, political commissar, applied only when the officer concerned was equal to the military commander and had the authority to countermand his orders. They definitely warranted this title when first established in 1919, although the officer at company level was called a political leader (*politruk*), rather than commissar.

Political officers were appointed in 1919 to ensure that former tsarist officers in the newly created Red Army did not deviate from the party line. These commissars were removed from 1925 onwards, only to be restored in May 1937 at the time of the purge, only to be withdrawn again in 1940, and then restored once more in the great panic stemming from the German attack in 1941. Once again their existence was not long and in October 1942 they were withdrawn yet again and replaced by a deputy commander for political work (*zampolit*) who was subordinate to the commander. Then in 1943 the position of zampolit at company level was removed, although they remained at battalion level and above. At all levels from regiment upwards the political officer was supported by a Special Section, composed of ultra-loyal Party workers. In general, the task of these political officers was to ensure that the Soviet Army, both collectively and individually, remained loyal to the Party, as well as maintain good discipline and give advice and welfare support to individuals.

above Newspapers such as *Pravda* and *Izvestia* and magazines such as *Ogonek* and *Krokodil* were largely propaganda sheets intended to raise the morale and determination of the country.

left Officers being briefed by their commander in 1942. At this stage in the war the Commissar is also present and able to countermand or overrule the military commander's decisions.

NKVD

The Soviet Union's "People's Commissariat for Internal Affairs", or *Narodnij Kommisariat Vnutrennih Del* (NKVD) was the most powerful and ruthless secret police organization in the Soviet Union. NKVD personnel ran the prison camps, guarded the borders, hunted dissidents (real and imagined), carried out espionage and counter-espionage as well as other tasks necessary to maintain the Soviet dictatorship.

Military NKVD units up to division size operated alongside the Red Army. Their main role was to provide security in the rear areas and to stiffen the resolve of front-line units. They often did this by placing blocking detachments just behind the front lines to catch deserters and shoot at units and individuals who had been forced to retreat.

NKVD units were also deployed in the front line, in the hope that their dedication and ruthlessness would translate into excellent fighting capability. They often did fight well, although they were usually hampered by their low allocation of heavy weapons and lack of infantry training.

The NKVD also created hastily formed militia divisions of men and women, not of military age or fitness, to defend their cities, districts or factories. These units were poorly equipped and trained and usually died quickly in large numbers when committed to combat.

Some 500,000 men and women served in NKVD combat units throughout the war

left and right The blue crown on the cap and blue piping on the shoulder-boards indicates that this officer is a member of the NKVD. His neatly tailored tunic has a high collar and pleated pockets. He wears a leather Sam Browne-style belt with a documents case and pistol.

below The green star on this sidecap is the badge of the NKVD border troops – the first soldiers to meet the German assault.

RANKS AND INSIGNIA

The tsarist system of rank names and insignia underwent a series of sweeping changes following the Communist takeover in 1917. The word "officer" was banned and the whole array of ranks, insignia and, in particular, the shoulder-board, were abolished. They were replaced by a system in which the individuals were known by their appointments; i.e., 'Army Commander A...,' 'Battalion Commander B...', 'Squad Leader C...,' and so on. These appointments were indicated by colored collar patches. The years 1937–38 saw the Stalinist purges of the armed forces and in 1938–39 there were brief wars against Japan and Finland, both of which ended in Soviet successes. However, it was clear that there was a need for greater discipline and morale in the army, so Stalin restored ranks for generals on 13 July 1940,

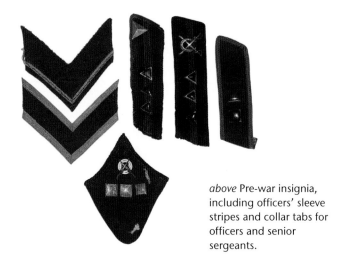

above Pre-war insignia, including officers' sleeve stripes and collar tabs for officers and senior sergeants.

followed by all the remaining military ranks on July 26, 1940. Then, in the aftermath of the German invasion of the USSR, even the hated shoulder-boards were reinstated (January 6, 1943). The ranks for the remainder of the war were then as shown in the table.

SOVIET INFANTRY RANK BADGES (POST JAN 1943)

Shoulder (Officers)

 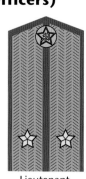    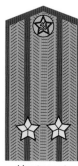 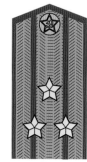

| Junior Lieutenant | Lieutenant | Senior Lieutenant | Captain | Major | Lieutenant-Colonel | Colonel |

Shoulder (NCOs)

| Private | Corporal | Junior Sergeant | Sergeant | Senior Sergeant | Sergeant Major |

above and left 1943 saw the reintroduction of shoulder-boards for denoting both NCO and officer rank.

Category	Soviet Ranks	Translation	US Army Equivalent
General officers	*Márshal Sovietskovo Soyuza*	Marshal of the Soviet Union	General of the Army
	Generál Ármii	General of an army	General
	Generál-Polkóvnik	Colonel-General	Lieutenant-General
	Generál-Leytenánt	Lieutenant-General	Major-General
	Generál-Mayór	Major-General	Brigadier-General
Field Grade Officers	*Polkóvnik*	Colonel	Colonel
	Podpolkóvnik	Lieutenant-Colonel	Lieutenant-Colonel
	Mayór	Major	Major
Company Grade Officers	*Kapitan*	Captain	Captain
	Starshiy Leytenant	Senior Lieutenant	Lieutenant
	Leytenant	Lieutenant	
	Mladshiy Leytenant	Junior Lieutenant	Second Lieutenant
Sergeants	*Starshina*	Sergeant Major	1st Sergeant
	Starshiy Serzhant	Senior Sergeant	Staff-Sergeant
	Serzhant	Sergeant	Sergeant
	Mladshiy Serzhant	Junior Sergeant	Corporal
Soldiers	*Yefreytor*	Lance-Corporal	Private First Class
	Ryadovoi	Private	Private

In addition to their badges of rank, Soviet Army officers and soldiers also showed their arm-of-service colors, which appeared as piping on the hat, jacket and, from January 6, 1943, on the shoulder-boards.

below Shoulder boards showing various ranks. Those with metal symbols denote arm of service (armor, artillery etc). The infantry one have red piping and are on a khaki background.

Arm of Service	Parade			Field		
	Base color	**Piping**	**Metallic**	**Base color**	**Piping**	**Metallic**
Infantry	Red	Black	None	Khaki	Red	None
Tanks	Black	Red	Tank		Red	Tank
Artillery	Black	Red	Crossed barrels		Red	Crossed barrels
Engineers	Black	Black	Crossed axes		Black	Crossed axes
Cavalry	Dark blue	Black	Crossed sabers		Dark blue	Crossed sabers
Airborne	Light blue	Black	Parachute/ aircraft		Light blue	Parachute/ aircraft

RIFLE BATTALION

As did all armies, the Soviets knew that the rifle battalion was the key to success, but it proved difficult to get the right balance of manpower, weapons, firepower and resilience. Equipment shortages and a lack of trained junior commanders forced the army to adopt a very simple battalion organization in the early months of the conflict. Over time, equipment supplies and hard-won experience allowed a more-balanced structure to evolve, as shown by the early 1945 version described here. The figures shown are the official "book" figures; however, for much of the time frontline units fought significantly understrength.

The total strength (on paper) of the battalion was about 600 all ranks, broken down approximately into 30 officers, 1 political officer and about 570 men, somewhat smaller than the US and British equivalent, but with significantly higher firepower, except in anti-tank weapons. The battalion was divided into three rifle companies, a machine gun company and a mortar

below The Red Army was expected to improvise river crossings, as shown here by the mixture of rubber dinghy, tire inner tube and wooden boat used by this group. They are equipped with Mosin-Nagant rifles and a DP light machine gun.

above The Soviet Army very quickly learned how to fight using combined arms tactics. Here infantry assault a village, closely supported by a T34 tank.

company, there being neither a headquarters company nor a support weapons company. The number of headquarters, logistics and administrative personnel was considerably less than in a US or British infantry battalion, despite the very large number of automatic weapons. It should be noted that by this stage, political officers had been withdrawn from the company level.

BATTALION HQ

A small command element comprised 3 military officers, the political officer, and the signal section of 1 officer and 10 men, the small size of the latter indicating the dearth of communications facilities available. The Anti-Tank Platoon (1+22) consisted of three squads, each with three 14.5 mm AT rifles, either the PTRD or the PTRS. There was also a Supply Platoon (1+11), whose primary task was the provision of ammunition, and a Medical Squad of 5 men.

MACHINE GUN COMPANY

This sub-unit provided a remarkable amount of support firepower for an infantry battalion. With 5 officers and 52 men it comprised three platoons (1+17), each with three SG-43 machine guns, while Company HQ was 2 officers and 1 man.

MORTAR COMPANY

The battalion Mortar Company (5+55) had three platoons, each of three squads, the latter comprising 6 men and a single 82 mm mortar each.

above A near miss detonates close to this machine gun crew. They are wearing M40 helmets and have their bedding rolls over their shoulders. Note how the sub-machine gunner grips the magazine to steady his weapon.

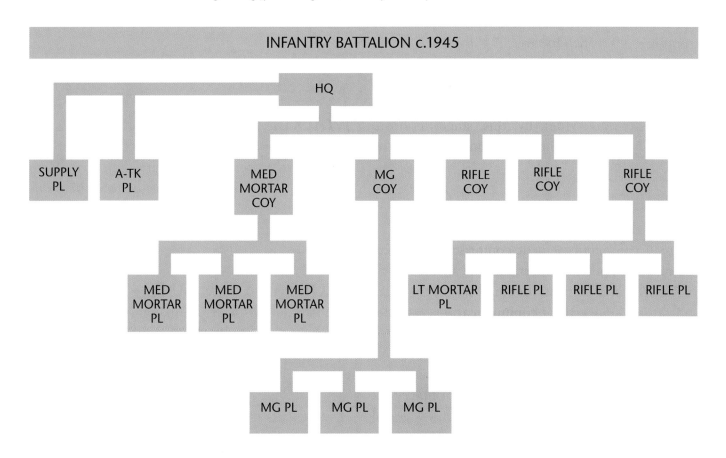

INFANTRY BATTALION c.1945

left A sergeant-major operating a radio to contact a reconnaissance unit. Soviet units became excellent at radio security and keeping transmissions to a minimum, especially before a major offensive.

right A mobile reconnaissance unit moves forward on motorcycle/sidecar combinations.

below Food supplies were always scarce in the Red Army, with supply space being mainly given over to ammunition and fuel. This runner has an insulated can on his back, carrying hot food from the company kitchens to his platoon.

THE RIFLE COMPANY

above These men are wearing snow camouflage suits, although they are taking cover in a ruined building and there appears to be no snow on the ground.

right Advancing over open ground these men are being protected by a smoke screen. Their rifles are not at the ready position so it seems that no immediate contact is expected.

The battalion had a fighting strength of 3 Rifle Companies (each 6 officers and 138 men), each of which consisted of three Rifle Platoons (each 1 officer and 39 men) and a Mortar Platoon (1 officer, 9 men).

The Rifle Platoon had a very small HQ (1 officer, 4 men) and four Rifle Squads each of 9 men: a commander (PPSh-41), two LMG teams (each one DP, with gunner and ammunition number, who carried a PPSh-41), and four riflemen (Mosin-Nagant M1890/30). The platoon HQ consisted of 1 officer in command, an assistant, a runner, and 2 snipers, each armed with a sniping rifle (these snipers may have been placed under company control).

The Mortar Platoon (1 officer, 7 men), consisted of an officer and assistant, plus two teams each of 3 men and one 50 mm mortar. There was also a Medium Machine Gun Squad of 4 men plus one machine gun; this small sub-unit may have been added to the mortar platoon to give the officer a reasonable span of command. Finally, Company Headquarters comprised 2 officers and 7 men, plus a Medical Squad of 5 men.

PUNISHMENT UNITS

Punishment battalions and companies were a special category of infantry unit established by the Soviet Army as a method of dealing with those who had, for one reason or another, fallen foul of the military system, principally by failing in a command task, retreating without authority, or deserting. In addition, ex-prisoners-of-war who had been captured by the Germans and then released by the Soviets were mostly sent to these units, while inmates of the gulags could "volunteer." The term of service was related to the sentence meted out by the court martial and specified in a tariff, but was usually between one and three months, following which, if he survived, the individual was returned to a normal unit and his crime was considered to have been totally paid for. Those serving in such units were eligible for decorations for bravery in the normal way and a

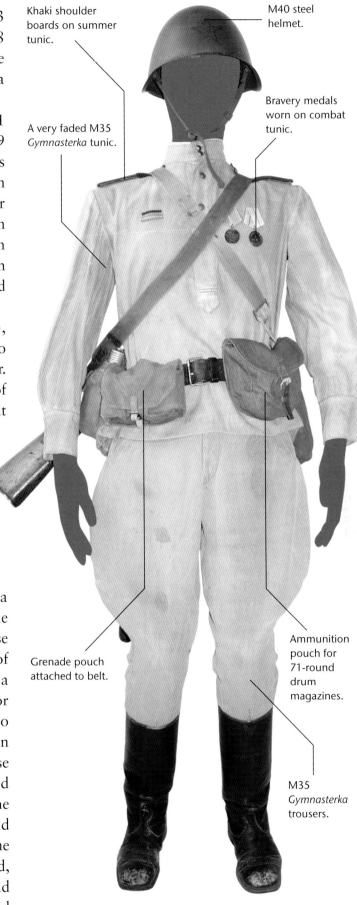

Khaki shoulder boards on summer tunic.

M40 steel helmet.

A very faded M35 *Gymnasterka* tunic.

Bravery medals worn on combat tunic.

Grenade pouch attached to belt.

Ammunition pouch for 71-round drum magazines.

M35 *Gymnasterka* trousers.

above An infantry sergeant sub-machine gunner in the spring/summer of 1944.

above This attacking group is armed with Mosin-Nagant rifles and DP light machine gun, while the man in the foreground has an SVT semi-automatic rifle. The SVT was often issued to the best shots in the squad as a sniper weapon.

combat wound could earn remission. The first of these units was formed at Stalingrad in August 1942.

There were two types of unit: punishment battalions (shtrafbats) and punishment companies (shtrafnaya rota). The battalions were around 7–800 strong and consisted mainly of former officers, particularly commanding officers and even some political officers; while the companies were 150–200 strong and consisted of former NCOs and privates. There was, of course, a cadre to provide command and guard functions.

It was deliberately intended that service in such punishment units would be hazardous, as it was an alternative to a sentence of death or long imprisonment. Thus, the main tasks were to attack enemy positions where other units had failed, reconnaissance by drawing enemy fire, and forming rearguards during a withdrawal. The total number to pass through such units is thought to have been about half-a-million, but since the men and entire units were considered expendable – cannon fodder in every sense of that term – no precise figures were kept. It is difficult to separate myth from reality where these notorious units were concerned. Some were deliberately sent over minefields, their bodies marking the cleared paths, and it is also reported that many men were sent into combat without weapons or ammunition and told to get them from dead comrades or enemy as they advanced.

above The mail arrives. Envelopes were scarce so note how the letters are just folded sheets of paper.

above In a foxhole perched on a hillside these men are wearing wet-weather capes over their equipment.

left A weary squad during the Stalingrad fighting. The machine gunner keeps watch while the others rest as they can. As well as the DP light machine gun they have a Mosin-Nagant rifle, a PPSh sub-machine gun and an SVT semi-automatic rifle.

COMBAT UNIFORM

The Soviet Army's combat uniforms and equipment were, as with those of the Japanese, the most basic and practicable of any army. And as with the Japanese, there was always a struggle to equip a large army from a disrupted and comparatively poorly-resourced industrial base. But after the first few months of the war the Soviet soldier was, on the whole, kitted out with clothing that, while it might not win any fashion awards, did the job it needed to.

The basic summer uniform was the M1935 *Gymnasterka*, a shirt-like tunic worn outside the trousers and which had long sleeves, two-button cuffs, a stand-and-fall collar and placket front (i.e., buttoned opening extending only about 9 inches). These shirts sometimes had breast pockets with button-down flaps. Officers eventually wore shoulder boards (*pogoni*), soldiers a dark brown epaulette; both carried

rank insignia and were piped in arm-of-service colors. As with all Soviet uniform items, color, cut and quality varied considerably from batch to batch and as factories struggled to overcome shortages of materials and labor.

Trousers (*sharovari*) were the same color as the tunic and were tucked into either the high boots or

above The M35 *Gymnasterka* had two chest pockets and a partially opening front

left An M35 tunic as worn by a lieutenant of automotive troops with the pre-1943 rank badges.

right and far right An *efreitor* (lance-corporal) in the Summer of 1942.

M40 steel helmet.

Bedding roll carried over shoulder.

Leather ammunition pouches for the Mosin-Nagant rifle.

Mosin-Nagant rifle and bayonet.

Pilotka side cap worn in this view.

M41 pack: a simple sack with shoulder straps.

Entrenching tool and holder.

Large "3-man" mess tin.

Puttees worn with short boots.

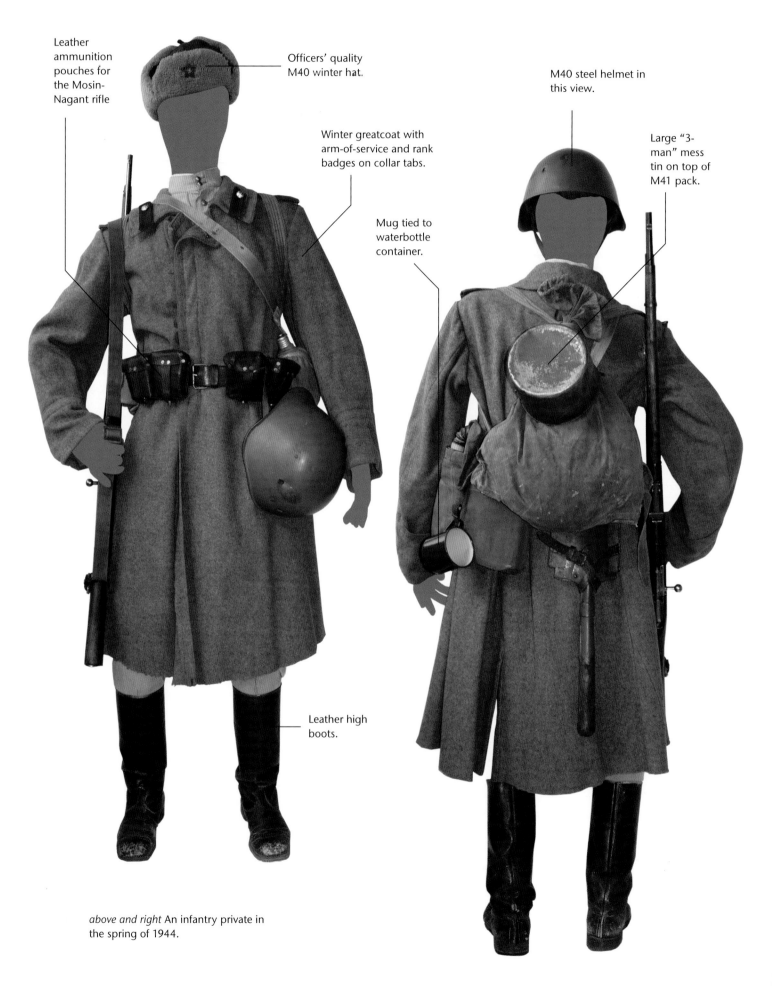

Leather ammunition pouches for the Mosin-Nagant rifle

Officers' quality M40 winter hat.

Winter greatcoat with arm-of-service and rank badges on collar tabs.

Mug tied to waterbottle container.

M40 steel helmet in this view.

Large "3-man" mess tin on top of M41 pack.

Leather high boots.

above and right An infantry private in the spring of 1944.

puttees. In particularly hot regions there was an even lighter shirt and trousers made of lightweight khaki cotton. This was worn with a floppy brimmed hat of the same material (with a cloth Red Star), similar in design to a British or American jungle hat.

below Officers' grade M35 trousers made from better-quality material.

above and top Soldiers' grade M35 *Gymnasterka* tunic and trousers. Note the variation in color.

left An officer entertains his men with a song at an impromptu field concert. Note the variety of headgear and uniform styles present.

OFFICERS' TUNIC

Even in this (theoretically) most egalitarian of armies, officers had special items. A tunic (*mundir*) was introduced for field wear by officers in 1943. This was single-breasted, with a stand-up collar with throat patches in arm-of-service color. There were also a gold bar on the collar patch and a spool on the cuff: with one bar for company-grade officers, two for field-grade officers. The tunic had brass buttons and piping in arm of service colors. Shoulder boards showed rank and arm-of-service.

above Officers' leather gauntlets.

left The M43 officers' tunic had a buttoned front, colored piping on the collar cuffs, and shoulder-boards with arm-of service piping.

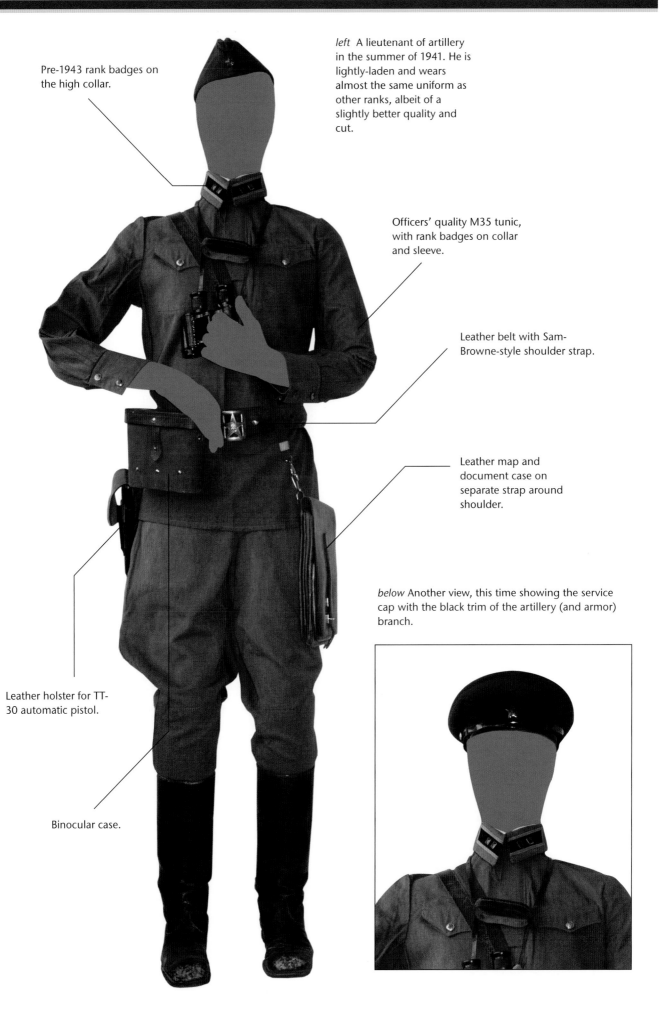

Pre-1943 rank badges on the high collar.

left A lieutenant of artillery in the summer of 1941. He is lightly-laden and wears almost the same uniform as other ranks, albeit of a slightly better quality and cut.

Officers' quality M35 tunic, with rank badges on collar and sleeve.

Leather belt with Sam-Browne-style shoulder strap.

Leather map and document case on separate strap around shoulder.

below Another view, this time showing the service cap with the black trim of the artillery (and armor) branch.

Leather holster for TT-30 automatic pistol.

Binocular case.

HEADGEAR

There were four main types of headgear. The service cap (*fourashka*) was made of khaki cloth with piping and capband in arm-of-service color (red for infantry), a black leather peak and a metal red star in the center of the capband. Chinstraps were brown or black leather except for general officers, who had two strands of gold braid. These caps were frequently worn by officers in the forward areas when not actually under fire.

left Woolen service cap as worn by officers and NCOs, trimmed in the colors of the infantry. Russian style was often to wear the cap at a jaunty angle perched at the back of the head.

right Interior view of the service cap, complete with the original wearer's initials inked into the lining.

below Side view of the same cap. Other ranks wore a similar cap but made from cotton material.

The sidecap (*pilotka*) was usually worn level on the head by all ranks. It was made of a cheap khaki cloth with arm-of-service piping and a Red Star in the front center.

right The M35 *pilotka* sidecap was comfortable, easy to carry and cheap to make. This interior view shows the headband and the maker's imprint.

left and right Soldier's cotton *pilotka* on the left and NCOs and officers version on the right.

left A display of M35 *pilotkas* showing a wide variation in color and material.

In cold weather there was the fur-lined Ushanka cap, and the Model 1927 Budionovka, described later.

In combat, all wore a steel helmet, mainly the Model 1939 or Model 1940 (*shtalui schlem obr.40*), stamped out of steel sheet and with a very characteristic raised and curved front brim. Helmets were painted green (white in winter) and, in some units, had a red star in the front center. Some soldiers were still equipped with the earlier Model 1936 helmet, which had a different, more dome-like profile with more of a flare to the rim.

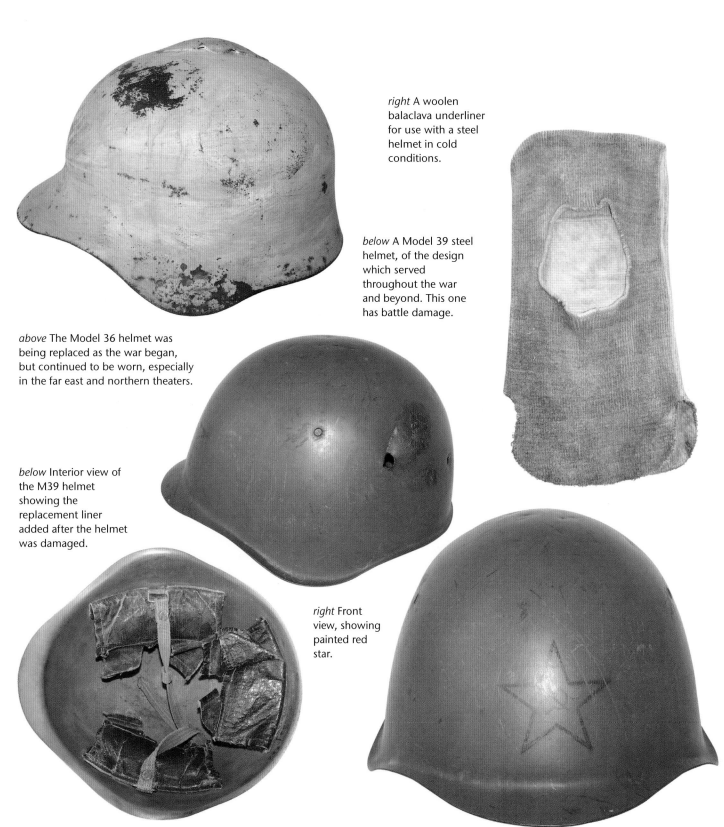

right A woolen balaclava underliner for use with a steel helmet in cold conditions.

below A Model 39 steel helmet, of the design which served throughout the war and beyond. This one has battle damage.

above The Model 36 helmet was being replaced as the war began, but continued to be worn, especially in the far east and northern theaters.

below Interior view of the M39 helmet showing the replacement liner added after the helmet was damaged.

right Front view, showing painted red star.

right An M40 helmet with scraped and faded paintwork. The shape gave good protection to the neck and side of face.

below Interior view showing the simple canvas liner.

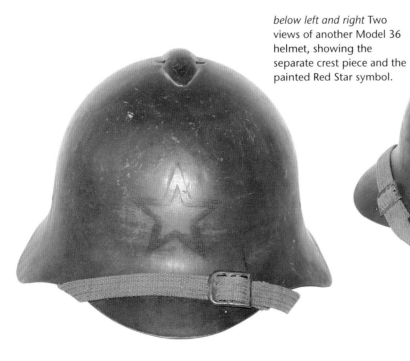

below The front edge, with the strap looped over it to keep it out of the way.

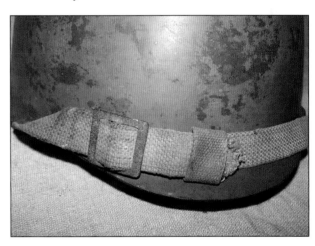

below left and right Two views of another Model 36 helmet, showing the separate crest piece and the painted Red Star symbol.

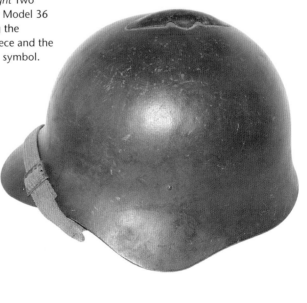

FOOTWEAR

The standard Boot (*sapogi*) was laceless, reached up to about 6 inches below the knee, and made of black leather. It was strong and durable, but towards the end of the war could not be manufactured in sufficient quantities so that black leather ankle boots and long, khaki puttees were issued instead.

For several centuries Russian soldiers had worn footcloths (*portyanki*) instead of socks and this continued into the Soviet Army-era. These were rectangular, approximately 46 x 14 in (118 x 36 cm), and made from flannel in winter, cotton in summer, and which had to be wrapped and tied-off in a very precise manner. They were undoubtedly useful but if the boot was too large or the cloth not tied properly they tended to slip down, causing blisters and calluses. Despite being washed once a week (at least in theory), the smell was dreadful.

above Most soviet soldiers wore these high leather boots, which were tough, hardwearing and reasonably comfortable.

above Leather boot and footcloths. Worn instead of socks, these cloths were wrapped around the foot before the boot was put on.

above When supplies of the high boots couldn't keep up with demand, short boots such as these were issued instead.

above Cloth puttees were worn with short ankle boots, the cloth being wound around the calf to just below the knee.

right Felt overboots (*valenki*) were worn over the normal boots in snow conditions and were effective at keeping the feet reasonably warm.

COLD WEATHER UNIFORM

Russia's invaders always found themselves fighting against the dreadful winter, whereas Russian soldiers had many centuries experience of living with it. Even so, the Finnish War exposed shortcomings in training and equipment for winter, many of which were being fixed when the Germans invaded.

So even as the army retreated and grappled with shortages and supply difficulties there was very rarely any problem with winter clothing,

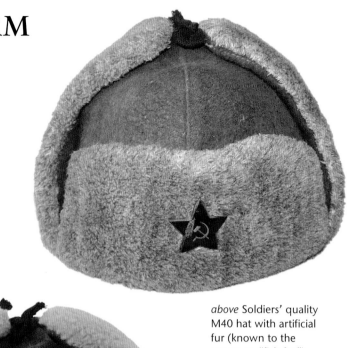

above Soldiers' quality M40 hat with artificial fur (known to the troops as "fish fur").

right Officers' quality M40 winter hat with fur-lined flaps (here tied in the raised position).

below The M27 winter felt hat with downturned flaps.

right Interior view of the M40 winter hat with flaps turned up.

left Interior view of the M40 winter hat with flaps turned up.

268

since commanders knew that this was essential to their men's fighting efficiency.

The normal winter headgear was the gray cloth cap (*ushanka*) with gray/brown fleece front, usually with metal Red Star, and neck and ear flaps. There was also the obsolescent Model 1927 *Budionovka* worn by many soldiers in the first months of the war. This was a lined felt cap with fold-down sideflaps and a central peak or "spike", intended to recall the design of spiked armored helmets worn by mounted warriors in Russian history.

The greatcoat (*shinel*) was made of stiff, coarse, grayish-brown cloth and was double-breasted with a large collar, which could be raised and buttoned against the cold. Rank and arm-of-service were shown by collar patches. When not being worn the greatcoat was rolled into a tube inside the *plash-palatka* (see below) and carried over the left shoulder

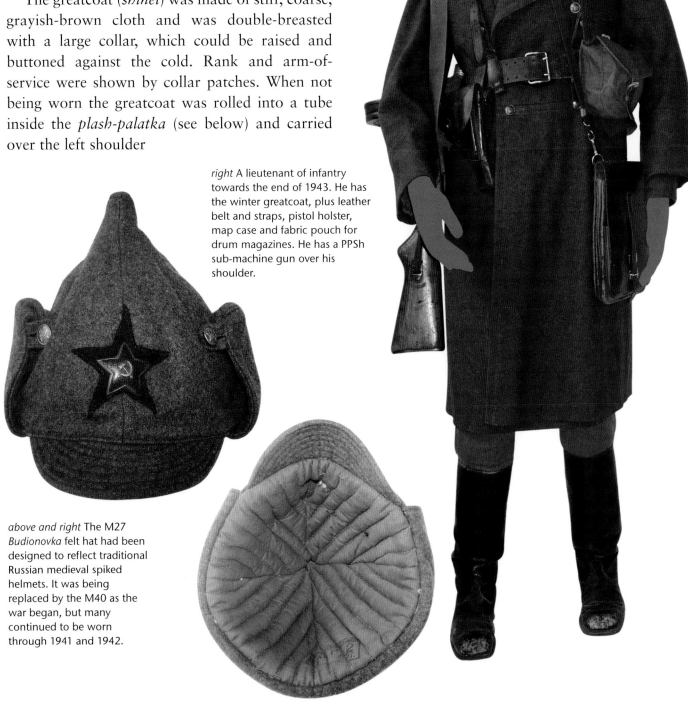

right A lieutenant of infantry towards the end of 1943. He has the winter greatcoat, plus leather belt and straps, pistol holster, map case and fabric pouch for drum magazines. He has a PPSh sub-machine gun over his shoulder.

above and right The M27 *Budionovka* felt hat had been designed to reflect traditional Russian medieval spiked helmets. It was being replaced by the M40 as the war began, but many continued to be worn through 1941 and 1942.

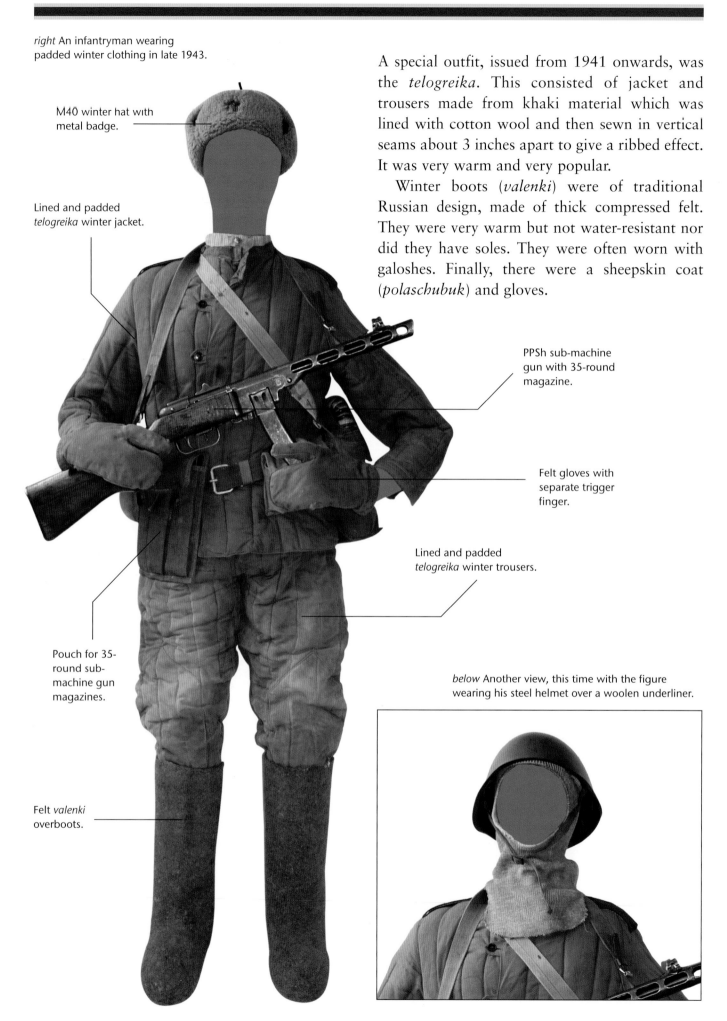

right An infantryman wearing padded winter clothing in late 1943.

M40 winter hat with metal badge.

Lined and padded *telogreika* winter jacket.

Pouch for 35-round sub-machine gun magazines.

Felt *valenki* overboots.

A special outfit, issued from 1941 onwards, was the *telogreika*. This consisted of jacket and trousers made from khaki material which was lined with cotton wool and then sewn in vertical seams about 3 inches apart to give a ribbed effect. It was very warm and very popular.

Winter boots (*valenki*) were of traditional Russian design, made of thick compressed felt. They were very warm but not water-resistant nor did they have soles. They were often worn with galoshes. Finally, there were a sheepskin coat (*polaschubuk*) and gloves.

PPSh sub-machine gun with 35-round magazine.

Felt gloves with separate trigger finger.

Lined and padded *telogreika* winter trousers.

below Another view, this time with the figure wearing his steel helmet over a woolen underliner.

above Winter gloves, soldier's pattern on the left and officer's pattern on the right.

M27 felt hat with flaps turned down.

Canvas pouch for 71-round drum magazines.

Sheepskin winter overcoat.

PPD-40 sub-machine gun with 71-round drum magazine.

Binoculars case with separate strap.

below Padded *telogreika* jacket with padded winter trousers underneath.

right Lieutenant of automotive troops wearing winter clothing at the end of 1941.

Leather map/document case.

271

COMBAT EQUIPMENT

Soviet infantry did not have an equivalent to the complicated system of belts, straps, pouches and haversacks used by Western armies, such as the British 37-pattern webbing. Instead, all soldiers wore a waist belt (poyas) with two double-pouches (patronaya sumka) either side of the buckle for ammunition clips. Both belt and pouches were made of leather until wartime shortages mean that they had to be made of synthetic materials.

The pack (veschmeshok) was a simple sack made of strong khaki-colored cloth with shoulder straps. Every soldier also had a waterproof rain cape (plash-palatka): a rectangular sheet of green or camouflaged material which could be used as a groundsheet, shelter-half or rain cape. The collar/hood was in one corner and when worn it reached halfway down the shins. It was cut generously to fit over the soldier's equipment and had two slits for his arms.

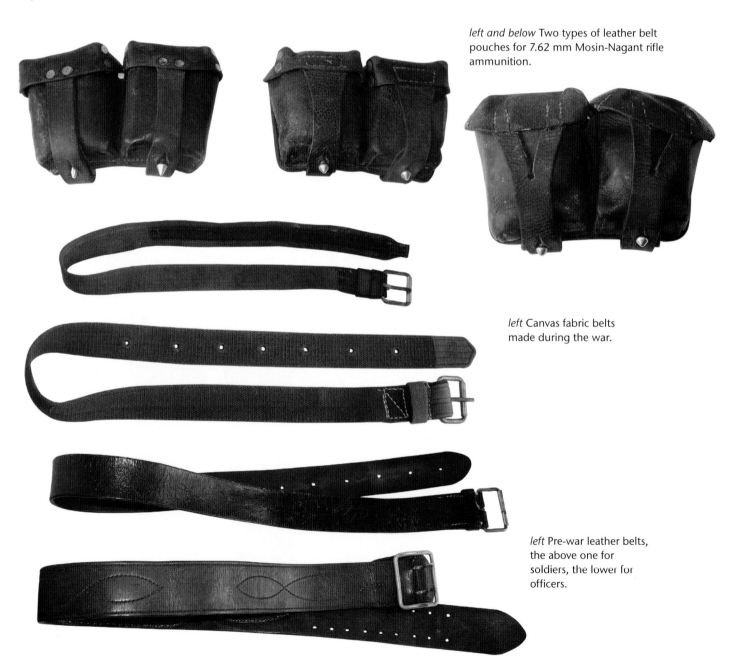

left and below Two types of leather belt pouches for 7.62 mm Mosin-Nagant rifle ammunition.

left Canvas fabric belts made during the war.

left Pre-war leather belts, the above one for soldiers, the lower for officers.

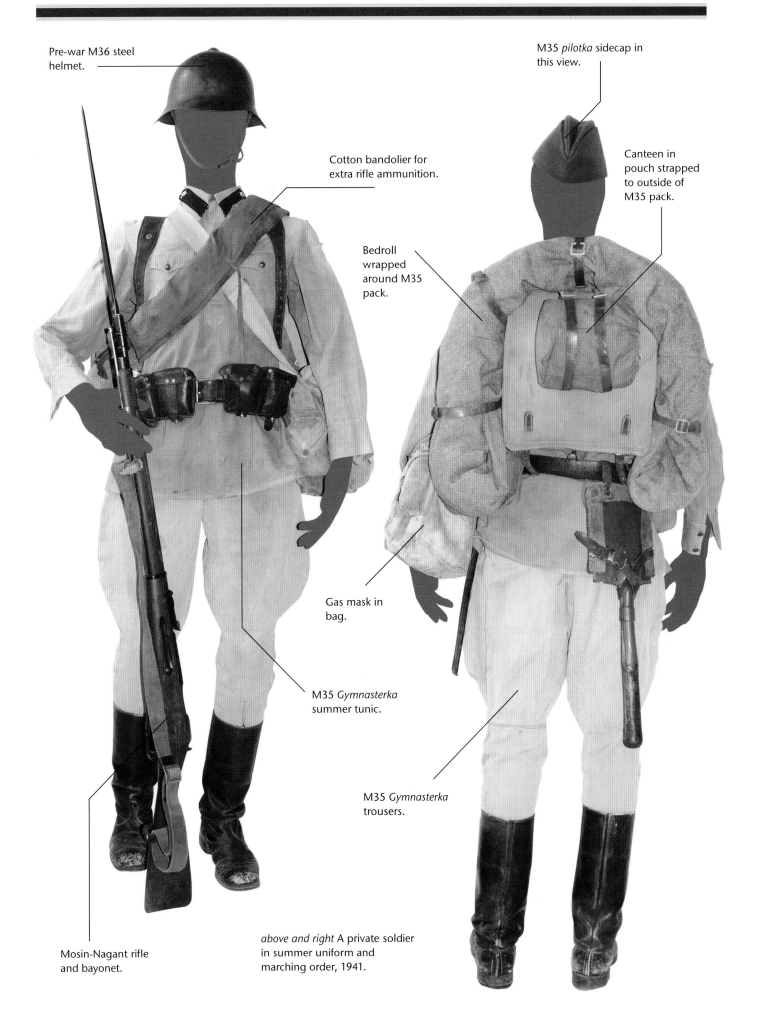

Pre-war M36 steel helmet.

M35 *pilotka* sidecap in this view.

Cotton bandolier for extra rifle ammunition.

Canteen in pouch strapped to outside of M35 pack.

Bedroll wrapped around M35 pack.

Gas mask in bag.

M35 *Gymnasterka* summer tunic.

Mosin-Nagant rifle and bayonet.

M35 *Gymnasterka* trousers.

above and right A private soldier in summer uniform and marching order, 1941.

below M35 backpack opened out to show contents, which include: soap, shaving equipment, matches and tobacco, washing cloths, tinned food, mug and eating utensils. The mess tins are below in a separate pouch. The Soviet soldier made do with much less comfort and fewer personal possessions than most allied troops.

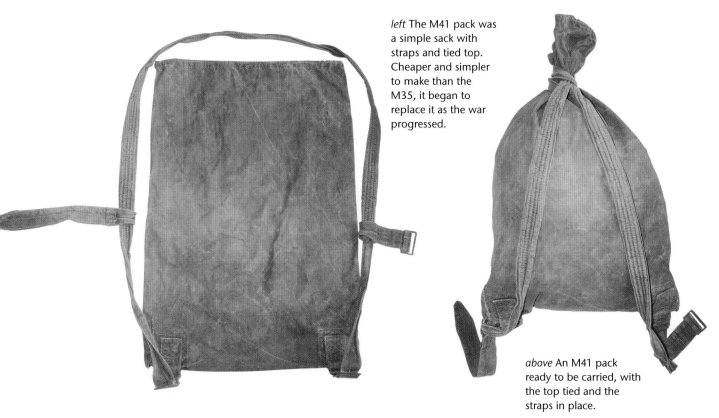

left The M41 pack was a simple sack with straps and tied top. Cheaper and simpler to make than the M35, it began to replace it as the war progressed.

above An M41 pack ready to be carried, with the top tied and the straps in place.

below the M35 pack was a similar design to the German *Tonister*, with a back flap that doubled as a "lid".

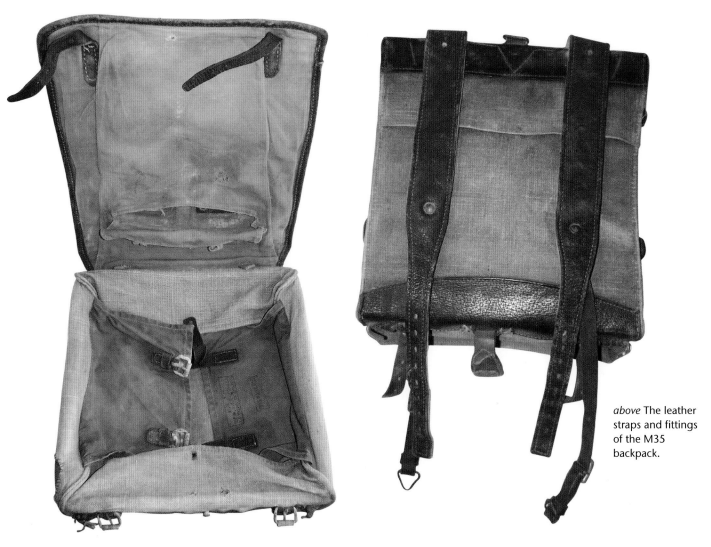

above The leather straps and fittings of the M35 backpack.

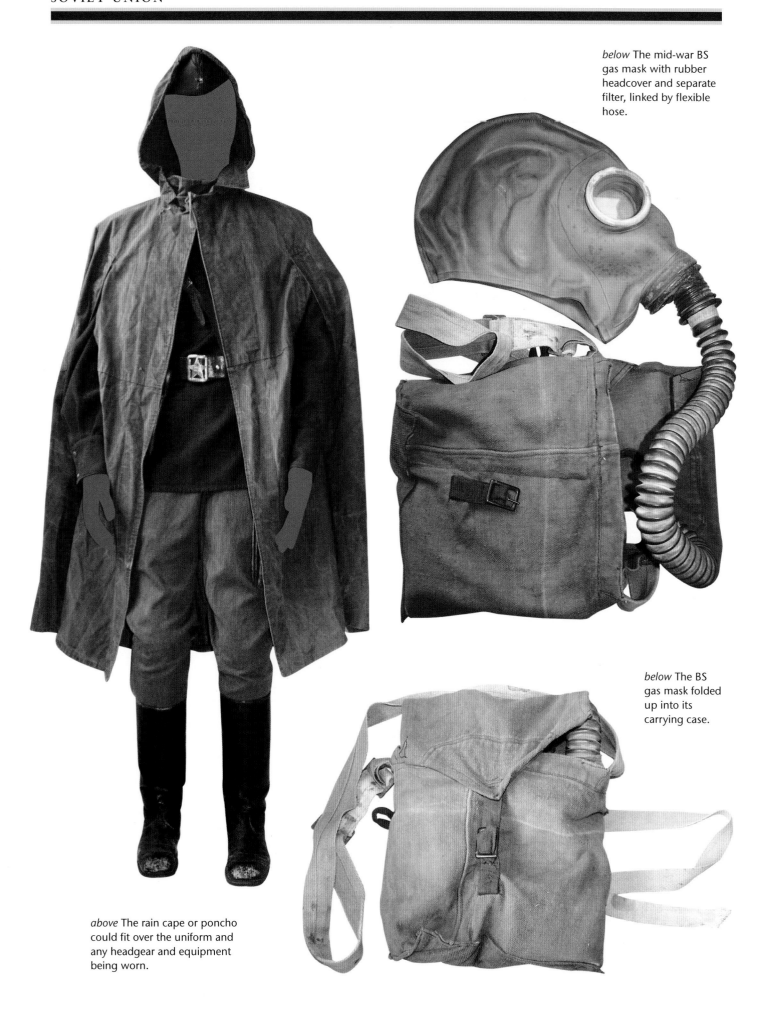

below The mid-war BS gas mask with rubber headcover and separate filter, linked by flexible hose.

below The BS gas mask folded up into its carrying case.

above The rain cape or poncho could fit over the uniform and any headgear and equipment being worn.

right The early-war BN-Tch gas mask and filter.

left Carrying case for BN-Tch gas mask and filter.

above Typical soldier's belt-gear. The leather belt holds: two pairs of leather ammunition pouches; water bottle and canvas holder; canvas grenade pouch and entrenching tool and carrier.

The gas mask was carried in a special haversack with a sling over the right shoulder, although examination of the bags would have shown that many soldiers had discarded the mask and carried personal items, particularly food, instead. Hanging from the belt in individual canvas containers were: bayonet (*styk*); entrenching tool (*lapata*) and canteen (*flyaga*)

below M38 bread bag for carrying food and other personal possessions.

left and above The entrenching tool was a simple shovel, attached to the belt by a canvas holder.

left Entrenching tool and carrier ready to attach to belt.

below A simple canvas bandolier which could be slung over the shoulder and could hold extra rifle ammunition.

right Wire cutters for clearing a path through enemy defenses.

SPECIAL OUTFITS

There was a curious individual amphibious outfit consisting of waterproof overalls up to the armpits held up by suspenders, a circular, inflatable flotation device and short paddles. All Soviet troops were capable of operating in winter conditions, but there were also special ski units who wore a very loose fitting white two-piece oversuit with a very bulky hood.

below Long sword bayonet and metal scabbard for Mosin-Nagant

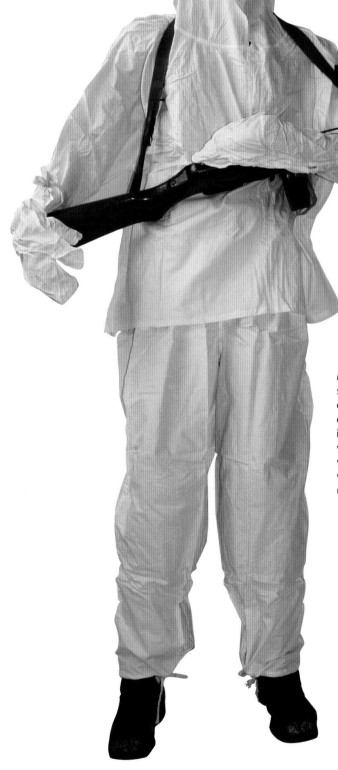

left This simple white snowsuit was for camouflage only and didn't provide much in the way of extra warmth. The soldier would still have to wear winter clothing underneath it.

OFFICERS

The 1935-pattern leather equipment for officers comprised a leather belt, square metal buckle with Red Star, cross strap over right shoulder, leather pistol holster and ammunition pouch, and leather map/document case. All leather was in brown. A new 1943 pattern was introduced during the war, but this was mainly because of the need to use cheaper raw materials, such as alloy buckles and inferior quality leather or even synthetic substitutes.

below NCO's leather map case.

left Officer's belt buckle and leather belt.

below right The NCO's map case with the top flap open.

below A selection of leather pistol holsters. The one on the right is for the Nagant revolver; the other two for smaller automatics.

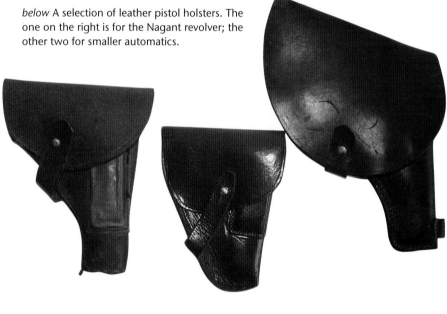

below Officer's wrist compass on leather strap.

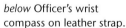

right Officer's leather map/document case.

280

left Two signaling flare pistols and a fabric pistol case.

below Another pair of binoculars and their case.

below Sand-painted binoculars and their leather case.

right Close-up of binoculars, showing Soviet markings and eyepieces.

MEDICAL EQUIPMENT

above Soviet military medical facilities were primitive, although they improved as the war progressed. Here stretcher-bearers hurry a wounded man down a Berlin street in 1945.

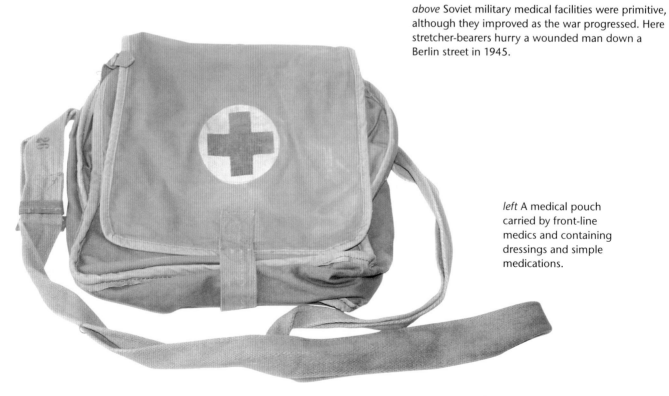

left A medical pouch carried by front-line medics and containing dressings and simple medications.

below A selection of field dressing, bandages and decontamination cloths as used by Soviet medics during the war.

above Soviet soldiers were expected to keep fighting with wounds that would have incapacitated other allied soldiers. Here a medic applies a dressing to a wounded man while the battle continues around them.

MAKING LIFE EASIER

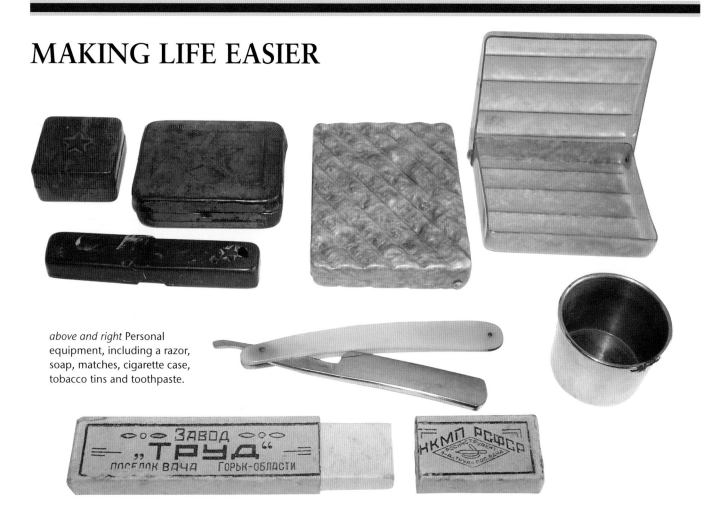

above and right Personal equipment, including a razor, soap, matches, cigarette case, tobacco tins and toothpaste.

below A cake of coarse army soap.

above and left Smoking equipment, including matches, tobacco, papers and pouch.

right A pristine washing cloth.

above A selection of soap, soap dishes and shaving equipment.

above Postcards and letters were as vital to the Soviet soldier as to the men of any other army. The postcards shown here display a selection of uplifting and patriotic images.

TRENCH ART

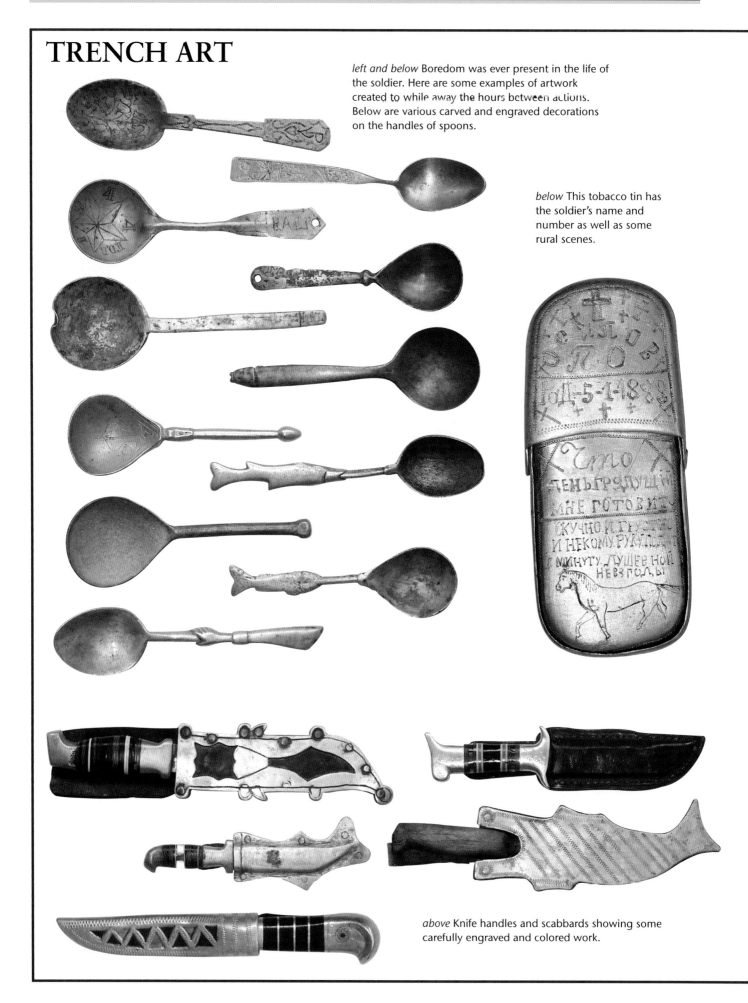

left and below Boredom was ever present in the life of the soldier. Here are some examples of artwork created to while away the hours between actions. Below are various carved and engraved decorations on the handles of spoons.

below This tobacco tin has the soldier's name and number as well as some rural scenes.

above Knife handles and scabbards showing some carefully engraved and colored work.

above and right Soap and tobacco containers gave scope for some extremely elaborate and ornate decoration.

below A selection of tobacco containers with designs ranging from the crudely drawn to finely carved.

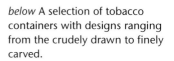

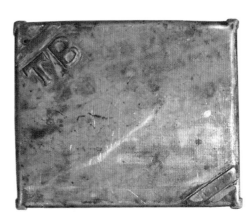

EATING AND DRINKING

left Various enameled cups and tin spoons.

below Many men were issued with this large mess tin, ostensibly designed to feed three men at once.

below Alcohol such as this Estonian vodka was hard to get hold of but was popular with front-line soldiers, if not their commanders.

left Metal plates were a luxury, but one which could make a tiny difference to the living conditions of the soldier.

left Various water bottles, including an enameled one and a glass bottle, this last being perhaps of limited use in the rough and tumble of the front line.

right Two-part mess tins based on the German design, complete with a canvas holder.

below Food supplies were erratic and unpredictable in the front line. Here a group of men enjoy a simple meal, probably of buckwheat porridge (*kasha*), accompanied by rough bread.

left A mess tin set in its canvas carrier.

below Water bottles in their carriers, the one on the left having a separate strap.

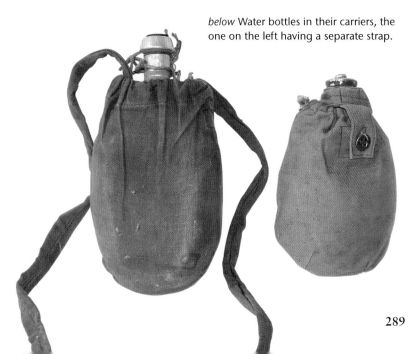

SOVIET WEAPONS

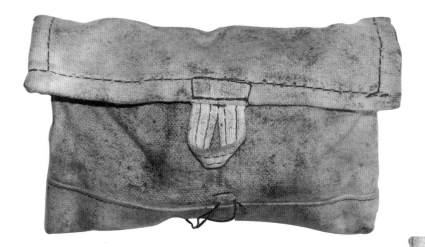

left, right and below
Cleaning kit for a Mosin-Nagant rifle, including pouch, oil bottles and screwdriver/combination tool.

S oviet infantry weapons were a blend of obsolete and advanced technology, of sophisticated design and desperate improvisation. Most infantrymen were equipped with an obsolescent bolt-action rifle of nineteenth-century design, but others had a modern and effective magazine-fed semi-automatic.

Desperate shortages in the early days meant that units had to make do with whatever was available. But as production ramped up Soviet infantrymen became equipped with plentiful weapons, and combat units could deliver large amounts of fire compared to their equivalents in other armies.

One weapon taken up enthusiastically was the sub-machine gun. Initially seen as a production solution more than a tactical one, sub-machine guns enabled the hastily-trained soldiers of 1941 and 1942 to put down withering amounts of fire – as long as they got in close. Such close-range engagement was one way of negating the tactical flexibility of German units and their array of support weapons and airpower.

Even as Soviet operational skill improved, the army continued to give priority to the sub-

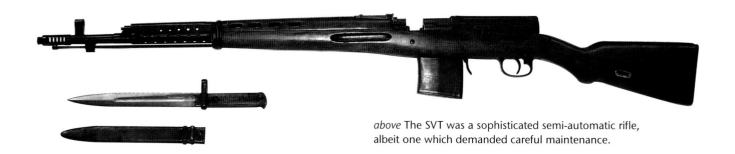

above The SVT was a sophisticated semi-automatic rifle, albeit one which demanded careful maintenance.

machine gun, equipping whole battalions with these simple, cheap but deadly weapons.

Soviet weapons at their best were tough, easy to use and effective. With them Soviet soldiers endured the disasters and retreats of 1941 and 1942, stopped the German advance at the gates of Moscow and at Stalingrad, then fought their way westwards to Berlin, the Reichstag and final victory.

left These men fighting in the ruins of Stalingrad demonstrate the usefulness of massed sub-machine guns in close-range combat. In this battle the Russians learned that if they stayed close to their enemies the Germans were unable to make effective use of their superior armor, artillery and airpower.

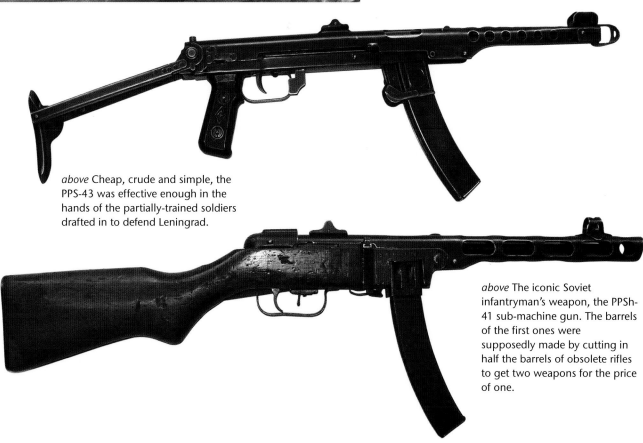

above Cheap, crude and simple, the PPS-43 was effective enough in the hands of the partially-trained soldiers drafted in to defend Leningrad.

above The iconic Soviet infantryman's weapon, the PPSh-41 sub-machine gun. The barrels of the first ones were supposedly made by cutting in half the barrels of obsolete rifles to get two weapons for the price of one.

RIFLES

MOSIN-NAGANT MODEL 1891/30 RIFLE

above The Mosin-Nagant rifle was long and cumbersome, especially when the spike bayonet was fitted.

above Another Mosin-Nagant, with no bayonet or sling.

Type: bolt-action rifle
Origin: USSR
Caliber: 7.62 mm
Cartridge: 7.62 x 54R
Weight (empty): 8.8 lb (3.95 kg)
Barrel length: 28.7 in (730 mm)
Feed: 5-round box

The Mosin-Nagant was a bolt-action, charger-loaded rifle, which was designed by Colonel Sergei Mosin of the Imperial Russian Artillery and a Belgian gun designer named Emil Nagant (who was also responsible for the Nagant M1895 revolver). The rifle entered service with the Imperial Russian Army in 1891 and was its principle weapon during World War I, when many millions were produced. It continued to serve in the Red Army during the Revolution and the subsequent Civil War. A version incorporating a few minor changes appeared in 1930. The main difference was a slightly shorter barrel – 28.74 in (730 mm) compared to 32.3 in (820 mm) – although weight was only marginally reduced. Both versions accepted a socket bayonet.

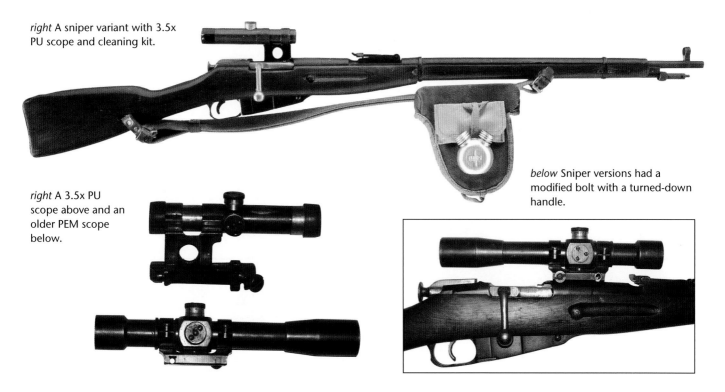

right A sniper variant with 3.5x PU scope and cleaning kit.

right A 3.5x PU scope above and an older PEM scope below.

below Sniper versions had a modified bolt with a turned-down handle.

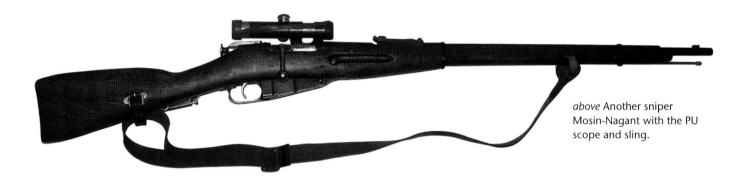

above Another sniper Mosin-Nagant with the PU scope and sling.

right The Soviet Army was enthusiastic about snipers, using them to target leaders and key personnel. A well-trained sniper can have a dramatic effect out of all proportion to the number of enemies they actually kill. Whole units can be pinned down, with soldiers unwilling to move or reveal their position. The effects on enemy morale can also be powerful.

The Red Army also made extensive use of female soldiers in both support and front-line roles, as demonstrated here. The picture shows two female snipers with their modified Mosin-Nagants and one-piece camouflage suits.

MOSIN-NAGANT MODEL 1944 CARBINE

Type: bolt-action carbine
Origin: USSR
Caliber: 7.62 mm
Cartridge: 7.62 x 54R
Weight (empty): 8.9 lb (4.0 kg)
Barrel length: 520 mm (20.5 in)
Feed: 5-round box

A slightly shorter and lighter version of the M1891/30 was introduced as the Model 1938 carbine, which accepted the same bayonet as the rifle. In 1944, however, a new carbine version appeared in which the bayonet was permanently attached, hinging back alongside the barrel when not in use. A consequence of this was that the carbine, while still shorter than the M1891/30 rifle was actually slightly heavier, with a lot of that weight forward. A curious claim to fame is that this was the last bolt-action rifle to enter large-scale production for any major army.

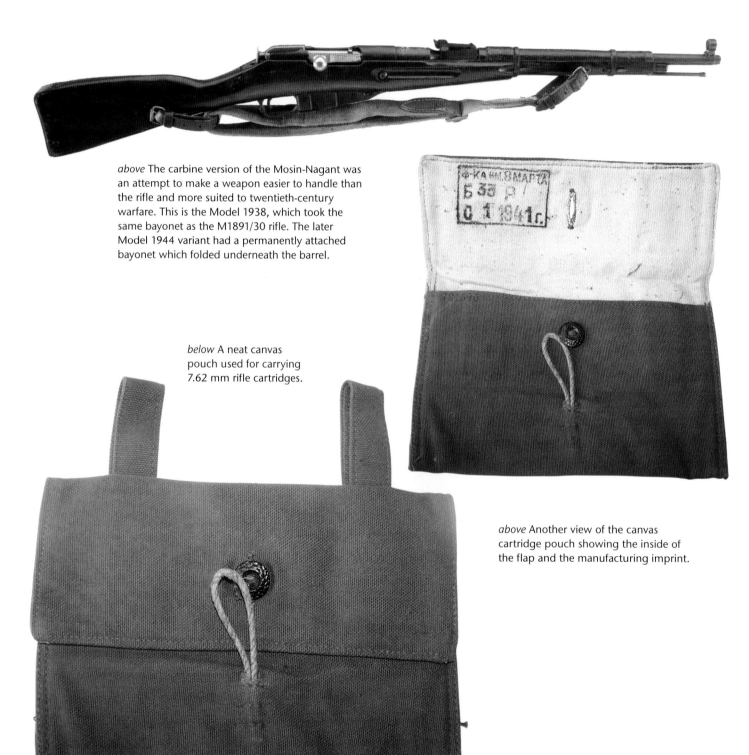

above The carbine version of the Mosin-Nagant was an attempt to make a weapon easier to handle than the rifle and more suited to twentieth-century warfare. This is the Model 1938, which took the same bayonet as the M1891/30 rifle. The later Model 1944 variant had a permanently attached bayonet which folded underneath the barrel.

below A neat canvas pouch used for carrying 7.62 mm rifle cartridges.

above Another view of the canvas cartridge pouch showing the inside of the flap and the manufacturing imprint.

SVT-38, SVT-40, SKT-40

Type: gas-operated, semi-automatic rifle
Origin: USSR
Caliber: 7.62 mm
Cartridge: 7.62 x 54R
Weight (empty): 8.6 lb (3.95 kg)
Barrel length: 25.0 in (635 mm)
Feed: 10-round box
(Specifications are for SVT-38)

Designed by Fyodor Tokarev, the Samozariadnyia Vintovka Tokareva (SVT) was a gas-operated, semi-automatic rifle, with a selective fire facility. It was fully stocked, with a three-quarter length slotted handguard, leaving muzzle and gas-cylinder partially exposed. It was fitted with a muzzle-brake and had a short, curved, box magazine, holding ten rounds. The later SVT-40 had a few minor improvements, and a variant, the fully automatic AVT-40 was tested in prototype form but not put into production.

A more radical version of the SVT-40 was the SKT-40 carbine, which did not have a muzzle brake, thus shortening the barrel to 18.5 in (470 mm). Like the Mosin-Nagant Model 1944 carbine, this Tokarev weapon also had a permanently attached bayonet which, in this case, folded back under the barrel.

These three weapons were perfectly satisfactory and went on to give many years of service in the post-war period. It is, therefore, surprising that the Red Army did not make greater use of them in World War II, although one reason was probably that the bolt-action was in service in such vast numbers and was so well liked that replacing it in wartime would have been simply too much effort. Another reason may have been that the SVT was a little too complicated for the millions of conscript soldiers who would have to use it. As it was, the SVT-40 tended to be issued to a few men in each company. A sniper version was also produced.

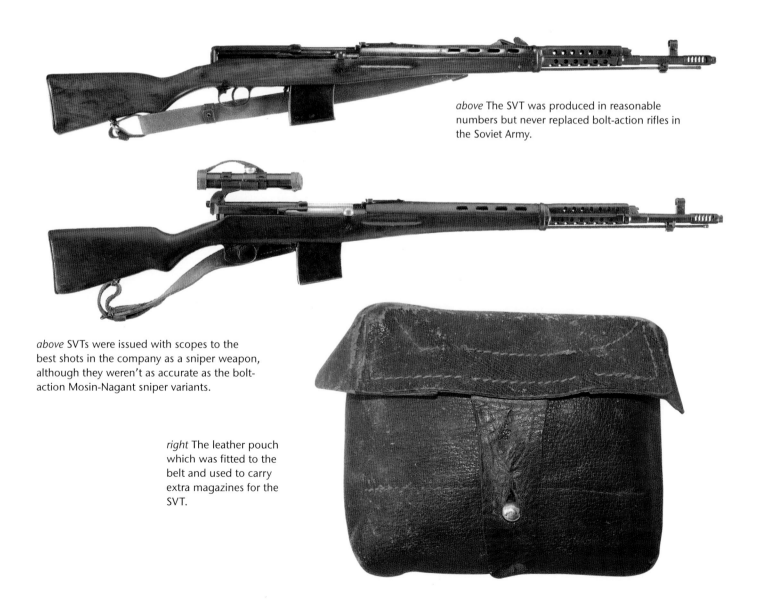

above The SVT was produced in reasonable numbers but never replaced bolt-action rifles in the Soviet Army.

above SVTs were issued with scopes to the best shots in the company as a sniper weapon, although they weren't as accurate as the bolt-action Mosin-Nagant sniper variants.

right The leather pouch which was fitted to the belt and used to carry extra magazines for the SVT.

PISTOLS

NAGANT M1895 7.62 MM REVOLVER

Type: revolver
Origin: USSR
Caliber: 7.62 mm
Cartridge: 7.62 x 38R Nagant
Weight (empty): 28 oz (.81 kg) loaded
Barrel length: 4.5 in (114 mm)
Feed: seven-round cylinder

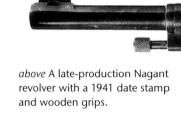

above A late-production Nagant revolver with a 1941 date stamp and wooden grips.

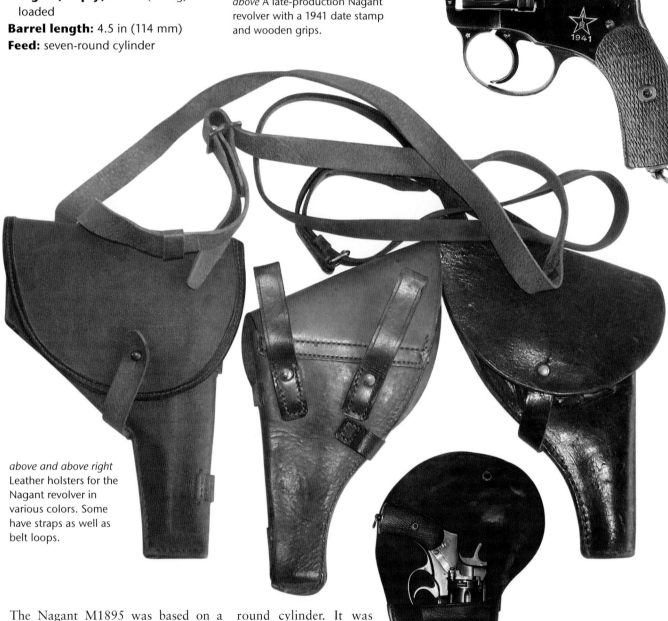

above and above right Leather holsters for the Nagant revolver in various colors. Some have straps as well as belt loops.

left The Nagant revolver in its holster.

The Nagant M1895 was based on a Belgian design with a solid-frame and double action. It used a gas-seal system in which when the trigger was pressed the cylinder moved forward a very short distance before the firing-pin struck the base of the round. Most unusually in a revolver, it had a seven-round cylinder. It was supposed to have been replaced by the TT-30/33 automatic but its total reliability and powerful round made it popular and it remained in service through to the end of World War II.

Tula–Tokarev Model 1933 (TT-33)

Type: semi-automatic pistol
Origin: USSR
Caliber: 7.62 mm
Cartridge: 7.62 x 25 mm Soviet pistol
Weight (empty): 27 oz (0.76 kg)
  loaded 29.3 oz (0.83 kg)
Barrel length: 4.5 in (114 mm)
Feed: eight-round box magazine

This pistol was named after the Tula State Arsenal where it was made and Fyodor Tokarev, its designer. It was first introduced as the TT-30 in 1930 and, as is clear from its appearance, its design owed a lot to the Colt 1911 and the Browning HP. It also had some improvements, including an improved ammunition feed system and the facility to remove the lock as a complete unit to facilitate cleaning. It was an effective weapon but its round was very powerful, with a muzzle velocity of 1,427 ft/sec (435 m/sec), which made it difficult to control. The TK-33 incorporated minor changes which were intended to ease and speed the production process, and was marginally larger and heavier. Both versions were in service throughout World War II.

above The TT-33 was a tough, reliable pistol firing a powerful cartridge. This one has molded bakelite grips with the Soviet star.

above Another wartime TT-33, this time with wooden grips fitted. The TT-33 followed similar design principles to Browning and Colt pistols.

above A TT-33 in a leather holster, complete with belt attachment. Note the pocket on the holster for a spare 8-round magazine.

SUB-MACHINE GUNS

PPD-34/38 AND -40

Type: sub-machine gun
Origin: USSR
Caliber: 7.62 mm
Cartridge: 7.62 x 25 mm Soviet pistol
Weight (empty): 3.74 kg (8.3 lb)
Barrel length: 10.8 in (272 mm)
Cyclic rate: 800 rpm
Feed: 71-round drum magazine

Designed by Vassily Degtyarev and based generally on the German Bergmann 9 mm MP28, the PPD-34 (Pistolet Pulyemet Degtyarev) differed in having a selective fire lever (the MP28 fired only automatic) and either a box holding 25 rounds, or a drum holding 71 rounds compared to the MP28's maximum of 32. It was a blowback weapon, had chromed bore and chamber and a prominent, full-

length barrel jacket with longitudinal slots. It was used in the Finnish War and remained in service during the equipment shortages of 1942–44. The PPD-40 was an even further improved version, adapted to take a new magazine which was based on that used on the Finnish Suomi SMG, which the Soviet Army had encountered and admired in the recently-concluded war.

above A PPD-40 with a 71-round drum magazine. It could also be fitted with a 25-round box.

PPSн-41

above The PPSh-41 was cheaper and simpler to make, yet just as effective as the PPD-40. Millions served during the war and beyond.

below Another view of the PPSh-41 and the stamped receiver and barrel jacket.

Type: sub-machine gun
Caliber: 7.62 mm
Cartridge: 7.62 x 25 mm Soviet pistol
Weight (empty): 8.0 lb (3.63 kg)
Barrel length: 10.6 in (269 mm)
Cyclic rate: 900 rpm
Feed: 35-round box or 71-round drum magazine

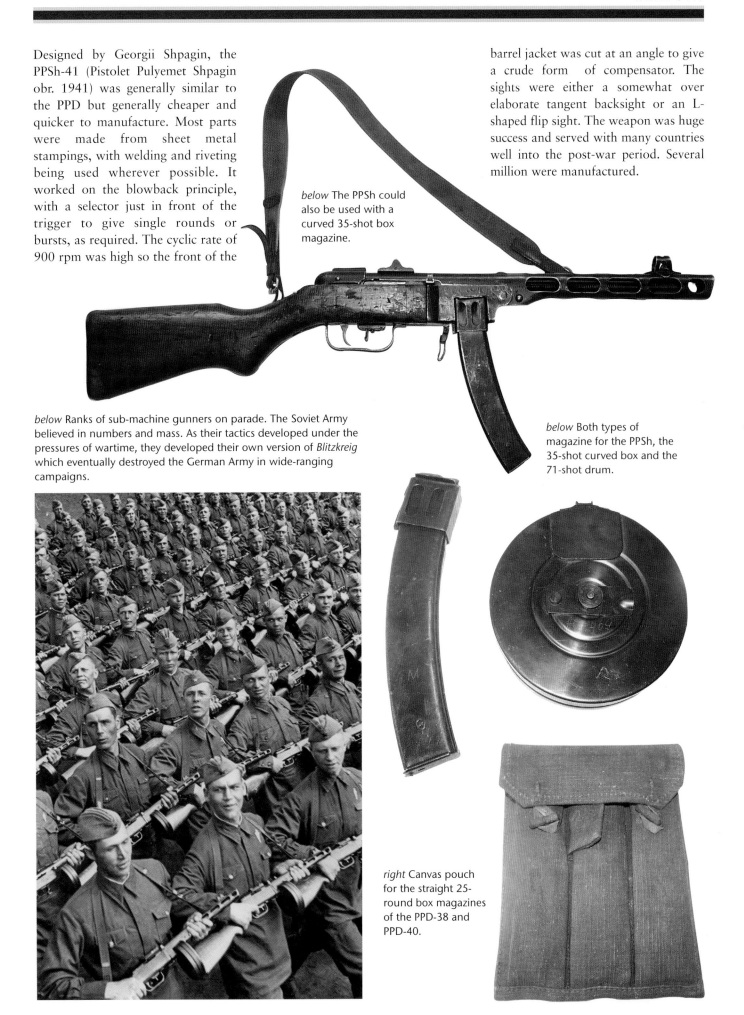

Designed by Georgii Shpagin, the PPSh-41 (Pistolet Pulyemet Shpagin obr. 1941) was generally similar to the PPD but generally cheaper and quicker to manufacture. Most parts were made from sheet metal stampings, with welding and riveting being used wherever possible. It worked on the blowback principle, with a selector just in front of the trigger to give single rounds or bursts, as required. The cyclic rate of 900 rpm was high so the front of the

barrel jacket was cut at an angle to give a crude form of compensator. The sights were either a somewhat over elaborate tangent backsight or an L-shaped flip sight. The weapon was huge success and served with many countries well into the post-war period. Several million were manufactured.

below The PPSh could also be used with a curved 35-shot box magazine.

below Ranks of sub-machine gunners on parade. The Soviet Army believed in numbers and mass. As their tactics developed under the pressures of wartime, they developed their own version of *Blitzkreig* which eventually destroyed the German Army in wide-ranging campaigns.

below Both types of magazine for the PPSh, the 35-shot curved box and the 71-shot drum.

right Canvas pouch for the straight 25-round box magazines of the PPD-38 and PPD-40.

left The 71-round drum magazine for Soviet sub-machine guns used a wound spring system to feed the cartridges into the gun. This soldier is carefully checking his before going into combat.

below Russian weapons such as this PPSh-41 had to be able to operate in extremes of weather - and on the whole, they did.

left Body armor was occasionally produced, often locally, and had some use in close combat such as in Stalingrad. The man at the rear has a ROKS-2 flamethrower, with the firing tube disguised as a rifle.

left An officer with a Nagant revolver leads his sub-machine gunners forward through the smoke of a burning building.

PPS-42

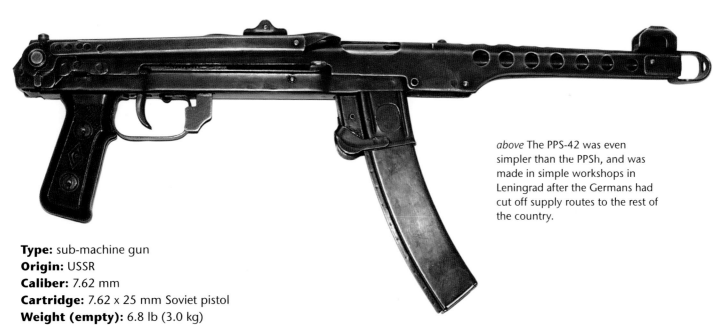

above The PPS-42 was even simpler than the PPSh, and was made in simple workshops in Leningrad after the Germans had cut off supply routes to the rest of the country.

Type: sub-machine gun
Origin: USSR
Caliber: 7.62 mm
Cartridge: 7.62 x 25 mm Soviet pistol
Weight (empty): 6.8 lb (3.0 kg)
Barrel length: 10.8 in (275 mm)
Cyclic rate: 700 rpm
Feed: 35 round box

Based in Leningrad during the German siege, Alexei Sudaev designed the PPS-42 (Pistolet Pulyemet Sudaev obr. 1942) in response to an emergency operational requirement for a weapon that was reasonably effective, but, most importantly, could be put into production in the city immediately. The result was one of the cheapest and simplest SMGs ever, being made entirely from stamped sheet steel except for the bolt, two wooden handgrips and a tiny piece of leather used as a bolt buffer. It was soon being produced in the city's workshops and the guns were being issued at once and put to use in action within hours. The PPS-42 had a folding two-strut butt and also several unusual features including a semi-circular compensator to keep the muzzle down when firing automatic (its only mode). The magazine was the same 35-round box as used on the PPSh-41, but it did not accept the drum magazine. It served in parallel to the PPSh-41. A slightly improved version, the PPS-43, entered service from 1943 onwards, the changes all being aimed at easing manufacture yet further. Again, it was manufactured in millions and was latter adopted by the Chinese People's Liberation Army as the Type 54.

301

MACHINE GUNS

DEGTYAREV DP 7.62 MM MACHINE GUN

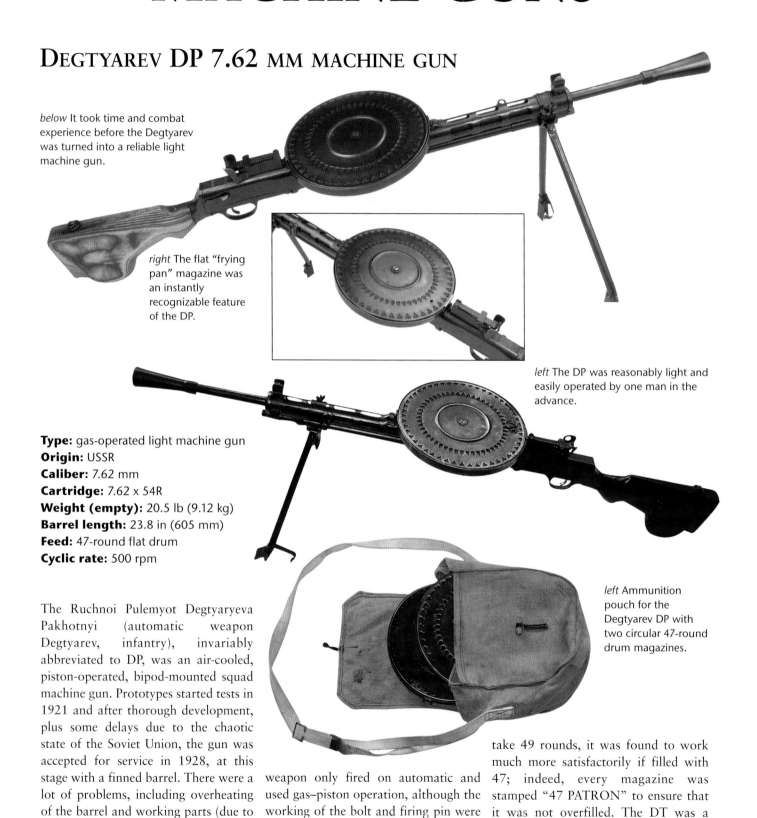

below It took time and combat experience before the Degtyarev was turned into a reliable light machine gun.

right The flat "frying pan" magazine was an instantly recognizable feature of the DP.

left The DP was reasonably light and easily operated by one man in the advance.

Type: gas-operated light machine gun
Origin: USSR
Caliber: 7.62 mm
Cartridge: 7.62 x 54R
Weight (empty): 20.5 lb (9.12 kg)
Barrel length: 23.8 in (605 mm)
Feed: 47-round flat drum
Cyclic rate: 500 rpm

left Ammunition pouch for the Degtyarev DP with two circular 47-round drum magazines.

The Ruchnoi Pulemyot Degtyaryeva Pakhotnyi (automatic weapon Degtyarev, infantry), invariably abbreviated to DP, was an air-cooled, piston-operated, bipod-mounted squad machine gun. Prototypes started tests in 1921 and after thorough development, plus some delays due to the chaotic state of the Soviet Union, the gun was accepted for service in 1928, at this stage with a finned barrel. There were a lot of problems, including overheating of the barrel and working parts (due to friction), and sensitivity to dirt. It was widely used in the Spanish Civil War (1936–39), as a result of which many improvements were made, and it gave good service in World War II. The weapon only fired on automatic and used gas–piston operation, although the working of the bolt and firing pin were slightly unusual. The flat circular magazine made the weapon instantly recognizable and was, in effect, one round thick. It was powered by clockwork and although designed to take 49 rounds, it was found to work much more satisfactorily if filled with 47; indeed, every magazine was stamped "47 PATRON" to ensure that it was not overfilled. The DT was a tank-mounted version, with a mounting block at the front of the receiver. Some of these were issued to the infantry during the war to make up for a shortage of DPs.

Maxim M1910

Type: medium machine gun
Origin: USSR
Caliber: 7.62 mm
Cartridge: 7.62 x 54R
Weight (empty): 52.55 lb (23.8 kg);
  on 2-wheeled carriage: 70 lb
  (31.8 kg)
Barrel length: 28.3in (718 mm)
Feed: 250-round cloth belt
Cyclic rate: 550 rpm

right The Model 1910 was a typical Maxim design: heavy, water-cooled, tough and reliable.

right below A Model 1910 on its distinctive wheeled carriage with armored shield.

left A Maxim crew in action in open ground. This gun doesn't have the shield fitted to the carriage.

The machine gun, Maxim, Model 1910 (Pulemet Maksima Obrazets 1910), was produced under license at the Tula Arsenal in Imperial Russia. It was a modified version of the Belgian M1905, with a smooth-surfaced water jacket, a robust wheeled carriage, designed in Russia by a man named Sokolov, and slight improvements to the feed mechanism. There were various minor changes over the years, including a corrugated surface water jacket, and a much larger filling cap, enabling snow to be stuffed inside in extreme conditions. The M1910 was a tough, reliable, effective weapon and remained in use throughout World War II.

Goryunov SG-43

Type: gas-operated medium machine gun
Origin: USSR
Caliber: 7.62 mm
Cartridge: 7.62 x 54R
Weight (empty): 30.4 lb (13.8 kg)
Barrel length: 28.4 in (720 mm)
Feed: 250-round cloth belt
Cyclic rate: 650 rpm

The designer, Piotr Goryunov, died in the same year as this weapon entered service, but his name lived on in the Stankovii Pulemet Goryunova obrazets 1943 (SPG-43). The Maxim M1910 was a popular weapon but was complicated and expensive to manufacture and production could simply not keep pace with demand. This weapon was therefore designed: a simple, belt-fed, gas-operated gun, utilizing a piston in a cylinder beneath the barrel. Operation of the bolt was somewhat complicated, but worked well and the heavy, chrome-lined barrel was very easy to change, so that the weapon could go on firing for protracted periods. When used by the infantry the SG-43 was normally mounted on a two-wheeled carriage, which initially was fitted with a metal anti-splinter shield, although this was both heavy and of limited value, and was soon discarded. The SG-43 could also be mounted on a tripod.

GRENADES AND FLAMETHROWERS

GRENADES

RG-33

When the war began the standard Soviet hand grenade was the RG-33 anti-personnel type. It was a stick grenade, with a shorter and thicker handle than German designs and a cylindrical metal container for the charge. The steel shell produced a quantity of fragments, although they didn't have much of an effective radius. An extra steel sleeve

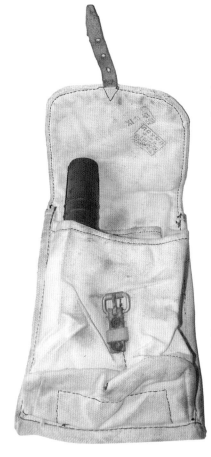

left Two RG-33 grenades and a canvas carrying pouch.

below The three main hand grenades in Soviet military service. Left is the RG-33, center is the simplified RG-42 and right is the F-1 "pineapple" pattern.

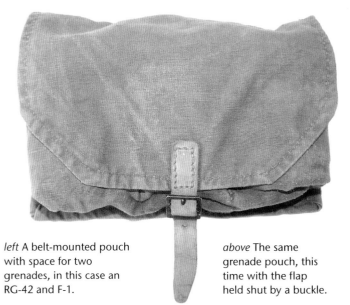

left A belt-mounted pouch with space for two grenades, in this case an RG-42 and F-1.

above The same grenade pouch, this time with the flap held shut by a buckle.

could be slid over the casing to give a much greater fragmentation effect over a larger distance. The RG-33 contained 2.8 oz (80 g) of explosive, weighed 27 oz (770 g) with the fragmentation sleeve attached and was some 7.4 in (190 mm) long.

RG-42

The RG-33 was time-consuming and expensive to make, so this crude and simple 1942 design was in an effort to get grenades into the hands of the troops as quickly as possible. It was in essence a tin can containing about 7 oz (200 g) of explosive and a simple fuse. Total weight was about 18 oz (500 g). Crude it may have been but it was an effective enough weapon.

F-1

The F-1 was introduced later in the war and went on to serve with many armies and guerrilla groups after 1945. Following a similar pattern to British and American fragmentation grenades, it comprised a steel egg-shaped casing with an engraved pattern and containing some 2.1 oz (60 g) of explosive. It used the same fuse as the RG-42, weighed about 21 oz (600 g) and was supposedly nicknamed the limonka or "lemon".

ROKS-2 AND ROKS-3 FLAMETHROWERS

Weight: Empty 33 lb (15 kg); operational 55 lb (25 kg)

Operator's firing unit: length 44 in (111 cm); weight 8 lb (3.6 kg)

Capacity: flammable liquid 2.6 gal (10 liters)

Weight: fuel tank 18.7 lb (8.5 kg); propellant (nitrogen) tank 6.2 lb (2.8 kg)

Range: 33–38 yd (30–35 m)

Bursts: 6–8 at 1 sec; 6 sec constant

Like other armies, one of the lessons of World War I learnt by the Red Army was that as soon as a man appeared on the battlefield equipped with a flamethrower (ranzewij ognemjot) he immediately became the target of everything the enemy could throw at him. The Soviets adopted a novel approach to overcome this by deliberately disguising their ROKS-2 equipment. The operator's firing unit had the same size and appearance as a Mosin-Nagant M1891/30 rifle and the canisters were disguised as an infantryman's backpack, the only giveaway (prior to firing) being the tube linking the two. There were varying mixes of fuel depending on the temperature. The ROKS-3 was essentially similar to the ROKS-2.

BAYONETS AND KNIVES

The bayonet for the Mosin Nagant 1891/30 rifle was a typical nineteenth-century design, having a cruciform-section blade (more of a spike) some 16 in (407 mm) long. It attached to the end of the muzzle using a socket mount. Unusually, the bayonet was issued without a scabbard, leaving the soldier to find his own way of attaching it to his kit using a strap or other method. As with other such rifle/bayonet combinations, the long bayonet made the already cumbersome rifle even more awkward to handle.

When the later Model 44 carbine entered service, it came with a cruciform bayonet permanently attached and able to fold back alongside the rifle. This meant that the bayonet was always available, but it also made the rifle muzzle-heavy and detracted from its shooting accuracy.

The Red Army also made use of sword- and knife-type bayonets, mostly on the SVT series of automatic rifles. This style of bayonet could at least be used as a general tool for all the other things a soldier needed a knife for, such as cutting foliage and preparing food.

Short combat knives such as the M40 fighting knife were also sometimes issued to specialist troops such scouts and reconnaissance soldiers, paratroopers and marine infantry.

top Socket fittings for the original spike bayonet for the Model 1891/30 Mosin-Nagant rifle.

left A selection of sword bayonets and their scabbards. The top one is for the Mosin-Nagant while the lower two are shorter and for the SVT semi-automatic rifle.

MORTARS

50 mm Mortar (50-PM 40)

Type: light mortar
Origin: USSR
Caliber: 50 mm
Weight (with bipod, sight): 20.5 lb
  (9.3 kg)
Barrel length: 24.8 in (630 mm)
Range: 875 yd (800 m)
Bomb: HE – 1.87 lb (0.85 kg)

The 50 mm (1.97 in) mortar entered service in 1940 and was originally fitted with a very light, pressed steel bipod, and a simple sight. These were, however, subsequently discontinued and, like the very similar British 2-inch mortar, one crewmember simply held the barrel and pointed it in the right direction at what looked like the correct angle, while the other man dropped the bomb down the barrel. The bomb was very light by Soviet standards and the mortar was not very highly thought of, but the Germans liked the weapon, which they captured in large numbers and pressed it into service as the 5cm Garanatwerfer 205(r).

82 mm Mortar (82-PM 41)

Type: medium mortar
Origin: USSR
Caliber: 82 mm
Weight (with bipod, sight): 99 lb
  (45 kg)
Barrel length: 52 in (132 cm)
Range: 3,390 yd (3,100 m)
Bomb: HE, smoke 7.5 lb (3.4 kg)

The original 82 mm mortar was a direct copy of the very successful Brandt mortar Mle 27/31 which entered Soviet service as the 82-PM36.

The Soviets then developed a modified version with springs to reduce the load on the bipod, the 82-PM 37, followed by the 82-PM 41 which made greater use of stampings to reduce production time and costs. In yet a further refinement the 82-PM 43 had a simpler bipod, designed to ease towing by hand. All three versions were captured in large numbers and adopted by the German Wehrmacht as the 8.2 cm Granatwerfer 274(r).

above An 82 mm mortar team in action. Mortars demanded much less specialist training than conventional artillery, an important consideration for a country creating a mass army from such a diverse population whilst under immediate threat of destruction.

left The Red Army used mortars in large quantities, appreciating their simplicity, cheapness and their ability to deliver lots of fire very quickly.

ANTI-TANK WEAPONS

DEGTYAREV PTRD-41

below The PTRD was a large and cumbersome anti-tank rifle, but was more effective than most of its counterparts and remained in service throughout the war.

Type: bolt-operated anti-tank rifle
Origin: USSR
Caliber: 14.5 mm
Cartridge: 14.5 x 114 mm
Weight (unloaded): 38.1 lb (17.3 kg)
Barrel length: 48.3 in (122.7 cm)
Feed: bolt-action, no magazine

The ProtivoTankovoye Ruzhyo Degtyaryova (PTRD) was a battalion and company anti-tank weapon that entered service in 1941, employing the Soviet-developed 14.5 x 114 mm rimless, necked, tungsten-cored round. This round could penetrate armor plate up to 1.56 in (40 mm) thick at a range of 100 meters. This performance proved inadequate for the newer generation of German tanks, so Soviet gunners concentrated on firing at periscopes, tracks and engines, in order to immobilize the tank which could then be dealt with by other means. The PTRD was bolt-operated but did not have a magazine, being reloaded one round at a time. The cartridge caused a large muzzle flash, making it relatively easy for an enemy to locate it, and also left a considerable residue. Despite its limitations against tanks, it was very effective against trucks, light tanks, self-propelled guns and armored cars.

SIMONOV PTRS-41

The PTRS-41, designed by Sergei Simonov, was intended to meet the same requirement as the PTRD-41, firing the same round, but was a semi-automatic. The weapon was loaded by inserting a five-round clip in the opening underneath the receiver, which was then held in place by a cover which swung backwards and held it in place, with a spring pushing the rounds upwards for loading. The PTRS-41 and its ammunition suffered from the same faults as those described for the PTRD, but the weapon remained in service for the rest of the war.

Type: semi-automatic anti-tank rifle
Origin: USSR
Caliber: 14.5 mm
Cartridge: 14.5 x 114 mm
Weight (unloaded): 44.8 lb
  (20.3 kg)
Barrel length: 48.0 in (1219 mm)
Feed: 5-round clip (see text)

above The semi-automatic PTRS held 5-rounds in its box magazine.

below A PTRS team engaging a tank target. To have any real chance of killing a mid-war tank the PTRS had to have a shot against the thinner side armor, ideally behind the suspension.

above A Red Square military parade with what appears to be a whole regiment of anti-tank riflemen marching past. Even if the anti-tank rifle wasn't particularly effective against tanks, it did help preserve morale by give the infantry some way of hitting back against apparently invulnerable enemy armor.

below An anti-tank rifle protects a machine gun position in the snow. While marginal against tanks, the PTRD was much more effective against light armor such as troop-carrying half-tracks.

RPG-43 Anti-tank Grenade

The RPG-43 shaped-charge grenade was developed in 1943 in an effort to give an anti-tank capability to the ordinary infantryman and improve on the marginal capability of the PTRS and PTRD anti-tank rifles.

Weighing some 2.9 lb (1.3 kg) it had a 3.7 in (95 mm) diameter warhead on top of a short throwing stick. When thrown, the grenade streamed fabric strips behind it, attached to a light metal cone which helped stabilize it in flight and ensure it would land with the top face against the target.

If the grenade hit the target square on it had reasonable penetrative power, but its weakness was its short range, and the fact that it depended on a courageous thrower getting to within a few feet of the target.

The RPG-43 did provide the

below A shaped-charge warhead gave the RPG-43 some anti-armor capability but it needed a brave thrower to get close enough to the target.

infantryman with some means of attacking armored vehicles though, and served, together with the later RPG-6, throughout the war and afterwards.

45 mm M1942 Anti-tank Gun

Type: semi-automatic anti-tank gun
Origin: USSR
Caliber: 45 mm
Elevation: -8° to 25°
Traverse: 60°
Weight: traveling 2,756 lb (1,250 kg);
combat 1,378 lb (625 kg)
Rate of fire: 15–20 rounds per minute
Feed: semi-automatic

The first significant Soviet anti-tank weapon was the 45 mm M1937, which consisted of a new 45 mm barrel on a modified 37 mm M1931 anti-aircraft gun carriage. It continued in production until 1943, and was deployed in the anti-tank platoons of infantry battalions. As soon as the Germans invaded in 1941 it was clear that the M1937 was inadequate so a hasty upgrade was developed, which had a longer barrel and more powerful shell, which entered service as the 45 mm M1942. This remained in production until 1945, but was only effective against the sides and engine compartments of the latest German tanks, but very effective against trucks and other soft targets. Ammunition types included: armor piercing, armor-piercing capped, fragmentation, high explosive, canister and smoke. The AP projectile weighed 3.2 lb (1.43 kg) and in theory could penetrate 0.25 in (61 mm) armor plate at 547 yd (500 m).

Marginal against tanks, the M-1942 did, however, achieve some use late in the war when it proved of value as an infantry gun firing high explosive shells in the final battles in the dying Third Reich.

left The 45 mm M42 anti-tank gun remained in service as a general support gun long after its effectiveness against the latest German tanks became marginal.

right The Russian 76 mm regimental gun was an artillery piece but also had a formidable anti-tank capability. The Germans also appreciated its combination of ruggedness, light weight and firepower, and put into service many of those they captured in the frontier battles of 1941.

above The 57 mm anti-tank gun had better armor-penetration capability than the 45 mm gun. Anti-tank guns on the defense couldn't move or retreat - the crews had to stand and fight. They would either win or die. This position is extremely exposed, with no camouflage or protective cover of any kind.

PARATROOPS

In the 1930s the Red Army became the world leader with airborne forces. Parachute training started in 1928, leading to the first battalion-sized drop on August 2, 1930. Then they staged a major demonstration near Kiev in 1936, where an international audience saw 600 transport aircraft drop a complete airborne regiment of 1,800 men, including its integral light artillery battalion. One of the unintended effects of this dramatic demonstration was to send German observers home determined to develop

their own airborne units, thus giving birth to the Fallschirmjäger.

The Soviet Airborne troops (Vozdushno-Desantnye Vojsa or VDV) eventually formed ten airborne corps, with numerous smaller independent units, but, rather surprisingly, were only rarely employed in their primary role. Their first airborne operations were in January 1942 when IV Airborne Corps was sent in small groups to support partisans in the Smolensk area in their efforts to disrupt the predicted German summer advance. In the event, the operations against the Germans were not particularly successful, but it also proved impossible to recover the paratroops, with the result that IV Airborne Corps ceased to exist.

The only other significant airborne operation on the Eastern Front occurred in September 1943 when three airborne regiments were dropped north-west of Kremenchug, some 25 miles (40 km) behind German lines. The aim was to set up secure bases and then actively disrupt German lines-of-communication until relieved by the advancing 30 Guard Tank Army and 40th Army. Unfortunately, the standard of training had dropped considerably following the dissipation of IV Airborne Corps and the pilots dropped the troops over a widely scattered area. Then, instead of concentrating, the scatted groups simply dug in and sat tight. So unimpressed were the Germans that they did not even bother to redeploy any front-line divisions, but sent in reserve and security divisions to deal with the problem.

In the Far East there was an uneasy stand-off between the USSR and Japan

left and right Paratroopers, snipers and reconnaissance troops wore hooded camouflage smocks such as the two-piece design shown here. A one-piece variant was also used. Note the captured German fighting knife tucked into the belt of this man. He carries a PPS-42 sub-machine gun.

left Moving cautiously through the woods, these camouflaged men undertake a stealthy reconnaissance. Such patrols were commonly used to gather intelligence, scout enemy positions and even snatch prisoners for interrogation.

from 1939 to when the Soviets declared war on August 9, 1945. The Japanese surrendered on August 18, 1945, when the Soviet High Command became concerned about what might happen if the Japanese submitted to the local civilian authorities. So, they quickly sent in paratroop units and between August 18 and 24 VDV units landed in Chyangchun, Dalny, Harbin, Kirin, Port Arthur and Pyongyang, and on 23–25 August undertook three separate landings, each by a group of 35 paratroops, on Japanese-held airfields on Sakhalin Island.

UNIFORM

As with paratroop units in other armies, the uniform evolved as experience was gained, and by 1944 Soviet paratroopers wore: dark-blue Air Force pilotka with light blue piping and red star; M43 tunic with Air Force shoulder-boards; M43

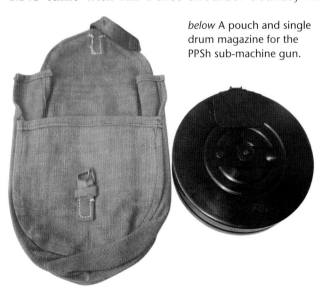

below A pouch and single drum magazine for the PPSh sub-machine gun.

trousers; Air Force embroidered sleeve patch,; and belt with canteen and cover, and combat knife. The great majority were armed with PPSh-41 SMGs, so on their belt they carried a single leather pouch for the 71-round drum magazine. They also wore a sniper's one-piece camouflaged coverall, high boots and the paratroopers', close-fitting leather helmet.

Soviet paratroops carried two parachutes, the main chute being an Irvin-type but with a square canopy, which gave a smooth descent but could not be maneuvered in the air by the parachutist. In the early 1930s, the men would climb out onto the wing of the very slow flying Tupolev ANT-06 aircraft then let go of the handholds and free-fall for a short distance before pulling the ripcord. After 1936, however, they used the more usual static-line method.

FRANCE

France had never truly recovered from her terrible losses in World War I, an experience that colored her whole military and strategic approach in World War II. Relying on a defensive strategy and without adequate mobility, training and modern equipment, the French Army in Europe was overrun in 1940 in a rapid, aggressive campaign by an enemy that moved, planned and fought to a completely different tempo.

When the home country was defeated many men stayed in service with the rump Vichy state. Others, however, mainly serving overseas, turned towards Britain and the Free French forces forming up there.

These men fought in many campaigns, initially in British uniforms but later equipped and armed with American equipment. And in one of those ironic twists of war, when Allied operations were launched to recapture French colonies, Free French attackers ended up fighting Vichy French defenders.

The war ended with French units taking part in the liberation of their own country as part of the multi-national Allied forces. Overseas, French forces also tried to reimpose colonial rule as their Japanese and German enemies surrendered – actions that set the scene for France's next wars in the 1950s and '60s.

FRENCH INFANTRY

above A Colonel inspects his troops in the winter of 1939. They are carrying Lebel rifles and wearing greatcoats. Some have the fronts of their greatcoats pinned back in a style unique to the French Army.

The outbreak of World War II found France with military commitments around the world, the army being split into two major elements. The metropolitan army was responsible for the defense of France and also had overall responsibility across the empire. Associated with this was the colonial army, which raised units in virtually every French-ruled territory, most of which could be moved to different territories at the orders of the high command.

During the "Phoney War" (August 1939–May 1940) the French prepared for the coming conflict and also dispatched a task force to the unsuccessful defense of Norway. The defense of France in Spring 1940 was spectacularly unsuccessful, except for the victory over the Italians in the southeast. The French signed an armistice on June 22, 1940, under which the government, now located in Vichy, retained responsibility for civil affairs throughout the whole of metropolitan France while the Germans took over military responsibilities in the north and west. Meanwhile, Colonel de Gaulle had escaped to London from where he broadcast on June 18, 1940 announcing the establishment of the Free French forces. From this point on every French citizen was faced with the choice of two loyalties.

The Vichy government was allowed to maintain an army of 94,200 volunteers in France, primarily to police the unoccupied zone. This *l'Armee de l'Armistice* had 18 infantry regiments and 11 horsed cavalry regiments, with a small artillery component, but no tanks. The army was always below its authorized strength and when the Germans took over the unoccupied zone on November 11, 1942 it simply faded away.

Although not included in the Armistice itself,

right The French Army had an international reputation for efficiency and modern thinking before the war. Scenes such as this parade, with a detachment of paratroopers being carried in a modern Citroen truck, only reinforced this impression.

below A soldier hands over weapons to his German captors during the surrenders of 1940. The French Army had been outmaneuvered and shocked into submission by the speed and violence of the German *Blitzkreig*.

above An officer and his men guard a key point in Paris during a pre-war alert in September 1938. The officer is wearing service dress with the familiar cylindrical *kepi* while the soldiers are wearing a mixture of barracks dress and full fighting order.

above French naval officers underwent infantry training to allow them to carry out expeditionary actions. The man on the ground is demonstrating how to create and camouflage a simple fire position.

Indian Ocean, Pacific, or the Far East. Some territories declared for de Gaulle, most for Vichy, while others sat, with increasing discomfort, on the fence.

A joint British–Free French force took Lebanon and Syria in July 1941 and, following the battle of Alamein and the Torch landings, the North African territories were rolled up by the Allies, culminating in the German withdrawal and surrender on May 12, 1943. The British and Free French also took Madagascar in a campaign lasting from May to November 1942.

In the Far East the French empire comprised Annam, Cambodia, Cochin China, Laos and Tonkin. The French colonial authorities were compelled by the Vichy government at home to allow Japanese forces to occupy parts of the empire in September 1940, and, perceiving French weakness, the Thais launched a brief war from October 1940 to May 1941. But otherwise the French in Indochina were quiescent until the Japanese suddenly took over the entire country on March 9, 1945.

the Germans and Italians subsequently laid down limits on French troops overseas: Algeria – 50,000; Lebanon/Syria – 40,000; Morocco – 35,000; Tunisia – nil. No limits were imposed on French territories elsewhere in central Africa,

above North Africa was where Frenchman ended up fighting Frenchman. Here a French unit of the Allied landing force marches towards a flag ceremony in a town. They are wearing sidecaps rather than helmets and are carrying Lebel rifles with the long sword bayonet.

above A weary column of straggling infantry retreats during the disastrous 1940 campaign. The men have obsolete Lebel rifles over their shoulders and the mules are laden with supplies and equipment.

right A Sergeant-Major wearing British battle dress but with a French-pattern sidecap trains with a Sten gun on a British beach. This target practice seems very relaxed, with the man behind leaning on his Thompson sub-machine gun and his comrade enjoying a cigarette.

The Allies liberated French overseas territories and later France itself, almost always with the active participation of Free French forces, and these campaigns often involved Frenchmen fighting against each other. Vichy French continued to use French equipment and uniforms, but the Free French were initially outfitted by the British, until late 1943 when they had received enough American clothing and equipment from the Americans under Lend-lease, following which they also adopted American organizations. Also at this point the Free French and ex-Vichy forces who had come across to de Gaulle were merged to form the *Corps Expéditionnaire Français* (French Expeditionary Corps - CEF). By the end of the war in May 1945, France had 1,250,000 troops, 10 divisions of which were fighting in Germany.

above Much French military strength came from soldiers recruited from the colonies, such as this Senegalese man demonstrating bayonet drill.

right An enameled badge typical of those worn by Free French soldiers and supporters wherever Frenchmen fought on after the armistice.

below Another patriotic badge showing the Cross of Lorraine.

left French soldiers operating with 7th US Army march into the German border town of Scheibonhard in March 1945. They are wearing a mixture of French and US equipment while the lead man has an M1 Carbine across his shoulders.

right Fighting in Karlsruhe at the end of 1944. This group from the French 1st Army are completely equipped with US clothing and weapons, including M1 Carbines, M1 Garand rifles and an M1917 machine gun.

below A Free French paratrooper in British battle dress uniform. He wears parachutist's wings above his right pocket and Special Air Service wings above his left.

right A Free French Commando unit in the UK, taking part in a Bastille Day parade in 1942. This officer is wearing 37-pattern webbing over his battle dress and is carrying the M1928 version of the Thompson sub-machine gun. His headgear is French, however, as is the beret of the man behind him.

above Free French soldiers in United States uniforms and equipment, alongside French Forces of the Interior (FFI), exchange fire with diehard Nazi supporters in Lyon in August 1944. The man standing behind seems unconcerned about the firing.

FRENCH ARMY INFANTRY RANK BADGES

NCOs
Service cap band

Cuff

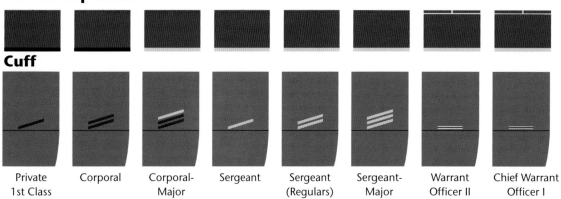

| Private 1st Class | Corporal | Corporal-Major | Sergeant | Sergeant (Regulars) | Sergeant-Major | Warrant Officer II | Chief Warrant Officer I |

Officers
Service cap band

Cuff

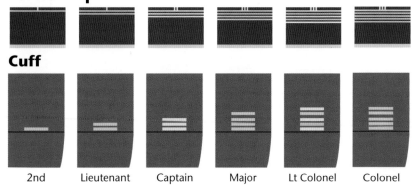

| 2nd Lieutenant | Lieutenant | Captain | Major | Lt Colonel | Colonel |

above French infantry ranks were mainly denoted by short stripes just above the cuff and by combinations of stripes on the service cap.

below The French officers' uniform was a well-tailored tunic, shirt and tie and a Sam Browne leather belt. The cylindrical *kepi* cap is a distinctively recognisable feature of French uniforms even today.

above Immaculately dressed instructors, including the Commandant of the training academy, work with young officer cadets during a field exercise.

Category	French Ranks	US Army Equivalent
General officers	*Maréchal de France*	General of the Army
	Général d'Armée	General
	Général de Corps d'Armée	Lieutenant-general
	Général de Division	Major-general
	Général de Brigade	Brigadier-General
Field Grade Officers	*Colonel*	Colonel
	Lieutenant-Colonel	Lieutenant-Colonel
	Chef de Bataillon	Major
Company Grade Officers	*Capitaine*	Captain
	Lieutenant	Lieutenant
	Sous-Lieutenant	Second Lieutenant
Warrant officer	*Adjutant-Chef*	Warrant Officer (1)
	Adjutant	Warrant Officer (2)
Sergeant-major	*Sergeant-Chef*	Sergeant-Major
Sergeant	*Sergeant*	Sergeant
Senior Corporal	*Caporal-Chef*	Corporal
Corporal	*Caporal*	
Soldiers	*Soldat de 1ère Classe*	Private First Class
	Soldat de 2ème Classe	Private

ORGANIZATION

above Bastille Day 1939, and an array of infantrymen march past, with their Model 1916 rifles shouldered. The Model 1916 was obsolescent by the time the war started, although many men went into combat with it.

French infantry organization, training and equipment in 1939–40 were very much rooted in 1918. The infantry were almost totally foot-mobile, virtually all supplies were brought forward by horse-transport, and tactics were inflexible and uninspired. The infantry battalion was organized rather differently from those in many other armies, particularly those of the United States and United Kingdom. The battalion was commanded by a major and comprised three rifle companies and a heavy weapons company; there was no headquarters or administrative company and there were many fewer officers.

BATTALION HEADQUARTERS

A small headquarters element comprised the commanding officer (major), adjutant (captain) and intelligence officer (lieutenant), plus a clerk and 5 messengers (3 on bicycles, 1 on a motorcycle, 1 in an automobile). The HQ also included the communications section (21 men) with a mix of radios and wire equipment; the medical section (doctor plus 20) and a supply section of 12 men plus a horse-drawn wagon.

left Paris was torn by political strife during the late 1930s, causing incidents such as this deployment of troops into the city in November 1939. This group is a machine gun crew, with the gun, tripod and ammunition being carried on the horses.

below Trenches manned in the winter of 1930. The men are wearing sleeveless sheepskin jerkins over their uniforms and balaclava helmets under their helmets.

HEAVY WEAPONS COMPANY

The Heavy Weapons Company had an HQ of 2 officers plus 7, and a supply squad of 12 plus the usual horse-drawn wagon. There were four heavy machine gun sections, each with two squads of 14 men plus two machine guns. There was also a mortar squad (two 81mm mortars) and gun squad (two 25mm SA-L Mle 34 AT Guns).

RIFLE COMPANY

The battalion's three rifle companies were each 6 officers plus 149 soldiers strong. Each company comprised four rifle platoons, plus a headquarters (2 officers, 11 men), a mortar section – one 60 mm mortar plus 6 men – and a supply section of 12 men plus a wagon.

RIFLE PLATOON

Each company had four rifle platoons, each commanded by a lieutenant or second lieutenant, with a sergeant, VB grenadier corporal, messenger and observer in the headquarters. The three rifle squads each comprised: a squad leader (sergeant), assistant squad leader (corporal), light machine gun team (Chatellerault M24/29 and gunner, loader, plus 3), plus a rifle team of 4 men, plus a VB grenadier. It was common practice to assemble the three VB grenadiers under the command of the VB Grenadier Corporal to maximize their barrage effect.

UNIFORMS AND EQUIPMENT

In 1940 the French soldier wore Model 1935 personal equipment. In combat he wore the M1926 Adrian helmet, which was stamped from a single piece of manganese steel. It had a metal flute attached to the top and a metal badge attached to the front, bearing a flaming grenade and the letters "RF" *(République Française)*. Both these were very ill-advised since any attachment weakens the structural integrity and may also act as a shell or splinter trap. When not actually under fire, officers and soldiers wore a French style of sidecap known as M1918 *bonnet de police*.

below Free French army and naval personnel in the UK, wearing a mixture of French and British uniforms. The French "Adrian" helmet with its central ridge on the crown is clearly visible as is the leather equipment on the central man.

Routine jacket was the tunic *(vareuse)* coupled with baggy trousers, black or brown boots (no toecaps) and long brown woolen puttees. The M1920/35 or M1938 greatcoat was often worn with, in a style confined to the French, the front ends of the skirt pinned back so that they did not restrict the legs when marching.

Round his waist he wore an M1892/1914 belt, with two pairs of pouches, each containing four ammunition clips, and straps passing over his shoulders to be secured at a ring between his shoulder blade, with a single strap down to the back of the belt, all of brown leather. He also wore

left The 1940 uniform with its heavy greatcoat, olive green shirt and "Adrian" helmet. Note also the brown leather belt, ammunition pouches and shoulder straps of the field order.

above An officer cadet in full marching order, with large pack on his back, musette bag on his waist, and a pick handle strapped to the whole assembly.

a large pack *(Pac superieur)* with a roll wrapped around the top and two sides, containing shelter-half, blanket and greatcoat. Fastened to the belt was a linen *musette* bag (haversack) for food, mess-tins, cup, and daily necessaries. Also suspended from the belt were a 2-liter water-bottle, bayonet and a tool, either a spade, pick or saw.

ANP 31 GAS MASK

The standard French gas mask, carried by all officers and men, was the *Appareil Normal de Protection Modèle* 1931 (ANP-31). Like contemporary respirators in other armies, it consisted of a face mask, a long corrugated tube and a metal canister containing the filter, which, when in use, was worn on the left hip. The complete outfit had its own linen carrier bag.

WEAPONS

In the 1939–40 campaign, the French infantry was armed almost entirely with weapons of French design and manufacture. These remained in use with Vichy forces until the end, but Free French forces were progressively rearmed with British weapons in 1940–43 and American weapons from 1943 onwards. Below are the principle French-made weapons.

RIFLE, MAS MODÈLE 1936

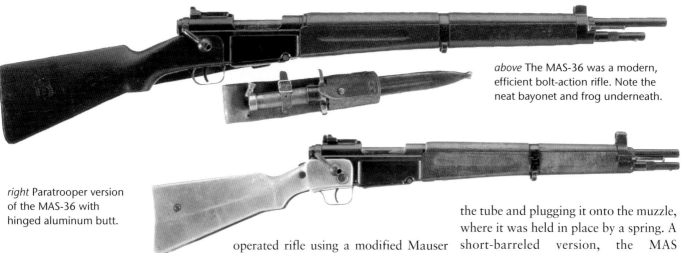

above The MAS-36 was a modern, efficient bolt-action rifle. Note the neat bayonet and frog underneath.

right Paratrooper version of the MAS-36 with hinged aluminum butt.

Type: bolt-action rifle
Origin: France
Caliber: 7.5 x 54 mm rimless
Weight (empty): 8.3 lb (3.8 kg)
Barrel length: 22.6 in (574 mm)
Feed: 5-round box

The MAS-36 (MAS = *Manufacture d'Armes de St Étienne*) was a bolt-operated rifle using a modified Mauser action, but with an unusual bolt lever which was angled forward in order to lock the bolt itself into the top of the body behind the magazine, which was an integral type holding five rounds. The weapon did not have a manual safety-catch. The bayonet was a rod type, with cruciform cross-section, which was carried in a tube under the barrel and fixed by removing it from the tube and plugging it onto the muzzle, where it was held in place by a spring. A short-barreled version, the MAS 1936/CR39 was accepted for service in 1939. Designed for use by paratroops and mountain troops, it had a hinged, aluminum butt which folded forwards.

The MAS-36 was in widespread service with the French Army by the time war broke out in 1939 although it had not fully replaced the antiquated Lebel in service, especially with colonial troops.

FUSIL-MITRAILLEUR MODÈLE 1924/29 (CHÂTELLERAULT)

Type: light machine gun
Origin: France
Caliber: 7.5 x 54 mm rimless
Weight (empty): 20.25 lb (9.12 kg)
Barrel length: 19.7 in (500 mm)
Cyclic rate: 500 rpm
Feed: 26-round box

above The effective Chatellerault had a similar configuration to the Czech ZB 26, although it made use of a unique dual-trigger system.

During World War I the French Army was armed with the Chauchat LMG, a notoriously poor and unreliable weapon. As soon as the war was over they started a search for a newer, better LMG, firing a more powerful round. The outcome was this weapon, designed and produced by the Châtellerault state arsenal. There were some early problems when financial restrictions led to efforts to production economies and poor build-quality, but once these were resolved it became a satisfactory squad-level weapon.

It was piston-operated and had two triggers – one for single rounds, the second for automatic – but as a safety measure the change lever had to be set to the required mode before the trigger could be pulled. The gun fired a new 7.5 mm round, but in 1929 this round was made marginally shorter and a revised weapon, the Modèle 1924–9 was produced to fire it. In this form the weapon quickly earned an excellent reputation for reliability and performance.

HOTCHKISS MODÈLE 1914

left Although it fed from an unusual rigid metal strip, the Modèle 1914 was made into a reliable machine gun that served through both world wars and beyond.

Type: heavy machine gun
Origin: France
Caliber: 8 mm rimless
Cartridge: 8 x 50R Lebel
Weight: gun (empty) 55.7 lb (25.3 kg); tripod 60 lb (27.2 kg)
Barrel length: 31.0 in (787 mm)
Cyclic rate: 500 rpm
Feed: strip

below The St Etienne heavy machine gun was largely supplanted by the Hotchkiss during Word War I, but some remained in service through World War II.

This weapon was designed in the 1890s and was one of the first to use a gas-piston system rather than the recoil mechanism typical of Maxim designs. Unlike most contemporary machine guns it was air- rather than water-cooled and this gave some trouble until five solid metal, 3.2 in (80 mm) diameter cooling discs were built into the breech end of the barrel, which completely solved the problem. An unusual feature was that the ammunition was fed in strips rather than box magazines or cloth belts. Somewhat surprisingly, the Hotchkiss was not selected for the French Army in a competition in 1907, but a slightly improved version was subsequently ordered in 1914 to make up for shortage in numbers. Designated the Modèle 1914, this had some minor changes, including steel as opposed to brass cooling discs, and quickly proved itself superior to other French machine guns. It became the standard French HMG, remaining in service until well after the end of World War II. It was also used by the British Army, in this case firing the 0.303 in round.

REVOLVERS AND PISTOLS

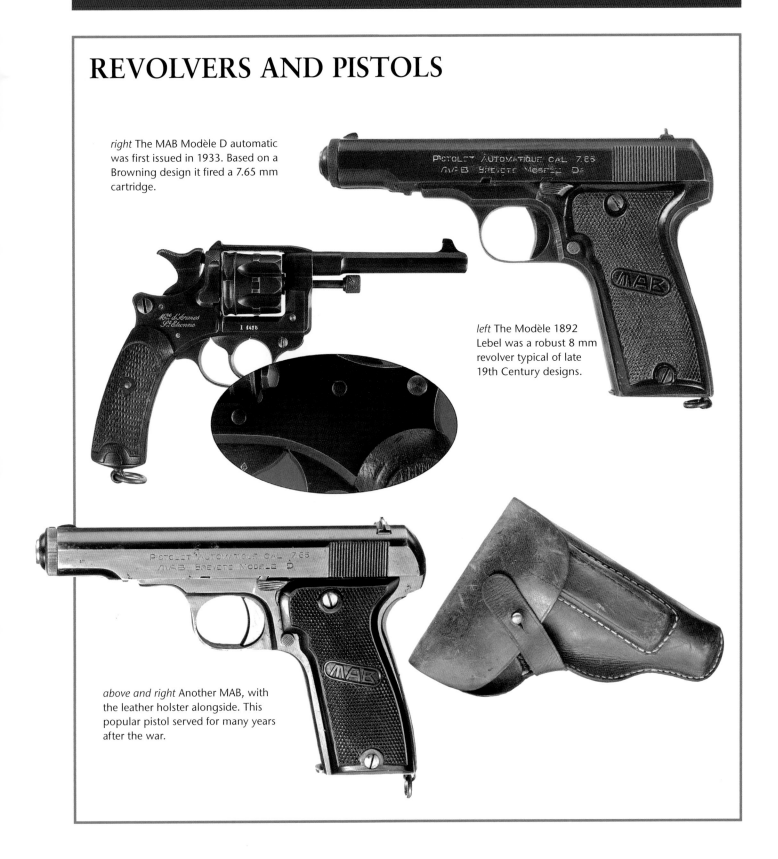

right The MAB Modèle D automatic was first issued in 1933. Based on a Browning design it fired a 7.65 mm cartridge.

left The Modèle 1892 Lebel was a robust 8 mm revolver typical of late 19th Century designs.

above and right Another MAB, with the leather holster alongside. This popular pistol served for many years after the war.

ANTI-TANK GUNS

In the 1940 campaign French infantry were equipped with two relatively modern anti-tank guns, but had nowhere near enough of them, so had to continue to use a World War I-vintage weapon, as well.

25 mm Modèle 1934 Hotchkiss/Modèle 1937 Puteaux

Type: anti-tank gun
Caliber: 25 mm
Length of barrel: M34 – 72 in (1.8 m); M37 – 76 in (1.93 m)
Weight: M34 – 1,058 lb (480 kg); M37 – 661 lb (300 kg)
Rate of fire: 15–25 rpm
Range: 875 yd (800 m) (see text)

These two weapons were virtually the same ordnance (the M37 tube was 5 in/13 cm longer) mounted on two different carriages, that of the M37 being considerably lighter. The gun was very accurate and in the 1940 campaign proved that it could penetrate German PzKpfw I, II and III tanks at 875 yd (800 m), although it had to allow the PzKpfw IV to approach more closely. The gun had a very low silhouette and was fitted with a flash suppressor, a combination which made it hard to locate, especially from within a tank.

It had several disadvantages. The first was that although designed to be towed, it proved susceptible to damage, so that wherever possible it had to be carried in the back of a vehicle. The second was that there was no HE shell for use against soft targets. During the "phoney war" period several hundred of these were exchanged with the British Expeditionary Force (BEF) for some Boys anti-tank rifles. The British called it the Anti-tank gun 25 mm Hotchkiss. The Germans captured a number in 1940 and put them into service, the Modèle 1934 becoming the 2.5 cm Pak 112(f) , and the Modèle 1937 the 2.5 cm Pak 113(f).

left The performance of the 25 mm anti-tank gun was just about good enough in 1940, but was rapidly being outclassed. This one is being used as cover by a despatch rider who is engaging enemy infantry with his carbine.

37 mm Modèle 1916 TRP

Type: anti-tank gun
Caliber: 37 mm
Length of barrel: 31.1 in (790 mm)
Weight: action – 238 lb (108 kg); traveling (including wheels) 353 lb (160 kg)
Rate of fire: 15–30 rpm
Range (effective): anti-tank 437 yd (400 m); soft target 1,640 yd (1,500 m)

This weapon was introduced into service in World War I as an infantry support gun, designated *Canon d'Infanterie de 37mm Modèle 1916 TRP*. It served in second-line divisions in 1940, but was popular because of its accuracy and high rate-of-fire, and also because it had an HE round for use against enemy infantry. For transportation it could be either towed on wheels or broken down into three loads. A number were captured by the Germans and put into service by them as 3.7 cm Infanterie Geschutz 152(f).

MORTARS AND GRENADES

The French made great use of mortars, particularly in 60 mm and 81 mm calibers. The 60 mm was little different from those used by other armies and the 81 mm Brandt was the prototype for virtually all models used in most armies during the World War II. The French also used the VB grenade launcher as a form of light mortar and their custom of assembling them in batteries was unique.

BRANDT 81.4 mm MORTAR MODÈLE 1927/31

Caliber: 81 mm
Length of barrel: 50 in (1.26 m)
Weight: complete – 126 lb (57 kg);
  barrel – 44 lb (20 kg); baseplate – 45
  lb (20 kg); bipod – 37 lb (17 kg).
Rate of fire: 18 rpm
Weight of projectile: 7.1/15.2 lb
  (3.25 kg/6.9 kg)
Range: 914–2,100 yd (1,000–1,900 m)

The celebrated Brandt 81.4 mm mortar entered service with the French Army in 1927, followed by an improved version in 1931. It was adopted, with virtually no changes, by many armies around the world. The weapon could be broken down into three loads – barrel, baseplate, bipod – for transportation. It had a crew of three men who fired it by dropping the bomb tail-first down the tube, where it hit the fixed firing pin which triggered the propellant. Maximum rate of fire was about 18 rounds per minute, although great care had to be taken to ensure that an overexcited mortarman did not drop a new bomb in before the previous one had left the tube.

left Moroccan soldiers (also known as *Goumier*) in Italy, operating an 81 mm mortar. They wear the striped overcoat often worn by Moroccans, the British steel helmet and US webbing gear.

left Grenade throwing from a slit trench. The thrower has another two hanging from his belt, ready for action. Note how the grenades have a smooth outer shell, typical of "offensive" grenades which rely on explosive power rather than metal fragments for their combat effect.

TROMBLON VIVIEN-BESSIÈRE (GRENADE DISCHARGER)

This device was unusual in itself and was also used in an unusual way. Designed in World War I by two officers named Vivien and Bessiere, the Tromblon VB consisted of a grenade cup which was fitted to the muzzle of a rifle, usually a Lebel Mle 1886 but also MAS Mle 1936.

Many other armies had similar devices, but in the French system the grenade launching process was initiated using a standard rifle round and not a ballistite (blank) cartridge. When the round was fired, the bullet traveled up the barrel and through the central tube of the grenade, lighting the 8 second fuze. The gasses released by firing the cartridge followed the bullet up the barrel but were then diverted into the lower chamber of the launcher, generating sufficient pressure to launch the grenade to a maximum distance of 186 yd (170 m) – the range depended on the angle of the rifle – with a minimum range of about 87 yd (80 m). The cast iron grenade body weighed 15 oz (415 g) and was marked with 40 grooves, which, unlike hand grenades, were designed to aid disintegration. The central tube passed through the entire body, so that the bullet would shoot through unimpeded. The other components were a fuze and a detonator

The VB launcher was normally used with the firer kneeling and the rifle butt resting firmly on the ground, but, if circumstances dictated, it could be launched from the hip or even from the shoulder. Rate of fire was between four and nine rounds per minute per launcher. Each company had about 16 launchers, the cups being carried in special pouches (etui). All French infantry platoons had a number of VB launchers and these men were often assembled as a group to fire a barrage of grenades, truly the platoon commander's own artillery.

below A squad of naval infantry demonstrate how French tactical doctrine was to often group VB grenade launchers into a miniature "battery" which could fire a barrage of high explosive.

THE FRENCH FOREIGN LEGION

The *Legion Étrangère* (Foreign Legion) suffered the same split loyalties as the rest of the French Army, a problem exacerbated by its heterogeneous composition. Immediately prior to the war, the Legion had a strength of six infantry regiments plus one regiment of cavalry. The infantry regiments, of two/three battalions each, were deployed in Syria, Indochina and Morocco. There were, as always, large numbers of Germans in the ranks, some of whom were suspected of being Nazi infiltrators. Several hundred of these were interned in 1939.

Seven new units were raised between August 1939 and June 1940, five of them in Metropolitan France rather than overseas. Three of these were for volunteers enlisting on a "hostilities only" basis; there were many Spanish Republicans in the ranks and numerous French reservists among the officers. All of the French-based units resisted the German attack in May 1940 and did well under difficult circumstances, sustaining heavy losses before disappearing in the general defeat.

By far the best of the new units was *13e Demi-Brigade Legion Étrangère* (13th Half-Brigade of the Foreign Legion = 13eDBLE) which was formed in early 1940 specifically for service in Finland from volunteers among all Legion units (a *Demi-Brigade* was a regimental-strength unit). The Finns capitulated before it could deploy, so it was sent to Norway where it performed heroically in the Narvik area but was then withdrawn. When France capitulated about half the unit chose to serve under Vichy but the remainder volunteered for de Gaulle's Free French. The unit retained its

left The French Foreign Legion fought for much of the war in North Africa and the western desert. This group, along with native auxiliaries, are celebrating their return from Lake Chad. The variety of uniforms is typical of the informal style adopted by most armies that fought in the desert, and includes solar topees, *kepi* hats, woolen cap comforters, scarves and berets.

title and was soon back to two battalion strength and in 1941 fought alongside the British in the East African campaign, then went into Vichy Syria where it found itself fighting against another Legion regiment in a campaign where both sides balanced military effectiveness against chivalric concerns for fellow legionnaires as soon as the fighting was over. 13eDBLE then went to the Western Desert where, with other Free French units, it fought in the epic action at Bir Hakeim. 13eDBLE remained with Eighth (BR) Army for the remainder of the campaign then landed in Italy with Fifth (US) Army and then in France as part of Operation Dragoon; it landed on August 16, 1944 and then fought its way as far as Arlberg in Austria by VE-day.

Once France had been defeated, German commissions visited all Foreign Legion units under Vichy control in an effort to recruit such well-trained soldiers for the Wehrmacht.

In 1940–41 some 2,000 German-born legionnaires were persuaded to transfer to the German Army, where they formed 361st Infantry Regiment and fought as part of Rommel's Afrika Korps. The regiment capitulated with other German units in Tunisia and its members were held as prisoners-of-war, although in 1945 many took the opportunity to re-enlist in the Legion.

The legion's fifth regiment (5e REI) spent the entire war years in the Far East. It had no choice but to acquiesce in the Japanese entry into Indochina in 1941, but when the Japanese took total control of the country in March 1945 they refused to give in and marched some 500 miles northwards into southern China, fighting their way through numerous Japanese attacks as they did so. They remained in China until early 1946, but when French troops returned to Tonkin in early 1946 they marched back again to return to French service.

LEGION UNIFORM, WEAPONS AND EQUIPMENT

Legion combat dress during the war went through three stages, although they always managed to retain some items to identify themselves as legionnaires. At the start, they wore standard French Army uniforms depending on the climate: temperate dress for Metropolitan France, desert uniforms for North Africa and Syria/Lebanon, tropical for Indo-China, and winter warfare for Norway. Vichy units wore French uniform until either they went over to the Allies, or were disbanded, but as other units came under British control they were outfitted with British Army weapons, uniforms and personal equipment. Then, from late 1943 onwards, they changed to US items.

Except when in actual combat (and sometimes even then) *legionnaires* below the rank of *sous-officer* wore the famous *kepi blanc* (white cap) with its stiffened cylindrical shape, although this was actually a blue kepi with a red crown with a white cover. They also retained a Legion badge, either in metal or cloth, and badges of rank.

above A more formal setting with everyone wearing the correct uniform at an inspection and awards ceremony after fighting in Syria.

COLONIAL TROOPS

The French had a vast array of colonial troops and in 1939 there were no less than twelve North African infantry divisions, many of which fought in the battle of France in 1940. The French government divided its troops into three broad categories: Metropolitan units; i.e., native Frenchmen from France; *troupes spéciales* who were indigenous troops in their own country; and colonial troops, from other parts of the Empire.

ZOUAVES

The *Zouaves* got their name from the Zouaoua tribe of Algeria from which they were originally recruited. The units later became a *corps d'elite* formed from indigenous volunteers from all over North Africa but in the 1870s this changed radically and from then on they were recruited from French settlers living in Tunisia and Algeria doing their compulsory military service, with any shortfall made up from men from southern France. They wore garish uniforms, prided

above Colonial cavalry, known as *spahis*, charge across an open hillside in North Africa. While seemingly anachronistic in a war of machine guns, tanks and aircraft, they still had a role as irregulars or security troops.

themselves on their *élan*, and were widely imitated in the American Civil War. Several *Zouave* units fought in the Tunisian campaign and in France in 1944–45.

TIRAILLEURS

Tirailleur can be translated as "sharpshooter" in French, but is more closely allied to the military term "light infantry." *Tirailleur* units were recruited from all over the French Empire and regiments used the name qualified by that of their recruiting area, for example: *Tirailleurs Annamites* (Indochina), *Tirailleurs Cambogiens* (Cambodia), *Tirailleurs Malgaches* (Madagascar), *Tirailleurs Marocienne* (Morocco), *Tirailleurs Tonkinois* (Tongkin), *Ttirailleurs Tunisiens* (Tunisia) etc.

left A Senegalese *Tirailleur*, a light infantryman in French colonial service, displays the unique national elements to his uniform.

left Many French colonial soldiers also ended up in the UK, alongside the Free French forces being constituted there. This North African bugler is wearing British battle dress and headgear

right Much French equipment changed hands more than once in the confusion of changing and conflicting loyalties. These obsolete 75 mm guns served the French in World War I then in the colonies in 1940. After a spell with Vichy colonial forces they ended up in Free French hands after the North African invasion.

PhilosophyofScience

CHASSEUR

Chasseurs (hunters) were troops trained for rapid action, and the term Chasseurs à pied (hunters on foot) was applied to certain elite light infantry units. They were originally recruited from hunters and were thus directly equivalent to the German *Jäger* units or British rifle regiments. Thus, the *battailons de chasseurs Libanais* (Lebanese Light Infantry Battalions) qualified for the *chasseur* cachet, while the Syrian *battailons du Levant* did not. *Chassseurs à cheval* (light cavalry) were not considered in the same elitist light and *Chasseurs d'Afrique*, for example, were recruited, like the *Zouaves*, from French settlers in North Africa doing their compulsory service.

GOUMIER

The French raised units of irregular indigenous soldiers in Algeria and Morocco in the early 20th Century, which were formed into battalion-sized units called a *tabor*, which usually consisted of three companies called *goums*, and whose members became known as *goumier*. Originally irregular, the units became permanent in 1911. In World War II regimental-size formations were formed, designated a *Groupe* which typically comprised three *tabors*. Initially, these were termed *Groupe de Supplétifs Marocains* (GSM) but this was later changed to *Groupe de Tabors Marocains* (GTM). Although these were redoubtable fighters in all types of combat, their specialty was night raids, when their silent, rapid movement, especially in mountainous country, and ruthless elimination of the enemy made them renowned among friend and enemy alike. Their first operations in World War II were against Italy in North Africa in 1939–40, but following

above French Moroccan troops in Alsace, near Colmar. Snow and mud have made many roads difficult, such that horses are useful for giving some mobility. They wear a mixture of US and British helmets.

Operation Torch they operated alongside the US Army, with whom they then moved to Sicily then Italy, where 4eGTM arrived in November 1943, followed by 3eGTM (January 1944) and 1erGTM (April 1944). In May 1944 these three GTMs were collected into the *Corps de Montagne*, which was part of *Corps Expéditionaire Français* (CEF). Meanwhile, 2eGTM took part in the invasions of Corsica (September 1943) and Elba (June 1944). 1er, 2e, and 3e GTM took part in the operations in southern France, fighting their way through the Vosges mountains and into southern Germany. 3eGTM was relieved by 4eGTM in April 1945, and 1e,2e and 4e fought their way across the hilly areas of southern Germany until the war's end. They returned to Morocco in early 1946.

Units of Indochinese and Malagasy machine gunners were also part of the 1940 garrison in the Maginot Line.

left Moroccan *Goumier* in Italy, operating on the 5th Army front. Their helmets are French, their belt and webbing gear US, and their striped coats Moroccan.

right A friendly gathering of French colonial, British and United States soldiers in Algiers, outside a hotel where Italian prisoners were being held. Not long before Frenchmen were shooting at other Frenchmen and their allies during the north African invasion.

COLONIAL UNIFORM

Colonial troops wore the same basic uniform as those from Metropolitan France but were permitted to wear certain traditional national distinctions, particularly headdress. For tropical and desert wear there was an outfit made of khaki drill, with either a shirt or jacket of a standardized pattern, worn with either very loose-fitting long trousers or with shorts. Khaki puttees were worn, but whereas other armies wore short puttees around the ankle with short trousers, the French colonial troops wore long puttees with shorts, either with or without long stockings underneath, which must have been very hot.

The *djellabah* was a traditional, very loose-fitting overgarment, designed for wear in the desert but frequently worn by North African troops in Italy and south-west Europe.

HEADDRESS

In combat, all ranks wore the Adrian helmet until it was replaced by either British or US models. The Adrian usually bore some special badges, including a crescent for Muslim units, an anchor for some European-manned colonial regiments, and the usual flaming grenade for the Foreign Legion and Chasseurs d'Afrique.

Many units wore a distinctive headdress. North African and Senegalese troops wore the *chechia*, which resembled a low-crowned, peakless kepi. While this was worn in various colors, for example, red for Tunisian units, it was almost always covered with a khaki cover in combat. Moroccans also wore a turban; there were various colors in peacetime, but in combat all were khaki.

below: The town square at Collobrieries, near Toulon, after liberation by a Free French unit. They wear a mixture of US clothing and French berets and side caps, while one officer wears a striped Moroccan coat.

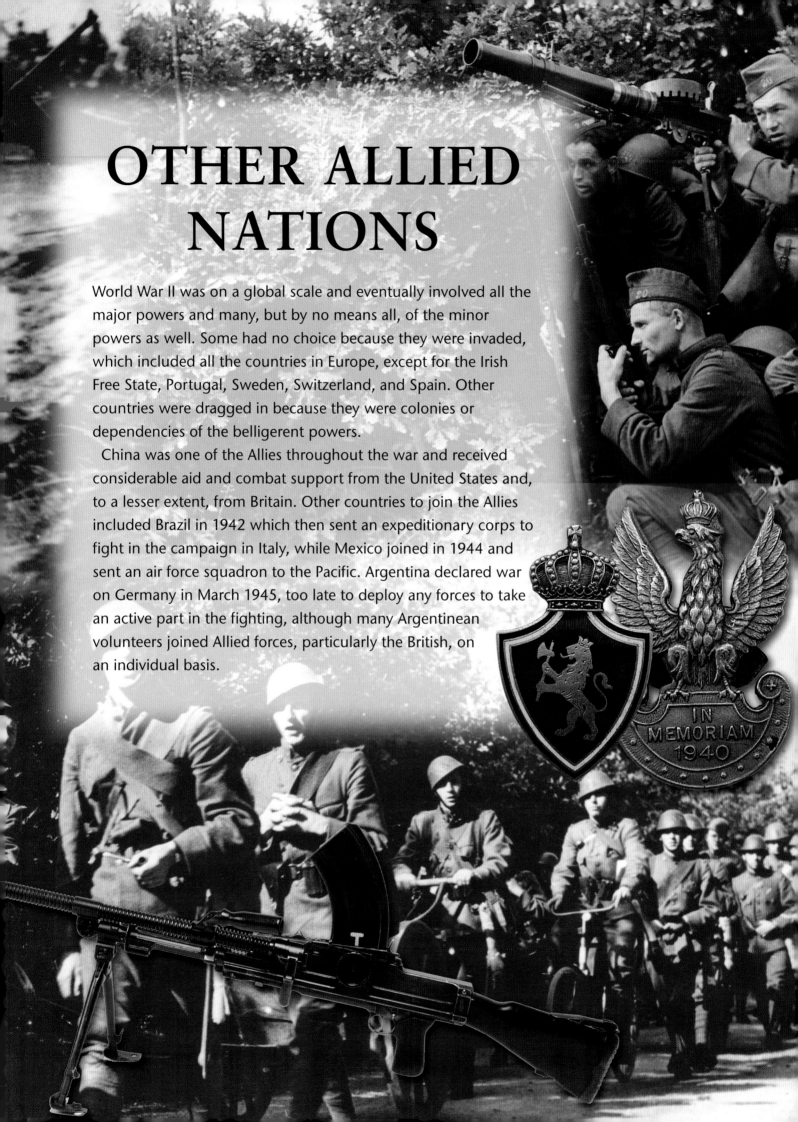

OTHER ALLIED NATIONS

World War II was on a global scale and eventually involved all the major powers and many, but by no means all, of the minor powers as well. Some had no choice because they were invaded, which included all the countries in Europe, except for the Irish Free State, Portugal, Sweden, Switzerland, and Spain. Other countries were dragged in because they were colonies or dependencies of the belligerent powers.

China was one of the Allies throughout the war and received considerable aid and combat support from the United States and, to a lesser extent, from Britain. Other countries to join the Allies included Brazil in 1942 which then sent an expeditionary corps to fight in the campaign in Italy, while Mexico joined in 1944 and sent an air force squadron to the Pacific. Argentina declared war on Germany in March 1945, too late to deploy any forces to take an active part in the fighting, although many Argentinean volunteers joined Allied forces, particularly the British, on an individual basis.

CHINA

The collapse of the Imperial Chinese Government in 1912 was followed by 40 years of conflict in China; partly against the invading Japanese but also between the Nationalists led by *Generalissimo* Chiang Kai-shek and the Communists, led by Mao Tse-tung. The strategic problem was that China was so huge and the population so vast that the Japanese would never be able to control it all, while the Chinese never achieved sufficient cohesion to enable them to drive the hated Japanese into the sea.

From 1922 a German military mission was influential in Chinese strategy, tactics, organization and weapons procurement until the Japanese persuaded Hitler that its activities were incompatible with German–Japanese friendship and the mission was withdrawn in 1938. By that time, eight Nationalist infantry divisions – out of 134 divisions and 36 separate brigades – had been trained and equipped to German standards.

right A young Nationalist Chinese officer wearing the padded tunic and German steel helmet with the Nationalist sun symbol on the side.

NATIONALIST CHINESE

above This well-equipped detachment are wearing long tunics, lightweight sun helmets and high puttees, with leather Sam Browne belts holding cartridge pouches. Note the white gloves and the drawn Mauser pistols.

The National Revolutionary Army (NRA) divided the country into 12 military regions, while the field army was made up of army groups, armies and divisions. In 1937 the German-trained infantry divisions had a strength of about 14,000 each, divided into two infantry brigades, each of two infantry regiments, each of three battalions, with proper artillery, engineers, signals and logistic support at all levels. The other divisions had a strength of about 6,000, their structure based on the order of three: three teams in a squad, three squads in a platoon, three platoons (plus a few administrative personnel) made a company, and three companies a battalion. At the higher level, there were three battalions in a regiment, three regiments in a division and three divisions in an army.

Category	Kuo Mintang Ranks	US Army Equivalent
General officers	*T'e chih shang chiang*	General of the Army
	I chi shang chiang	General
	Chung chiang	Lieutenant-General
	Shao chiang	Major-General
Field Grade Officers	*Shang hsiao*	Colonel
	Chung hsiao	Lieutenant-Colonel
	Shao hsiao	Major
Company Grade Officers	*Shang wei*	Captain
	Chung wei	Lieutenant
	Shao wei	Second Lieutenant
Warrant Officer	*Chun wei*	1st Sergeant
Sergeant-Major	*Shang shih*	Staff-Sergeant
Sergeant	*Chung shih*	Sergeant
Corporal	*Hsia shi*	Corporal
Soldiers	*Shang teng ping*	Private First Class
	Erh teng ping	Private

INFANTRY COMBAT UNIFORM

The infantry combat uniform was based on an outfit made popular by Dr Sun Yat-sen, namely the *Zhongshan* suit. This was made of light, khaki cotton and consisted of a long-sleeved jacket with five buttons and a stand-up/fall-down collar, four external pockets, and a pair of long trousers. A similar outfit for winter was blue and made of padded cloth. Soldiers wore canvas shoes and junior officers leather shoes, all with long puttees wrapped from the foot upwards and tied-off just below the knee.

Some elite units were issued with German-style belts, ammunition pouches and packs, and later in the war others received either British or US clothing and webbing. The vast majority, however, used cloth ammunition bandoliers and simply tied on equipment and grenades by a system of cloth straps. All had water-bottles and some form of haversack in which to carry rations. Some, but by no means all, were issued with a gas-mask.

HEADGEAR

The usual hat was made of cotton and similar in design to the German *Feldmütze*, but with a flatter top, two buttons at the front and the Chinese Nationalist cockade. This cap was khaki with summer uniform and blue with winter uniform. For helmets, in the 1930s the usual wear was the British Brodie helmet, but this was replaced in many units by the German Model 1935 *Stahlhelm*, while for a lucky few there was the US Army M1.

top right Chinese troops fought the Japanese for many years before Pearl Harbor, often without success but usually with dogged determination. This cheery group are posing with trophies and Japanese dead.

right An infantry unit in the light cotton summer uniform with canvas shoes, long puttees and simple peaked cap. They have cotton bandoliers tied around their waists and blanket rolls around their shoulders.

COMMUNIST CHINESE

The Communist forces were nominally allied with the Nationalists against the Japanese and cooperated to a certain extent, but retained their independence. Their two main formations, numbered in sequence within the National Revolutionary Army were the New Fourth Army, which operated south of the Yangtze River, and the Eighth Route Army, whose operating base was in north-west China. There were also many independent regiments, battalions and smaller units, including many bands of guerrillas scattered around the country.

Very approximate strengths were: squad – 15; platoon – 50; company – 160; battalion – 550–600. Control by the Communist Party was very tight and all commanders at platoon level and above were Party members, while there were political officers on the Soviet model.

below Communist fighters cross a stream in a training exercise. Two men are carrying Sten sub-machine guns while the third has an M1928 Thompson. They are otherwise lightly equipped and wear a typical mixture of military and civilian clothing.

UNIFORMS AND EQUIPMENT

During the period 1939–45, regular Communist troops wore similar field uniforms and rank insignia to Chiang's men. Headgear comprised a soft visored kepi in either blue or khaki, a wool-lined winter cap similar to a Russian *ushanka*, or, once relations with the Nationalists broke down, a "Mao-style" cap. Equipment comprised a belt, usually of leather, cartridge pouches or a cloth bandolier and a "food-tube" slung over one shoulder. Uniformity was achieved wherever possible but the main emphasis was on making the best use of what was available – which was usually not very much. The basic premise was that the Communists took whatever weapons, ammunition and military equipment they could lay their hands on. In the 1920s and 30s they captured weapons from the Nationalists and then increasingly from the Japanese. The latter ranged from rifles and machine guns to sufficient tanks to form whole armored units.

above A group of Communist Chinese pause during the Long March north. Note the two officers wearing military uniform while the rest are wearing civilian clothes with headscarves and soft hats, and with blankets and cloth "food tubes" over their shoulders.

CHINESE WEAPONS

Both Nationalists and Communists used weapons from a wide variety of sources, some produced in country, some supplied from overseas, and many captured from the Japanese. State arsenals produced both weapons and ammunition, usually to foreign design, sometimes under license, sometimes not, but always slowly. Quality was variable, ranging from as good as the originals to

24, a locally-made Maxim. The heaviest anti-tank guns were the German-supplied *3.7 cm Pak 36* and the Solothurn 20 mm anti-tank rifle. Mortars, the heaviest being 81 mm, came from a variety of European companies but were all based on the Brandt; in theory there were six per division. The range of weapons used was vast and those which follow are just representative.

above A Japanese Arisaka rifle in Chinese service. Many Chinese weapons were captured from the Japanese.

below Taking aim with a stocked Mauser. Obsolescent and out of service elsewhere, the Mauser pistol was popular with Chinese soldiers.

so bad that the weapon was as dangerous to the user as to the target. Among the known products were the Hanyang rifle, Generalissimo rifle, Mauser C/96 7.63 mm pistol and M1917 Browning machine gun. Many weapons were also purchased in quantity from abroad.

The scale of issue of machine guns was far short of international standards, with, perhaps, one light machine gun per platoon and a single water-cooled medium machine gun per battalion . An attempt was made to standardize on the Czech 7.92 mm ZB-26 but many other models were also found. The battalion machine gun was the Type

MAUSER MODEL 1912

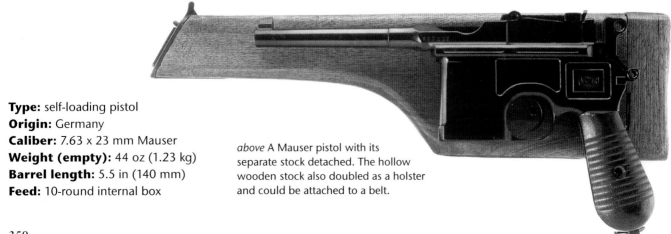

Type: self-loading pistol
Origin: Germany
Caliber: 7.63 x 23 mm Mauser
Weight (empty): 44 oz (1.23 kg)
Barrel length: 5.5 in (140 mm)
Feed: 10-round internal box

above A Mauser pistol with its separate stock detached. The hollow wooden stock also doubled as a holster and could be attached to a belt.

The famous C96 "broom-handle" pistol was introduced in 1896 and upgraded over the years. It was a short-recoil weapon, in which, on firing, the barrel and bolt moved rearwards for a short distance before the latter was unlocked then continued to the rear, extracting and ejecting the empty cartridge case and compressing the return spring inside the bolt. The spring then took over, driving the bolt forwards, picking up a round from the magazine and chambering it. The Mauser had a 10-round fixed magazine loaded from above using a clip.

The Model 1898 introduced a removable shoulder stock, which enabled it to be used for aimed fire at ranges of up to 766 yd (700 m), although effective range was much shorter. This was, in effect, a light carbine although it was only capable of firing single rounds. The Model 1930 had a longer barrel, while the Models 711 and 712, introduced in 1930 and 1931, were capable of automatic fire and had a removable 20-round magazine. Many of those used in China had the detachable stock.

below Mauser with stock attached. There was even a burst-fire version with a larger magazine.

RIFLE, .30 CAL, MODEL OF 1917

Type: bolt-action rifle
Origin: USA
Caliber: .30-06 in rimless
Weight (empty): 9.0 lb (4.1 kg)
Barrel length: 26.0 in (660 mm)
Feed: 5-round internal box

One weapon to reach the Nationalists in quantity was the Model 1917, bolt-action rifle supplied by the United States. This weapon started life in Great Britain in 1910 as a potential replacement for the 0.303 in Short Magazine Lee-Enfield (SMLE) but was designed to use a new 0.276 in rimless round. This rifle was accepted for service as the Pattern 1913 when World War I broke out, when the order was cancelled. The British were, however, desperately short of rifles, so they asked the Winchester Company in the United States to adapt the design to take the British standard 0.303 in round, and this was then produced as the Pattern 1914. When the United States entered the war they had nowhere near sufficient rifles so the Pattern 1914 was rechambered to accept the US .30-06 in round and over two million of the Model of 1917 were produced, being known throughout the US Army as "the American Enfield." At the end of the war they were placed in storage. On the outbreak of World War II a large number were supplied to China.

The Model 1917 had a Mauser-type bolt and an integral magazine which could not be removed and had to be reloaded by a charger from above. The British judged it too large – it was 2 in (5 cm) longer and 8 oz (227 g) heavier than the SMLE, and subject to excessive fouling. However, it did turn out to be exceptionally accurate, which is why it was often used as a sniper rifle.

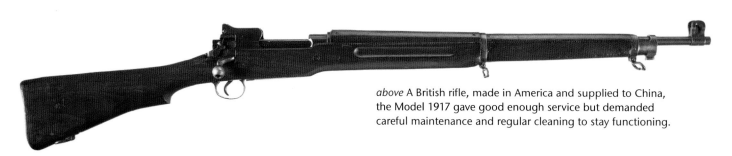

above A British rifle, made in America and supplied to China, the Model 1917 gave good enough service but demanded careful maintenance and regular cleaning to stay functioning.

RIFLE, 7.92 MM, HANYANG MODEL

Type: bolt-action rifle
Origin: Hanyang State Arsenal
Caliber: 8 x 57 mm rimless
Weight (empty): lb (3.9 kg)
Barrel length: in (743 mm)
Feed: 5-round internal box

below Taking up a fire position on a ridge, these men are equipped with American weapons and padded winter uniforms. Note the array of loads carried on their backs.

This rifle was produced in the Hanyang arsenal when German weapons supplies ceased following the outbreak of World War I; production started in 1916 and peaked in the 1920s. The weapon was something of a hodge-podge, with the action based on that of the Mannlicher *Gewehr 88* but with various changes such as the removal of the barrel shroud and a revised bayonet lug. The loading system was the Mannlicher design using a clip which was held in place until the last round had been fired, when it fell through a hole in bottom of the magazine: good for rapid reloads but an unwanted entry-point for dirt. As with most other Chinese-produced weapons of this period it was poorly made. It was used by Chinese infantrymen in both Nationalist and Communist forces throughout World War II.

RIFLE, 7.92 MM, GENERALISSIMO MODEL

Type: bolt-action rifle
Origin: Hanyang State Arsenal
Caliber: 7.92 x 57 mm rimless (8mm Mauser)
Weight (empty): 9.0 lb (4.1 kg)
Barrel length: 23.6 in (600 mm)
Feed: 5-round internal box

This weapon was known variously as the "Chiang Kai-shek" or "Generalissimo" Model, and also as the Type 24, since it was accepted for service in 1935, which was the 24th year since the creation of the Republic of China. Like the Hanyang Rifle it was based on a German original, in this case, the Mauser *Gewehr M1898*, but with various Chinese improvements. Production standards were very variable, ranging from fully equal to the German original to those which were as dangerous to the user as the enemy. It

started to reach troops in 1936 and was replaced in the course of World War II by the M 1903 Springfield and the Model of 1917. The Generalissimo rifle had some advantages over the Japanese standard rifle, the Arisaka, primarily the much heavier bullet (7.92 mm compared to 6.5 mm) which gave greater stopping power, range and accuracy.

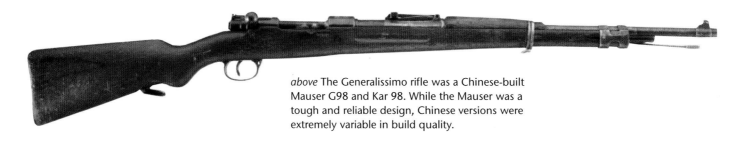

above The Generalissimo rifle was a Chinese-built Mauser G98 and Kar 98. While the Mauser was a tough and reliable design, Chinese versions were extremely variable in build quality.

BAYONET

The Japanese were very keen on the use of bayonets, one favorite tactic being to overcome resistance by firing one volley and then charging in order to get involved in hand-to-hand combat. The Chinese had no choice but to respond in kind and most riflemen were issued with a bayonet suitable for the weapon they carried. Many were imported, but one known to have been produced by Chinese State arsenals was the Hao Yang Model 1935 to fit the Generalissimo rifle. This bayonet had a 19 in (485 mm) blade and weighed 26 oz (0.75 kg).

DADAO

Many Chinese soldiers not only carried the traditional Chinese long sword, the *Dadao*, into battle, but used it as well. A typical example was 37.5 in (95 cm) long and weighed 35 oz (1 kg), with long handle and wide, curved blade with its weight well forward, making it suitable for either one- or two-handed use in cutting and slashing. Traditionally, the *Dadao* had no scabbard, but in military use it was usually carried in a simple container strapped on the wearer's backpack. The weapon was simple to manufacture by local blacksmiths, one popular source of the steel being redundant (or stolen) railroad tracks.

below A courageous warrior displays his sword prowess while his comrades take up positions more suited to 20th century warfare. Note the British-style steel helmets.

POLAND

above Polish soldiers at the border with Czechoslovakia during the 1938 German invasion of the Sudetenland.

Poland achieved independence in 1918, but this was followed by four years of boundary disputes and several wars including the Soviet–Polish War which was only settled in 1921. As a result, while Poland had a national army, it could not afford to equip it properly. Improvements started in 1937 but were by no means complete when Germany invaded (September 1, 1939), followed by the USSR (September 17, 1939). The Poles were ill-prepared for two such hammer-blows and their armed forces, albeit very brave, proved no match for them. The Poles also employed bad tactics, their infantry being committed to the offensive, while horsed cavalry faced armored formations. Polish resistance ended in October but without any formal surrender, following which the Germans and Soviets imposed their own forms of government, while a Polish "government-in-exile" was formed in Paris, but later moved to London.

Stalin's incorporated these captured territories into the USSR, one method of suppressing resistance being to remove almost the entire intelligentsia either by murdering them, for example, at Katyn, or by exile to Siberia. In the event some 1.5 million Poles were sent to Siberia but when the Germans invaded the USSR large numbers of these people were released to help fight the hated Germans, although only several hundred thousand made it out of Siberia alive.

right Polish alpine troops practicing rifle fire using their ski poles as a support.

below A woven cap badge worn by Polish officers.

Category	Polish Ranks	US Army Equivalent
Generals	Marszalek Polski	General of the Army
	General	General
	General broni	Lieutenant-General
	General dywizji	Major-General
	General brygady	
Field Officers	Pulkownik	Colonel
	Podpulkownik	Lieutenant-Colonel
	Major	Major
Company Officers	Kapitan	Captain
	Porucznik	1st Lieutenant
	Porporucznik	Second Lieutenant
Senior NCOs	Starszy Sierzant	Staff Sergeant
	Sierzant	Sergeant
Junior NCOs	Kapral	Corporal
	Starszy Szeregowiec	Lance-Corporal
Soldiers	Szeregowiec	Private

INTERNAL RESISTANCE

Throughout the war there were a number of groups within Polish territory with various political allegiances which undertook sabotage, attacks on key points and assassination of individuals. These included *Armia Krajowa* (Home Army), *Narodowe Sily Zbrojne* (National Armed Forces), *Armia Ludowa* (People's Army), several Jewish groups and *Bataliony Chlopskie* (Peasants' Battalions). Many Poles, however, managed to escape to continue the war under a variety of foreign banners.

left A soldier of the Polish Home Army and a desperate refugee family outside the ruined Warsaw Opera House. The Home Army was the largest resistance force that fought the SS during the 1944 Warsaw uprising. This soldier is well-equipped with steel helmet, uniform, pouches, bedding roll and a captured German Kar 98 rifle.

POLES IN FRANCE

A surprisingly large number of men escaped from Poland in 1939 and one of their principle destinations was France, which was both an ally in the war against Germany and also the home to a Polish émigré community. A reconstituted Polish army was formed in France and by mid-1940 it was some 80,000 strong, comprising four infantry divisions (two operational, two still forming) and a number of independent brigades, including one of mountain troops. A further group of Poles had escaped southwards to reach the French mandate of Syria where they formed the Polish Independent Carpathian Brigade, which subsequently ended under British command.

First Grenadier and Second Fusilier Divisions fought manfully during the German attack on France but were repeatedly left isolated by withdrawing French units on their flanks. Most Polish units were forced to disband and allow their troops to make their own way to England, although Second Infantry Fusilier Division managed to escape en masse to Switzerland where they were interned for the remainder of the war. The Polish Independent Highland Brigade took part in the Allied defense of Norway in May–June 1940 and then returned to France where it, too, had to be disbanded; most of its troops escaping to England.

Of the 85,000 Poles in France in 1940, some 55,000 took part in the fighting. Of those, 1,400

above After Poland fell many men fought in France during the German invasion there. Here a group of Polish soldiers share a break with men of the Welsh Guards.

above Many Poles ended up in Britain, where they were equipped with British uniforms and weapons. These men wear battle dress but with their berets in the Polish style.

died, 4,000 were wounded, 16,000 became prisoners-of-war, and 13,000 were interned in Switzerland. Somewhere between 20,000 and 30,000 reached England or Egypt and some remained in France, most of whom became involved in the Resistance.

POLES IN THE UK

One wave of Poles arrived in England after the fall of Poland and these were followed by a second wave following the fall of France. There were some 15,000 in uniform by late 1940, rising to 195,000 in mid-1944. They formed 1st Polish Corps, comprising 1st Polish Armored Division, which served in North-West Europe in 1944–1945 as part of 1st Canadian Army; 4th Polish Infantry Division; and 16th Independent Armored Brigade.

There was also the famous 1st Polish Independent Parachute Brigade, which was formed in Scotland in 1941. It was always understood by the Poles that its role would be to parachute into Warsaw to aid an uprising, but this never happened and it was committed to the battle of Arnhem, instead.

Two Polish military groups were formed in the USSR, one of which ended up under British command. In 1941, an agreement was reached

357

above Another group in Britain, this time with British-style sidecaps as well as battle dress and SMLE rifles. Note the Polish unit badges on the tips of their collars.

between the Polish government-in-exile and the USSR, a result of which was that the Soviets released Polish citizens, and allowed them to join what became known as the "Anders Army" after its commander. Stalin then agreed that this would form the occupation force in Persia so Anders took his force (about 40,000 troops plus 70,000 civilians) to Persia where they passed to British command. The British then moved the force to Palestine, where many of its Jewish members promptly deserted. The remainder were retrained and re-equipped by the British and as the 2nd Polish Corps played a very distinguished part in the Italian campaign, including the final capture of Monte Cassino.

The Polish Independent Carpathian Brigade was formed in April 1940 in French-mandated Syria from escaped Polish soldiers. It was organized and equipped as a French mountain brigade of two regiments and was about to go to

below The badge of the Free Polish 2nd Korps.

above Cap badge worn by Polish troops serving alongside UK forces.

358

Greece when that country capitulated. The French commander in Syria then decided to support Vichy, so the Polish brigade marched across the border into British Palestine, where it was reorganized, rearmed and re-equipped on British lines, and renamed the Polish Independent Brigade Group. In 1941 it held part of the perimeter during the Siege of Tobruk and when the siege was lifted the brigade operated as part of the British XIII Corps. It was withdrawn to Palestine in March 1942 where it married up with the Anders Army and was used as the nucleus of 3rd Carpathian Rifle Division, whereupon the brigade ceased to exist.

POLES IN THE USSR

When the Anders Army left, there was still another group of Poles in the USSR who formed the Polish People's Army (*Ludowe Wojsko Polskie*, LWP). The Polish I Corps was formed in 1943, which became Polish 1st Army in 1944, which formed part of the Soviet 1st Belorussian Front with which it re-entered Poland from the Soviet territory in 1944. In April–May 1945 it fought in the final capture of Berlin. The Polish 2nd Army formed part of the Soviet 1st Ukrainian Front and took part in freeing Czechoslovakia.

ORGANIZATION

In the brief campaign in September–October 1939, the Polish Army had approximately one million men under arms, the vast majority of whom were in 30 infantry divisions, plus a number of motorized and independent infantry brigades. Each of the infantry divisions comprised three infantry regiments, each of three infantry battalions. Once new units were formed under British, French or Soviet command, the Polish formations followed the organizational patterns of their hosts.

below Marching against the *Blitzkrieg* in 1940, a Polish infantry unit heads to the front. The speed, aggression and firepower of the German attack quickly overwhelmed the dogged resistance of the Poles.

UNIFORM

The combat uniform worn in 1939 was standard for all ranks. It consisted of a jacket and trousers in a deep olive green, with lace-up brown leather boots and the standard Polish steel helmet. Personal equipment was similar to that worn by the German Army, with pouches of leather but the remainder of a webbing material. Badges of rank were worn by all on their caps, and also on collar patches for officers and shoulder straps for other ranks. When not wearing the steel helmet all ranks wore the distinctive Polish, square-topped *czapka*. The only exceptions were officers and men of the Carpathian Mountain Division who wore a special hat and long khaki cape, derived from clothing worn by the people of the Carpathian mountains.

Once they had become part of the British, French or Soviet armies, Polish soldiers adopted the uniforms and equipment of their hosts but retained the cap-badge and rank distinctions of their own army.

above A stretcher bearer in 1940 displays the distinctive square-topped cap worn by Polish soldiers.

right The Polish helmet with separate crest and metal badge on the front.

left Uniform in 1940 was this woolen tunic and trousers, usually worn with high puttees. A greatcoat is rolled up over the pack while the brown leather straps and ammunition pouches are similar to the German design.

WEAPONS

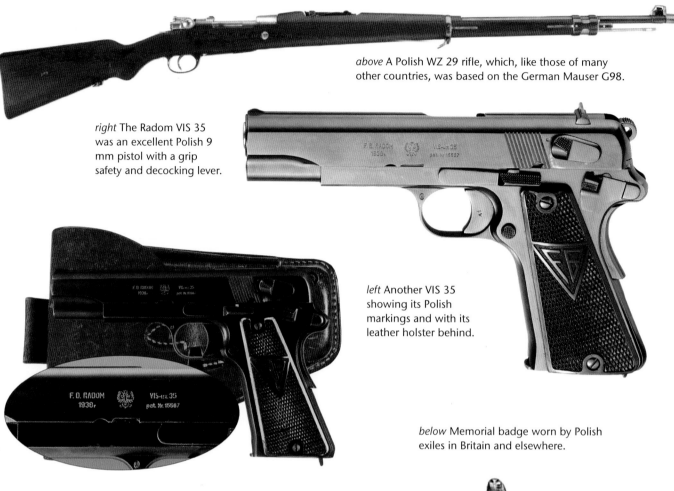

above A Polish WZ 29 rifle, which, like those of many other countries, was based on the German Mauser G98.

right The Radom VIS 35 was an excellent Polish 9 mm pistol with a grip safety and decocking lever.

left Another VIS 35 showing its Polish markings and with its leather holster behind.

below Memorial badge worn by Polish exiles in Britain and elsewhere.

In the 1939 campaign the Polish Army was armed with a mixture of small arms, including Mauser Model 1929 rifles, Mauser M1938 pistols. Browning M1928 LMG, and Browning M1930 HMG. As with the uniforms, they were rearmed by their hosts.

THE POLISH ACHIEVEMENT

Because of their rapid defeat in 1940 and the resulting split between a number of hosts, the achievements of Polish soldiers in the rest of the war has tended to be overlooked by historians. But the record shows that these soldiers, particularly the infantry, were as resolute and courageous as any, and their achievements at Tobruk, Monte Cassino, the Falaise Gap, Arnhem and the eastern advance into Germany mark them as among the finest infantry in any army.

NETHERLANDS

left Dutch infantry march past the Royal Palace in Amsterdam in 1940.

below Gas was seen as a genuine threat before and during the war, and most armies prepared to deal with contamination in some way. This scene is of a pre-war exercise where a slurry is spread to absorb any chemicals and decontaminate the road.

In 1940 the Netherlands was a rich country with substantial colonial possessions in the Far East and the Caribbean. The Dutch maintained their neutrality throughout World War I and hoped to do the same in World War II. In 1940 the army consisted of 1,500 officers and 6,500 NCOs, whose main task was training the annual intake of 65,000 conscripts in their mandatory 11 months full-time military training. On mobilization the field army was about 114,000 strong, plus about 150,000 in the longer-term reserve. These were organized into four army corps, each of two divisions plus supporting troops. The fighting strength of the division was in two infantry regiments, each of three battalions. However, these preparations were totally inadequate and did not deter the Germans who attacked on May 10, 1940, the conflict lasting just five days.

Category	Dutch Ranks	US Army Equivalent
Generals	*Generaal*	General
	Luitnant-Generaal	Lieutenant-General
	Generaal-majoor	Major-General
Field Officers	*Kolonel*	Colonel
	Luitenant-Kolonel	Lieutenant-Colonel
	Majoor	Major
Company Officers	*Kapitein*	Captain
	Eerste-luitenant	1st Lieutenant
	Tweede-luitenant	Second Lieutenant
Warrant Officer	*Adjutant-onder-officier*	Warrant Officer (I)
Sergeant-Major	*Sergeant-majoor*	Sergeant-Major
Sergeant	*Sergeant ter 1e klasse*	Senior Sergeant
	Sergeant	Sergeant
Junior NCO	*Korporaal*	Corporal
	Soldaat ter 1e klasse	Lance-Corporal
Soldiers	*Soldaat*	Private

above A Dutch infantry unit moves up to the front. Some men have bicycles while others push handcarts laden with heavy equipment.

DUTCH ARMY WITH BRITISH

Escaping Dutchmen arriving in the UK were concentrated at Haverfordwest in Wales, where they were joined by volunteers arriving from overseas. By late June there were sufficient to form an infantry battalion – "*Detachment Koninklijke Nederlands Troeper en Groot Brittania*" (Detachment of Royal Dutch Army in Great Britain). Following further increases in numbers, the title was changed in January 1941 to "*Koninklijke Nederlands Brigade Prinses Irene*" (Royal Dutch Brigade, Princess Irene) usually known as the "PIB"). From 1941 to 1944 the PIB performed coastal defense duties in East Anglia but on August 7, 1944 they returned to the Continent, via Juno Beach, and then fought as part of Montgomery's 21st Army Group, reaching their homeland and helping oversee the German surrender on April 5, 1945.

left Cap badge worn by Free Dutch troops who remained fighting overseas after the home country had surrendered.

COLONIAL TROOPS

The Dutch East Indies covered all of what is now Indonesia. The Dutch colonial government maintained a standing army, which in 1941 numbered approximately 7,000 ethnic Dutch (1,000 officers plus 6,000 NCOs) and 28,000 Indonesians. A few escaped but the vast majority became Japanese prisoners-of-war.

MARINES

Some Dutch marines escaped from continental Europe in 1940 to form the 2nd Dutch Commando Troop, which operated with British Royal Marines in Burma in 1943 and returned to Europe to take part in the Walcheren campaign in 1944/45. At the time of the Japanese attack in early 1942, there were also some 400 Dutch marines in the East Indies and in January 1942 a group of these were shipped to California, where they were armed, kitted-out and trained by the US Marine Corps. More volunteers joined and by 1943 the unit had reached brigade size, its intended mission being an amphibious landing against a target in Japanese-held Indonesia. The Japanese surrendered before the brigade could be employed, but it went to Indonesia, anyway.

right A Dutch group in 1940, equipped with rifles and a Lewis light machine gun.

COMBAT UNIFORM

In the 1940 campaign, the Dutch Army wore a combat uniform of jacket, knickerbockers, boots and long puttees. The uniform had started as a very pale green in color but by 1940 was almost gray. Normal headdress was a sidecap which bore a national cockade and piping in arm-of-service colors (blue for infantry). A curious feature of the soldiers' jacket was that the shoulder straps were stitched down, but incorporated a raised roll at the outer end to prevent straps from slipping off.

Soldiers wore an equipment assembly of ammunition pouches and suspender straps in brown leather, and a cloth pack. Water-bottle, bayonet and tools were suspended from the belt, and there were separate cloth haversacks for daily rations and a gas mask, both suspended by cloth slings. Officers and warrant officers wore a Sam Browne type belt, with shoulder-strap and leather pistol holster.

Once in England members of the PIB were issued with British uniforms and equipment. Their nationality was indicated by a flash on the left sleeve featuring the Dutch Lion with word "*Nederlands.*" The steel helmet was of an unusual shape with a high, almost pointed crown. A new design had been introduced in 1928 but the shape was changed in several respects to produce the M1934, which had slightly more extensive brims and was an apple-green in color.

Colonial troops wore a version of the standard Dutch uniform but cut rather more generously and made of a lightweight material. Officers wore a peaked service cap and Sam Browne belt, while soldiers wore a hat similar to the Australian bush hat, with the right brim pinned up and bearing the national cockade. Marines wore a straw hat with a wide brim which was turned up at the back with a black tally, bearing the words *Koninklijke Marine* (Royal Marines).

top In a field trench preparing to refight World War I, these men show the distinctive flared dome shape of the Dutch steel helmet.

right Dutch colonial infantry wearing slouch hats with the brims pinned up, in a similar manner to those worn by Australian soldiers.

WEAPONS

In the 1940 campaign Dutch infantry weapons were of old design and poor combat effectiveness. The Mannlicher 6.5 mm M1908 rifle was used throughout the Dutch forces; officers and warrant officers carried the FN M1903 pistol and the squad light machine gun was the venerable Lewis M1920.

right and below Dutch 9.4 mm Model 1873 revolver, a typical large and heavy 19th century design.

below A machine gun detachment in brush cover, showing the unique shape of the Dutch steel helmet. They have Mannlicher rifles and a Schwarzlose medium machine gun.

SCHWARZLOSE M.08/15

right The heavy Schwarzlose predated World War I but was still the standard Dutch machine gun when the Germans attacked in 1940.

Type: heavy machine gun
Origin: Austria-Hungary
Caliber: 7.92 mm
Cartridge: 7.92 x 57R Dutch
Weight (empty): 54 lb (24.5 kg); complete (plus tripod, water) 97 lb (44 kg)
Barrel length: 20.7 in (525 mm)
Cyclic rate: 400 rpm
Feed: 215-round cotton belt

below A Schwarzlose detachment operating in the anti-aircraft role. These is no ammunition box so the No. 2 has to guide the ammunition belt to the gun to prevent it twisting and causing a stoppage. Note the simple deflection sight on the barrel.

The Schwarzlose was the standard heavy machine gun of the Dutch forces in 1940. In 1900 there was a competition for a new machine gun for the Dutch which was won by this weapon, made by *Österreichische Waffenfabrik Gesellschaft, Steyr*. In terms of range, hitting power and rate-of-fire it was greatly inferior to its competitors, but it had three advantages: it shared its 6.5mm round with the Dutch rifle; it was exceptionally reliable and, most tellingly, it was under half the price of its nearest competitor. It entered service in 1908 but in World War I supply of both guns and ammunition dried up, so a new factory was built in Holland: *Artillerie Inrichtingen* (AI) at Hembrug. Complaints from commanders in colonial campaigns led to the adoption of the heavier 7.92 round for this weapon and by 1940 Dutch forces were equipped with new Schwarzloses made in the new caliber or older ones converted.

The M.08/15 was a water-cooled weapon with a much simpler operation than Maxim designs. Nevertheless, it was very heavy and its rate of fire slow. A machine gun company comprised four sections of three guns each with each weapon being carried on a cart towed by horses or the gun crew; there were no tractor vehicles at this stage.

BELGIUM

On mobilization in 1939 the Belgian Army was some 550,000 strong, of which approximately 400,000 were conscripts and recalled reservists. The country was difficult to defend and great (and misplaced) reliance was placed on massive fixed defenses such as the fortress at Eban-Emäel. Despite its small size Belgium fielded 22 infantry divisions in 1940; some of these had static duties, while six formed three army corps. There was also a light infantry force – the Ardennes Rifle Corps. Despite putting up strong resistance, these were overcome by the powerful German forces in just under three weeks. There was no official sanction for Belgians to escape from their country and those servicemen to reach England did so as private individuals. Nevertheless there were sufficient Belgians in England plus emigrés returning from abroad, to form a company in June 1940, expanding to a battalion and finally to an independent brigade group. Belgians also served with distinction in the Commandos and Special Operations Executive.

The Belgian Independent Parachute Company was formed in May 1942 and after intensive training and an attachment to the British 8th Parachute Battalion, moved to the SAS to become 5th (Belgian) Squadron, later expanding to

battalion size. There was also a brigade-sized formation which was raised from the *Force Publique* in the Belgian Congo and served in campaigns in North Africa and the Middle East.

UNIFORM

right A Belgian soldier in 1940 field order. His uniform resembles French designs, complete with ridged helmet and greatcoat with the front flaps pinned back. He has a Mannlicher M95 rifle and leather cartridge pouches.

below Another badge worn by Belgian exiles in Britain.

left Cap badge worn by Free Belgian forces who escaped to Britain.

The pre-1941 combat uniform for infantry soldiers was very similar to that for the French Army, including the Adrian helmet, leather accoutrements and a greatcoat with habitually turned back skirts, but with black boots and black leather leggings. Badges of rank for officers and warrant officers were on collar patches, while NCOs all had a plain collar patch. Rank was indicated by diagonal stripes just above the cuff. Arm-of-service was indicated by the color of the collar patch (red for infantry) and for officers by a crown on the service dress cap (crown for infantry).

The Free Belgian forces in the UK wore British uniforms and equipment, including British badges of rank. The only indication of nationality was a flash on the left sleeve embroidered "Belgium" in red, the base color matching that for the arm-of-service, and another thin flash on the right sleeve in the national colors of black, yellow and red. These national colors also appeared on the steel helmet, on the left side.

WEAPONS

In 1940, equipment and weapons were mainly of Belgian or French origin, but the standard rifle was the *Fusil Mle 1935*, a Mauser *Gewehr 1898* with some modifications, manufactured by FN at Herstal. Once in England, Belgian forces were armed with standard British and sometimes US weapons.

above A Belgian soldier in late 1944 wearing British uniform and equipment but with national flashes on his sleeve and helmet.

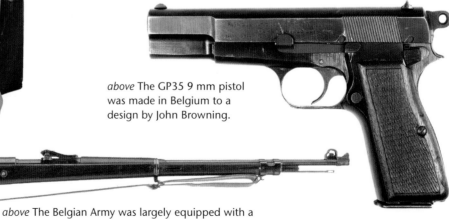

above The GP35 9 mm pistol was made in Belgium to a design by John Browning.

above The Belgian Army was largely equipped with a version of the Mauser G98 rifle.

BRAZIL

Germany and Italy objected when Brazil, ostensibly neutral, allowed the United States to establish a large airbase at Natal, as a result of which they allowed their U-boats to attack Brazilian shipping; 32 ships were then sunk between 1941 and 1943. Brazil declared was on the Axis in August 1942 and it was quickly agreed with the US government to form *Força Expedicionária Brasileira* (FEB), which would consist of one infantry division to be armed, trained and equipped by the Americans.

The original agreement was that the division would fight in a hot climate and lowland terrain as similar as possible to Brazil, so military logic dictated that it would be sent to Italy where it fought in the mountains in one of the worst winters on record.

The division played a full part in the operations in northern Italy between July 1944 and February 1945, operating in the mountains before descending into the Po Valley. A total of 25,445 men and women went with FEB, of whom 480 were killed, 34 were missing and 2,064 wounded. The other side of the coin was that they fought hard, gained a lot of ground and captured 20,573 prisoners before the end of the war.

ORGANIZATION, UNIFORMS AND EQUIPMENT

During the 1920s and early 1930s a French advisory team oriented the Brazilian Army towards French organizations and equipment, and taught them how to win World War I. For the deployment to Italy, however, organization was strictly on US lines, as were clothing and personal equipment.

WEAPONS

Prior to 1944 the Brazilian infantry was equipped with outdated weapons, including: Mauser C-96 and Luger M1908 pistols; Mauser M1908 rifles; and Hotchkiss Mle 1904 and Madsen machineguns. The most recent arrival had been the Czech ZB26 light machine gun, although a shipment of arms from Germany in 1939 had been intercepted at sea by the Royal Navy and confiscated.

above A Mauser C96, a popular automatic in the 1920s and 1930s.

above Brazil was one of the many countries to take the excellent Czech ZB26 light machine gun.

above A Mauser G98 in Brazilian service.

DENMARK

Denmark and its dependent territories were neutral in the World War I and hoped to remain so in the second, but this was not to be, as, unlike Sweden or Switzerland, the country did not maintain forces of sufficient strength to deter aggression. The German occupation (April 9, 1940) was swift and the government surrendered some two hours later, with Denmark becoming a "protectorate" of the Third Reich.

There was no Danish army in exile in the UK but a small force was raised in Sweden in December 1943 – *den Danske Brigade* – although it undertook no active operations until deploying to Denmark on May 5, 1945 to help take the German surrender. It was disbanded in July 1945.

The Royal Danish Army was a conscript force, theoretically two divisions strong on mobilization. The infantry component was: Jutland Division – four infantry regiments; Sjaelland Division – three infantry regiments. These regiments, each of three battalions, were about 3,000 strong.

COMBAT UNIFORM

Danish solders wore a gray combat outfit with brown leather accoutrements from 1915, but the German attack in 1940 found them in the middle of a change to a new khaki outfit with brown leather belt, pouches and haversacks. The most characteristic item was the unique M1923 steel helmet which had very low sides giving the wearer, especially when viewed from the front, a menacing appearance.

WEAPONS

The well-known Danish-based Madsen company provided most of the small arms for the army, including their light machine gun. Designed in 1903 and always known as "the Madsen" it was one of the earliest light machine guns and was adopted by at least 30 armies and even some police forces. The standard infantry rifle was the Krag-Jørgensen Model 1889/24, which although designed in Norway, was manufactured in Denmark for many years.

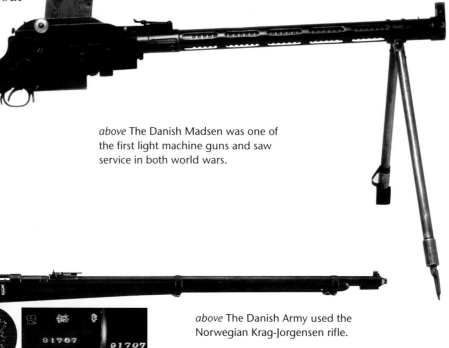

above The Danish Madsen was one of the first light machine guns and saw service in both world wars.

above The Danish Army used the Norwegian Krag-Jorgensen rifle.

GREECE

At the start of World War II, Greece was invaded twice, first by the Italians (October 28, 1940), and when they successfuly resisted then by the Germans (April 6, 1941). This time, despite British help, they were out-generaled and outfought and forced to surrender (April 20). The Germans went on to take the Greek islands, including their spectacular parachute assault on Crete.

Sufficient men escaped with the British to form independent units. Originally there were two brigades, armed and supported by the British, which fought in Syria and North Africa, but they were severely affected by the 1944 Greek mutinies and disbanded. The British took the reliable elements to form 3rd (Greek) Mountain Brigade, which fought with distinction in Italy before returning to Greece to help put down the Communist insurrection.

The Sacred Band (Leros Lothos) was formed in 1942 from Greek officers and cadets who had escaped to Egypt. Originally company-sized, it became part of the Special Forces and after training with the SAS undertook numerous actions alongside the British and French in North Africa and subsequently in the Greek islands, by which time it was regiment-sized.

UNIFORMS AND WEAPONS

Pre-war Greek Army combat uniforms were generally similar to British styles, but once in Egypt they were absolutely identical apart from the badges of rank and arm-of-service colors. Weapons included the Greek Mannlicher-Schönauer Model 1903/14 Infantry Rifle, a Steyr design which married the Mannlicher bolt action to an unusual built-in rotary magazine.

NORWAY

Norway achieved its independence from Sweden in 1905, was neutral throughout World War I and seemed set to keep out of World War II. Realizing the threat from Germany, Norway had only partially mobilized when the invaders struck on April 8, 1940 and the annual conscription cycle had only just begun. Aid from Britain, France and Poland failed to stem the tide and the government capitulated on June 9, 1940.

Sufficient men escaped to England to enable first a company and then a battalion to be formed and in March 1941 a brigade was formed, although it was under strength by British standards. Despite the arrival of small numbers of recruits the Free Norwegian Army never amounted to more than about 3,000 officers and

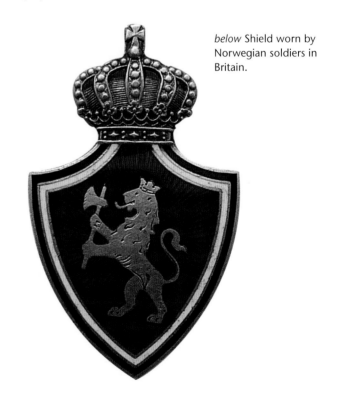

below Shield worn by Norwegian soldiers in Britain.

left They may look British but this unit exercising in England is actually Norwegian, formed from men who escaped to England as their country fell to the Germans.

below Cap badge worn by Free Norwegians in the UK.

men and it undertook no significant operations as a unit. A significant number of Norwegians served with SOE in the well-known Linge Company (Norwegian Independent Company Nr 1) which conducted daring operations in Norway; 530 Norwegians served in the unit of whom 57 were killed.

UNIFORM

Norwegians serving in Great Britain wore British uniforms with a shoulder flash "Norway" or "Norge" on the left arm and a small embroidered Norwegian flag on the right. They wore British headdress with Norwegian cap badges and national badges of rank.

WEAPONS

In the 1940 campaign, the Norwegian infantry was armed with Krag-Jørgensen 6.5 mm M1894 rifles, with 6.5 mm M1909 Madsen and M1929

Colt-Browning heavy machine guns. Very few weapons were taken to England where the Norwegian Brigade was armed entirely from British stocks.

above A Krag-Jørgensen carbine as used by the Norwegian Army during the 1940 campaign.

YUGOSLAVIA

A relatively new combination of different ethnic groups, the unstable Kingdom of Yugoslavia was overrun by the Germans in March 1941. They then divided the country into the quasi-independent states of Croatia, Serbia and Montenegro while other portions were simply taken over directly by neighboring Bulgaria, Italy and Hungary, as well as some by distant Germany. With the invasion of the USSR looming the Germans rushed the disarming of the Yugoslav army, leaving many soldiers free to take their weapons and join the partisans.

COMBAT UNIFORM

The combat uniform of the Royal Yugoslav Army was that of the earlier Serbian Army and consisted of a double-breasted jacket, pantaloons and puttees, all in a brownish-gray color, with black, lace-up leather ankle boots. Personal equipment consisted of a belt, pouches and pack in leather, with a bayonet frog and canteen. Badges of rank were worn on the shoulder boards (officers) and shoulder straps (other ranks) and also incorporated the arm-of-service color – purple for infantry.

The combat headdress was the French-style Adrian helmet, with the Yugoslav coat-of-arms. The soft hat worn by Yugoslav soldiers was not, as is usually described, a side-cap, but a lajkala, which had been the Serbian national headdress since the 18th century, when it originated with Serbian boatmen on the rivers Danube and Sava. Unlike the sidecap, the lajkala does not open out to form a cold-weather cap, and its shape resembles that of an inverted flat-bottomed river ferry. It was adopted as the headgear of the Serbian Army in World War I and its use then spread throughout Yugoslavia. The national cockade was worn at the front.

BRITISH SERVICE

A number of Yugoslavs made good their escape and joined British and other allied forces as individuals. There were also two units of Yugoslavs under British command. One was a complete infantry battalion, initially some 800-strong, which was formed in the Egypt and sent to garrison duties in Cyprus, but as there were no reinforcements its numbers dwindled until November 1943, when, with British recognition of Tito's Communists, it was quietly disbanded. The other was a group of two officers and 20 men who formed No 7 (Yugoslavian) Troop in 10th (Inter-Allied) Commando of the Special Services Brigade. Their primary mission was to conduct clandestine operations inside Yugoslavia.

CHETNIKS

The members of the Royal Yugoslav Army loyal to the deposed King Peter were organized into a partisan movement officially designated the "Royal Yugoslav Army in the Homeland," but more commonly known by a traditional Serbian title of "Chetniks," which was headed by Colonel (later General) Mihailovil. This was some 20,000 strong and organized on supposedly conventional military lines, with platoons, companies, battalions, brigades and corps. Some units were undoubtedly up to strength, but others were "on paper" only. The Chetniks were recognized by the Allies up to 1943, when they transferred their support to the Communists. The Chetnik badge, normally worn on the left breast, was a black skull and crossbones.

COMMUNISTS

The leader of the Yugoslav Communists was the party's general-secretary, Josip Broz, always known by his cover name as "Tito." He created the Yugoslav People's Liberation Army from

above Browning's Model 10 automatic was taken up by the Yugoslav Army as well as by others.

1945 Tito had reorganized his army, now some one million strong into four army groups and he cleared the Germans out of the country.

The Communists, like every other partisan army, wore whatever clothing came to hand, and, towards the end of the war this could even include items from the British Army. The Communists did, however, develop a khaki sidecap of their own, based on a Soviet Russian design but modified (allegedly) by Tito himself and with a red star at the front – it was universally known as a "Titovka" (Tito hat).

former soldiers in the Royal Army, together with arms and ammunition that the Germans and Italians had failed to capture. The Communist partisans steadily expanded, with the first "regular" unit being formed on December 21, 1941 although it was not until December 1942 that they were recognized by the Allies and it was not until June 1943 before they received their first air-drop of weapons and ammunition. By mid-1944 Tito had some half-million men and women under arms and the last British liaison mission had been withdrawn from the Chetniks. By January

WEAPONS

The rifle of the Royal Yugoslav Army was the 7.9 mm Mauser M1924, most of which were manufactured at the Voino Tekhniki Zavod (state arsenal) at Kraguyeval, However, some were imported from ZB in Czechoslovakia and Fabrique Nationale in Belgium. Once war was in progress both Chetniks and Communists made use of whatever they could lay their hands on. Modern British weapons delivered by parachute were especially highly valued.

ITALIAN CO-BELLIGERENT FORCES

Following the Italian armistice with the Allies on September 8, 1943, the first units of the new Co-Belligerent Army were formed on September 28. Designated I. Raggruppamento Motorizatto (1st Motorized Combat Group) it was immediately assigned to 5th (US) Army, where it fought well, and was then transferred to the Polish Army (Anders Army), which was on the left of the British 8th Army. Volunteers came forward in ever-increasing numbers and by April 1944 it was redesignated Corpo Italiano di Liberazione. The Co-Belligerent Army did much to rehabilitate the reputation of the Italian infantry and ended the war on a particularly high note with Operation Herring, a successful airborne operation which turned out to be the last parachute drop of the war.

UNIFORM AND WEAPONS

Initially men of the Co-Belligerent Army wore Italian uniforms, but these were soon exchanged for British battledress and personal equipment. Italian ranks and badges were retained, although officers moved their rank badges from the cuff to the shoulder-strap. All ranks also wore a square patch in Italian national colors (Tricolore) on the upper left arm, in which the central white strip carried the emblem of the combat group (division) to which the wearer belonged. These units used a mixture of Italian and British weapons.

ACKNOWLEDGEMENTS

Many people have helped us with this book, and its companion volume on Axis Forces. The following individuals and museums have been especially gracious, allowing us to show unique items from their collections to help us tell the story of the World War II infantryman. Without them this book would not have been possible.

Any errors in identification are ours.

MUSEUM OF THE PACIFIC

The Museum of the Pacific is a private, non-profit, research museum which was founded in 1995 by the owner, Tom McLeod. Sited in Texarkana, Texas, it has over 8,000 square feet of display space, housed in seven large rooms.

The core of the museum is its collection of World War II US and Japanese uniforms, equipment and weapons. But the collection has spread beyond this, and now includes some 300 fully dressed mannequins from the USA, Britain, Canada, Australia, New Zealand, France, Japan, Germany, Italy, Russia, China, North & South Vietnam and Sweden.

United States uniforms begin with the Spanish-American war, then cover all the conflicts that American fighting men took part in through to

right Military veteran, writer, collector and historian Tom McLeod outside his Museum of the Pacific.

Desert Storm. Figures display US Army, Navy, Marine Corps, Army Air Force, USAF and Coast Guard uniforms.

Japanese uniforms begin with the Menji Period and extend through World War II. Some special items include: the uniform of the emperor's veterinarian (Royal Household Horse Keeper), Lt. Honda, the uniform of the Akagi's Medical Officer, including a very rare "Pearl Harbor Book" given to the officers who participated in the raid, and the uniform of 3-star Admiral Junji Uozumi, of Yamamoto's staff.

The museum also has over 400 rifles and pistols, dating from the US Civil War through to Vietnam. The sniper collection is complete with every type of rifle and scope variation and includes a near mint Japanese sniper armor shield and machine gun shield, shown in the Axis Volume of this series.

There are over 80 Japanese military swords on display, as well as hundreds of other swords, knives, bayonets, and several thousand miscellaneous items. To further enhance the museum's usefulness to researchers there is an extensive library of books and original artwork. Many of the mannequins and artefacts shown in this book and its companion volume come from Tom's collection.

Museum of the Pacific
Texarkana, Texas
Tel 903-793-1452 (visits by appointment only)

www.pacificwrecks.com/restore/usa/museum/

DECEMBER 1944 HISTORICAL MUSEUM

The museum is situated in La Gleize, Belgium, a village set in the heart of the beautiful Ardennes. The village was the scene of some of the key battles of "the Bulge", when in December 1944 German forces tried to re-invade Belgium in an attempt to split the Allied armies and reach the strategic port of Antwerp.

La Gleize is where the SS "Kampfgruppe Peiper" were finally stopped by US resistance and where the survivors had to abandon most of their vehicles and equipment as they made their way back to German lines. Many historians believe that: "if the Americans won the Battle of the Ardennes in Bastogne, the Germans lost it in La Gleize"

The museum, owned by the local authorities, principally houses the collection of Philippe Gillain, who scoured the surrounding farms and countryside as a young man, collecting up vital artefacts left by the retreating German Army.

His collection takes the form of 15 dioramas, featuring 85 mannequins, dressed authentically and carrying the correct weapons of the period. Vehicles, equipment and personal items from both sides, together with archival photographs, complete the museum's story of those dramatic times.

left Philippe Gillain outside the museum he created.

A King Tiger tank, which was abandoned in the village square, now adorns the front of the museum. Many of the items shown in this book and its companion volume come from the museum's unique collection.

December 1944 Museum.
La Gleize, Belgium.
Tel: 0032 80/785191
Email: museum@december44.com

www.december44.com

above The December 1944 Museum in La Gleize with King Tiger 213 outside. The marks on the tank's front armor show how it was used for target practice for US anti-tank weapons after the fighting had stopped. Nothing penetrated the armor...

ESPENLAUB MILITARIA

This company, who has been especially generous in opening their archives to us, is operated and owned by Aleksandr Jarovoi and Dmitri Tihhonov. They are both collectors themselves, and that fact has made them passionate about their business of dealing in World War I and World War II militaria for over 20 years. Their main interest is World War II Soviet and German items and it is from this rich source that we are pleased to feature many rare artifacts, some of which have never been seen by collectors before, in our Soviet Union chapter.

Based in Estonia, Aleks and Dimas point out that they are near to where a lot of the real wartime action took place and ideally placed to search for interesting and rare items from the war, uncovering "new pages" of war history as they go. They are helped by their close friend and colleague, Pavel Smirnov, historian and archaeologist who graduated from St. Petersburg State University.

As they say: "We are firstly collectors – the guys who are interested in living history. When you deal with us, you deal with the collector who loves the subject..."

Espenlaub Militaria
Email: info@aboutww2militaria.com

www.aboutww2militaria.com

above Aleksandr Jarovoi.

above Dmitri Tihhonov.

above Pavel Smirnov.

BARRY JENKINS

Artist and graphic designer Barry Jenkins is the archetypal collector. Since his art college days on the south coast of England, Barry has been scouring antique shops, collectors' fairs and placing wanted ads in local papers seeking treasure troves of war memorabilia tucked away in attics. In the heady days of the late sixties there was still a steady supply of material surfacing from World War II. Perhaps a husband had passed away and their wives wanted to know what to do with the immaculate Japanese sword in the attic. or maybe Uncle Joe's medals were up for sale in the interests of clearing out the "old junk", as people often perceived mementoes from the war.

Barry's amazing collection, put together on a fairly careful budget over the years, has been widely featured in our Fighting Men series. Many of the quirky and unusual items are unique to his collection and we thank him for making them and his extensive knowledge available to us.

right Barry Jenkins

ED STOREY

Ed Storey has been collecting Canadian Army Militaria for over 30 years. Employing his extensive collection, he has authored several magazine articles as well as a book on Canadian 1937 Pattern Web Equipment.

Ed is also a Warrant Officer in the Canadian Military Engineers, Mapping and Charting Establishment, having started his military career in the Reserve Infantry in 1978 before transferring to the Engineers in 1982. He has undertaken four overseas deployments beginning in early 1993 when he was the first geomatics technician deployed to The Former Yugoslavia with the United Nations Protection Force. He has also served in Uganda and Honduras as well as making a return trip to Bosnia with NATO in 2000.

Ed resides in Ottawa, is married and has two teenage children. When not hunting for militaria he also enjoys travel and photography. Ed has supplied much of the material used in the Canada and Special Service Force sections of this book.

right Ed Storey in his Canadian Army uniform.

THE GURKHA MUSEUM

Based in Winchester, England, this museum commemorates the contribution of the Gurkha soldier to British and Indian military history. It is also an important source of material and information concerning the Indian Army and the British war in the Far East. We thank Gavin Edgeley-Harris, Gerald Davies and the staff of the museum for helping us with this book.

The Gurkha Museum
Winchester, Hampshire, England.

www.thegurkhamuseum.co.uk

ROYAL SIGNALS MUSEUM

The UK national museum of army communications, this museum's exhibits show how the British Army has communicated in all its campaigns and tells the story of the men and women that made it possible. We thank Cliff Walters and the staff of the museum for helping us with access to communications equipment and general British Army equipment.

Royal Signals Museum
Blandford, Dorset, England.

www2.army.mod.uk/ royalsignalsmuseum/

SASC WEAPONS COLLECTION

The British Army's Small Arms School Corps, based in Warminster, England, is the central school for training infantry soldiers in the essential skills of marksmanship, weapons handling and infantry tactics. As part of this function they maintain a training facility comprising probably the best collection of infantry weapons in the world. It is not a museum and is not open to the public, but they will occasionally allow access to serious researchers.

Index

CREDITS

Editing and Project Management: Graham Smith
Design: Cara Rogers
Original photography: Vincent Abbott; J. P. Bell
Historical images: Andrew Webb at the Robert Hunt Library
Color reproduction: Asia Graphic Printing Ltd